INDIAN ARMY IN EAST AFRICA

INDIAN ARMY IN EAST AFRICA

1914 - 1918

S.D. PRADHAN

NATIONAL BOOK ORGANISATION
(Publishers - Distributors)

First published in India in **1991**
by **Mrs. A.H. Marwah** on behalf of
National Book Organisation (Publishers-Distributers)
H-39 Green Park Extension
New Delhi- 110016 (INDIA)

ISBN 81-85135-53-3

Laser Set by

Laser Business Services
B-471 New Friends Colony
New Delhi- 110065
Phone : 6844675

Printed at Kay Kay Printers, Delhi-110007

CONTENTS

LIST OF SKETCHES

List of Abbreviations used in the present work

F.K.	Field-Kompagnie (Field Company, German)
fn.	Footnote.
G.S.B.	General Staff Branch
I.E.F.	Indian Expeditionary Force
K.A.R.	King's African Rifles (British)
M.D., H.S.	Ministry of Defence, Historical Section (Government of India)

PREFACE

War, unfortunately, still occupies a very important position in the society of nations and that is why, despite sincere efforts to outcast war, we have not succeeded in doing so. For every single year of peace in the world, history has recorded thirteen years of war, the reason being, according to a military thinker, Du Picq, that human nature, which is the starting point in all matters pertaining to war, has remained unchanged. It is perhaps due to this that even today, with so many organisations working for peace, wars persist. Understanding the nature of war and certain permanent basic principles of the game, which have remained unchanged in spite of developments in science and technology, with the help of military history continues to be relevant. Unfortunately, however, such an important subject remains neglected in India.

The present work is an analytical study of the East African Campaign during 1914-1918 with special reference to the role of the Indian Army. This campaign occupies an important position in military history. It explains the utility of the Fabian Strategy. It also clearly domonstrates that in a war, training and morale of troops, proper planning of military operations, proper execution of plans and good leadership are the most important factors. I hope that this study of the campaign will prove very useful for both soldiers and students of military history.

All the available records, pertaining to the campaign and the Indian Expeditionary Force (Force 'B') which was sent to German East Africa, have been consulted. The War Diaries of Force 'B' wherein the day to day actions of the force have been recorded has been invaluable. Unfortunately, the War Diaries of Force 'B' do not give every detail of the campaign. The details of the military operations, after the arrival of Smuts in February 1916, are also not available in the War Diaries. Only summaries of the military operations in German East Africa after February 1916 are available in the these Diaries or with the General Staff Branch. The gaps have been filled in by the Official History of the campaign to some extent. The Official History contains details up to September 1916. Other details have been gathered from the memoirs or books written by officers who took part in the campaign, specially the writings of Brigadier-General J.J. Collyer, Chief of the General Staff of Smut's force; Brigadier-General J.H.V. Crowe, Commander of the Royal

Artillery during Smuts's time; and Captain R.Meinertzhagen, the Intelligence Officer of Force 'B'. Besides, the contemporary writings of army officers in various journals provide relevant material for writing a cohesive history of the campaign. Some very useful information - based on personal interviews - about the military operations has been obtained from two surviving Indian soldiers - Lieutenant Colonel M.A. Singh and Captain Hazara Singh - who participated in this campaign. Other soldiers of the First World War have also been interviewed. They have given useful information about the organisation and the equipment of the Indian Army in 1914.

The memoirs and newspaper articles of von Lettow Vorbeck, Commander of the German force in German East Africa, present the German point of view. Besides, the Governor of German East Africa, Dr. Schnee's book has proved useful in understanding the German strategy.

The maps used in this investigation have been prepared with the help of those given in the Official History of the campaign, Collyer's book, Crowe's book and the War Diaries of Force 'B'. Where no north-point appears, the vertical margins of the sketch-map are true north and south. The spellings of some of the places differ in the different sources, but the spellings used in the present work are those given in the Official History. Those used in other sources are given in brackets.

It is my pleasure to acknowledge my indebtedness to late Dr. K.C. Srivastava, D. Litt., Professor in History, Lucknow University, for his valuable guidance and untiring help. I am deeply indebted to Dr. S.N. Prasad, Incharge of the War Studies Division, Ministry of Defence for his keen interest, valuable advice and suggestions, without which my work would not have been completed. The Research Fellowship awarded by the Historical Section, Ministry of Defence, Government of India, is gratefully acknowledged. The Section very kindly provided me xeroxed copies of the missing War Diaries of Force 'B' from the India Office Records, London. I wish to acknowledge my debt to Professor Dewitt Ellinwood, Director of the Asian Studies Programe in the State University at Alhany (New York) for making useful suggestions. I am also grateful to the Department of Arms Control, Disarmament and International Security of the University of Illinois (U.S.A) for granting me fellowship which enabled me to meet several experts on low intensity conflits in U.S.A. and obtain their views. In the end, wish to express my appreciation to Mr. Jaswinder Singh, Seniour Research Officer, War Studies Division, Ministry of Defence for his assistance throughout this undertaking.

Place : New Delhi, S.D. PRADHAN
Date : 9-12-1990.

INTRODUCTION

The First World War resulted from the interaction of various forces which had long been at work. Self-interest, nationalism and militarism were the dominant notes of the years immediately preceding the outbreak of the war. All these factors worked together to make nations narrow-minded in the beginning of the twentieth century. In addition, economic computations gave rise to militant competitive spirit among the nations. In such an atmosphere, the national press of the rival powers played its role by exaggerating and colouring political events, giving them a chauvinist slant. It sharpened the hostility among the nations. In such a tension-ridden atmosphere, it was quite natural for the European nations to take military steps for their defence. Nations having common interests welded together to form groups to protect their interests. In these circumstances, long before the outbreak of the war, two major groups - the Triple Alliance and the Triple Entente - came into existence. These blocks stood opposed to each other. The members of the Triple Alliance were Germany, Austria and Italy (though later, during the war, Italy joined the Allied Powers). Those of the Triple Entente were England, France and Russia. The rival alliances had decided to support their allies whenever their security was threatened.

In such a critical period, only a spark was required to trigger off the ever impending war. This spark was provided by the assassination of Archduke Francis Ferdinand, the heir-apparent to the Austrian throne, and his wife on June 23, 1914, by a Serb of Serajevo. Austria held Serbia responsible for the assassination and on July 23, issued an ultimatum to Serbia. On July 28, Austria declared war on Serbia. Within a week many other European Powers jumped into the fray and the hostilities of World War I began.

There were many factors responsible for England's entry into the war. Russia and France were arrayed against Germany and England, as a member of the Triple Entente, was expected to help its allies. There were other reasons as well. The rivalry between England and Germany for colonial power contributed significantly to the already prevailing tension between them.

After its industrial development, Great Britain, like other European nations, looked for new markets for its products, which could only be provided by the colonies. Besides, her colonies provided her the raw materials essential for industrial development. Britain could only turn to the still open African continent - Asia provided no new avenues and America was safe from European exploitation, though some European powers including Great Britain were economically interested in Latin America despite the 'Monroe Doctrine'. Therefore, Britain took keen interest in the scramble for Africa and secured the lion's share, the regions with greatest potential in the African continent. In the north, it controlled Egypt from where it extended its sway over Sudan. The acquisition of British East Africa, followed by the establishment of protectorate over Uganda, gave it a stretch of territory from the Indian Ocean to the Mediterranean Sea. At the southern end of the African continent, there was the Union of South Africa, consisting of four colonies, viz., the Cape, Natal, Transvaal and Orange River Colony. North of this was the protectorate of Bechuanaland and even further north was Rhodesia, touching the southern boundary of German East Africa. Thus, pushing northwards from the Union of South Africa, Britain came to control a continuous stretch of territory upto lake Tanganyika and, but for German East Africa, the British empire would have extended continuously from the Union of South Africa to Egypt. The other British possessions in Africa included Gambia, the Gold Coast, Sierra Leone and Nigeria on the west coast, and a part of Somaliland on the east coast.

In the beginning Germany was averse to colonial enterprise. However, later it realised that in its preoccupation with the European continent, it had been left lagging far behind in the race for acquisition of colonies. With the ascension of William II, Germany embarked upon its new policy known as "Weltpolitik'. Its national prestige, industrialisation and the growth of population demanded colonies, so Germany turned to the African continent. Within a short time, Germany had acquired Togoland, the Cameroons, German South-West Africa and German East Africa.

The outbreak of the war brought into sharp focus, for the warring camps, the urgency of retaining their respective colonies in Africa. German East Africa did not only cut the vital lines of British communication from the Cape to Cairo but also provided Germany with a naval base from where German ships could operate in the Indian Ocean and destroy British ships on routes to and from India. Consequently, the British Government, decided to capture German East Africa. Germany, on the other hand, wanted not only to retain German East Africa but also intended to distract Britain in the east by threatening India and the other colonies thereby reducing its enemy forces in the European sphere.

Under these conditions, the Indian Government was given the responsibility of capturing German East Africa. The Indian Government despatched its army to East Africa and so began the East African Campaign. Though the campaign was one of the subsidiary campaigns of the First World War, it was one of the most interesting because of the peculiar method of warfare adopted by the Germans, which gave them favourable results under unfavourable circumstances. In spite of great disparity between the resources and the manpower of the Allied forces and the German force, the latter was able to pin down a much larger number of the Allied troops, in German East Africa for a period of four years. Besides, the campaign was fought under conditions which rendered it unique in military history. For Force 'B' of the Indian Army, its typical composition of troops, its equipment and the unfamiliar terrain created unprecedented difficulties. Yet, in spite of these, the Force 'B' proved an invaluable asset to the Allies in this campaign.

1

The Indian Army Before the First World War

From advent of the British in the Indian subcontinent and the employment of Indians by them, for their own protection, originated the Indian Army. The East India Company, which started recruiting Indians to serve it, helped to enhance their military capability. The training and the drill imparted, the discipline and morale instilled by the British, made a world of difference to the Indian soldier. It was an interesting though humiliating to find that troops of Indian soldiers trained by the British on European lines could easily beat native armies not trained by Europeans. That is why most Indian rulers later employed Europeans to train their armies. The more efficient and improved organisation of the armed forces in India was one act of the British that gave stability and cohesion to their empire which helped in weathering all storms until the nation became independent.

The British came to India to trade and gradually acquired many trading stations in India. Initially, for the protection of their trading centres, they enrolled guards, who could be regarded as *chowkidars*. In 1668, the East India Company got possession of the island of Bombay. For its defence, the East India Company stationed a garrison there, consisting of 5 officers, 139 non-commissioned officers and men and 54 Topasses.[1] The Topasses were half-castes claiming descent from the Portuguese. This is the earliest force that can be regarded as the embryo of the Indian Army. The troops located in Madras and Bengal were negligible in number. The Bombay garrison was increased in 1683, being supplemented by two companies of Rajputs.[2] Each company was composed of 100 men and was commanded by its own Rajput officers. This small force may be considered the first regular native troop of the Indian Army.

In 1708, after the amalgamation of the new Company of Merchants and the London Company, three Presidencies, each distinct from the other and each absolute within its own limits, were formed: namely Bombay, Madras and Bengal.

These Presidencies gradually increased the strength of their armies. By 1741, the Bombay Army, besides some 700 so-called sepoys who attended on the civil servants of the Company in the capacity of peons, had a regular regiment consisting of 26 British officers, 166 Warrant and Non-Commissioned officers, 1,276 rank and file and 27 followers.[3] In 1748, the armies were reorganized on European lines. Each Presidency got one company of artillery consisting of 5 British Officers (BOs) and 110 Other Ranks (0Rs).[4] A Commander-in-Chief was appointed as the head of all the three Presidency armies. The first such appointment was given to Major Stinger Lawrence, 'the father of the Indian Army', who took various steps to improve the organisation of the Indian Army.

Shortly before the Battle of Plassey, Robert Clive re-organised the Indian troops, giving them the shape of regular battalions. These battalions were commanded by British Officers and were equipped on European lines. The first battalion organised on these lines was known as the '*Lal Pultan*' and was composed of 3 British Officers, several British Non-commissioned Officers, 42 Indian Officers and 820 Indian rank and file.[5] The battalion was divided into ten companies. Gradually many more battalions were raised on this pattern. Clive also introduced British Officers into the Indian units.

In 1796, some changes were introduced in the Indian Army. The number of British Officers in each unit was increased, Artillery battalions were created, and double battalion regiments were formed. Some of the alterations were, however, found defective. The battalions were linked only in theory and had no mutual interdependence or common bond or interest. The control of the Regimental Commanders was excessive, which made it difficult to administer the battalions. The increased number of the British Officers in units diminished the authority and dignity of the Indian officers, which caused discontent in the Indian Army and ultimately contributed to the Mutiny of 1857.

In 1824, the Indian infantry regiments, which had been formed by combining 2 battalions, were broken up again into single battalion regiments. In the same year, the number of Cavalry regiments was increased, partly by using regular regiments and partly by raising irregular troops. The irregular regiments were raised on the *Silladar* system. Under this system, the individual soldier supplied and maintained his horse, clothing, equipment and arms (other than rifle), receiving in return a higher rate of pay than the non-silladar soldier, whose needs were furnished by his employer.

In course of time, the East India Company acquired more territories, and for their protection increased the strength of the Indian Army. In 1861, as a result of the Mutiny of 1857, the Government disbanded some of the Cavalry and Infantry units and many others were amalgamated.[6] The artillery units, with the exception of four Mountain batteries, an irregular force (the Punjab Frontier Force) and the Native batteries in Bombay, were disbanded. In the same year, Staff Corps were introduced in all three Presidencies.[7] Prior to this, whenever the officers of the regimental cadres went an extra-regimental duties, the regimental establishment found it difficult to carry on its work. The institution of a Staff Corps removed this defect. It established a Corps of officers in each Presidency of sufficient strength to ensure the smooth working of regimental establishments in the absence of their officers. Certain steps were also taken to remove the disparity in promotions of officers of the different regiments.

In 1886, the Indian infantry regiments were linked in many groups. Each group consisted of 2 or 3 battalions and was given a permanent regimental centre where one of the battalions of that group was always stationed. A soldier of one battalion was made liable to serve in other battalions of his group. In the same year, a reserve force was created for the first time in the Indian Army.

In 1895, the separate Presidency Armies were abolished and the unified Indian Army was divided into four commands, viz., "Punjab, Bengal, Madras and Bombay, each under a Lieutenant-General who was responsible for the administration as well as for the training of troops in his command".[8] These commands were divided into many 1st and 2nd class Districts.

In 1902, Lord Kitchener was appointed Commander-in-Chief of the Indian Army. He carried out many important changes to improve the organisation of the Indian Army. He abolished the Indian Staff Corps and from that time onwards all officers belonged to a single corps - the Indian Army. He also abolished the Madras Command in 1904 and the army was divided into three Commands - Northern, Eastern and Western.[9]

On the recommendation of Lord Kitchener certain administrative powers were given to the divisional commanders to ensure quick disposal of routine matters. The retention of similar powers by the Lieutenant-Generals of Command, however, created confusion and delayed matters.

In 1907, therefore, the command system was abolished and "Indian Army was divided into two groups - Northern and Southern - each under a general officer, who was charged with command, inspection and training, but was not accorded any administrative responsibility."[10] These armies were divided into 9 divisions and these divisions were put directly under the Army Headquarters for administrative purposes. It was intended that each division would include one or more definite formations together with the garrison troops necessary for the internal security of that area in war. But as the reorganization involved considerable extra expenditure, it could not be completed before 1914.

By 1914, only 7 of the 9 divisions were ready for immediate mobilisation. The whole army was divided into two groups - Field Army and Internal Security Troops. The former consisted of Army Troops, 9 divisions and 8 cavalry brigades.[11] The latter consisted of 3 independent frontier brigades which were retained to prevent internal uprising.

The Recruiting Policy

In 1914, recruitment in the Indian Army was based on the theory of 'martial races'. This theory was introduced by Lord F.S. Roberts, who served as Commander-in-Chief of the Indian Army from 1885 to 1893. His intention was to create a strong army which could defend India from Russian attacks, which the British statesmen, under the strong influence of Russo-phobia were expecting. In his view all Indians could not be good fighters and the best men for the army were available only in certain castes of the Indian society. According to him, the long years of peace and security, resulting in properity in certain areas, had a softening and deteriorating effect on the fighting qualities of the people living in those areas.[12] Roberts' theory of 'martial races' formed the basis of the recruitment policy. General Sir O'Moore, Commander-in-Chief of the Indian Army from 1909 to 1914, also held this belief though he gave a different justification for it. According to him, the people living in the hot and plain regions were timid and unwarlike while people living in the cold and hilly regions were warlike.[13] A few specific races were declared fit to bear arms and recruitment was restricted to these 'martial races'. Some of the important 'martial classes' before 1914 were the Rajputs, the Dogras, the Pathans, the Gurkhas, the Garhwalis, the Kumaonis and the Sikhs. The British highlighted the particular characteristics of each of these classes which distinguished them from the other martial classes and the masses. These classes began to regard themselves as superior to other classes which were not allowed to join the army. The result of this feeling was that the flow of recruits from these 'martial classes' into the army increased markedly. The formation of separate units of each of these martial classes in the army led to a sort of competition among themselves. Each class desired to contribute more in terms of supplying manpower to the army in order to prove superior to others. The policy of segregation of the different 'martial classes' led to the formation of pure class or caste units in the army. In 1914, there were two types of units in the Indian Army - "class regiments" and "class company regiments". Class regiments were composed entirely of the same ethnic of caste group, class company regiments had different classes in its companies; the companies themselves were always pure, in the sense that they comprised of the members of a particular class, caste or community.[14] The system of promotion also differed in these two types of units. In the former, promotion was based on a general seniority list of the regiment while in the second type, each company had its own seniority list and whenever a vacancy occurred in a company, promotion was based on that company's seniority list. There were special provisions for the few regimental posts. No Indian officer was allowed to command any unit which was not composed of men of his caste or group.

On the whole, this system of recruitment worked well upto 1914. But when the First World War broke out, it proved inadequate because the base of recruitment was too narrow. It could not meet the insatiable demand for manpower for this war. Yet, the old system remained in existence during the first twenty-nine months of the war. During 1914-1916, recruitment was made partly by direct enlistment (whereby a young man whose family was connected with a certain regiment could present himself as a recruit at the Regimental Depot) and partly by 'class recruiting' (which meant recruitment by recruiting officers who were posted at different cantonments with a view to enrolling recruits of a particular class). In 1917, it was realised that the old system could not provide sufficient numbers of recruits for the military operations. A new system of recruitment was introduced. The 'class system' of recruitment was replaced by the 'territorial system'. In the new system, in each division a Divisional Recruiting Officer was appointed to make intensive efforts to recruit men from his assigned area. The divisional reçruiting officers were asked to prepare lists showing the potentiality of their areas for recruitment. They were asked to recruit men from 75 new classes which had now been declared eligible for recruitment in the army.[15] To coordinate the working of the Divisional Recruiting Officers, a Central Recruiting Board was established in June 1917. In each province, a Provincial Recruiting Board was established to coordinate the working of the Divisional Recruiting Officers under it. This new system worked well and a large number of recruits joined the army in 1917 and 1918. [16]

High Command

In 1914, India being a part of the British Empire, the British Government had a special responsibility and authority in regard to the military administration in India. The Secretary of State as one of the ministers of the British Government bore the responsibility for all Indian matters.

The Secretary of State's main adviser on Indian military affairs was the Secretary in the Military Department of India.[17] In addition, a retired officer of high rank of the Indian Army was a member of the Council of the Secretary of State. He advised the Secretary of State in the Council, whenever it took up matters pertaining to the Indian Army.

The Viceroy, being the head of the administrative machinery, exercised the same control on the administration of the Indian Army as he exercised in respect of the other government departments. There was an Army Department which dealt with new proposals relating to the Indian Army which required the decision of the Government of India. It was headed by the Army Member of the Viceroy's Council. To assist the Army Member the Secretary of the department was an army officer of the rank of Major-General.[18]

The military head of the Indian Army was the Commander-in-Chief. He was also the Army Member of the Viceroy's Council.[19] The commander-in-Chief in India was responsible for the administration of the Indian Army, the promotion and execution of the military policy of the Government of India, the maintenance of every branch, Combatant and Non-combatant, of the army and for supreme direction of any military operations based upon India.[20] The Commander-in-Chief had the Military Secretary on his personal staff to assist him.[21]

For the assistance of the Commander-in-Chief in his duties there was the Army Headquarters composed of the three Principal Staff Officers - the Chief of the General Staff, the Adjutant General and the Quartermaster General and the heads of the other minor departments which were not directly under the Principal Staff Officers.[22] These heads of the minor departments were the Director General of Ordnance, the Director General of Military Works and the Director of Medical Services. They functioned directly under the Commander-in-Chief.

The Chief of General Staff headed the General Staff Branch which dealt with military policy, plans of operations for the defence of India, the organisation and distribution of the army for internal security and external defence, in accordance with the policy of Government, the collection and distribution of intelligence, the supervision of the training of the army, war regulations, the education of soldiers and the inter-communication services.

The Adjutant General's Branch was responsible for all matters related to the raising, organising and maintenance of the military force, discipline, military and internal law, the welfare of soldiers, personal and ceremonial matters, prisoners of war, pay and pension questions, recruiting, mobilisation and dembolisation.

The Quartermaster General's Branch was concerned with the specification, provision, inspection, maintenance and issue of supplies, i.e., food, forage, fuel, clothing, armaments, ammunition, equipment, general stores and material, and reserves of these articles, transportation, movement and quartering of troops, military farms, military works, the remount and veterinary services, cantonment administration and regimental institutes.

Different Arms and Services

The Indian Army consisted of two branches - Combatant and Non-combatant. The Combatant branch consisted of the Infantry (including the Pioneers), Artillery, Cavalry, Sappers and Miners, and Signals. The Non-combatant branch consisted of the Supply and Transport Corps, Indian Medical Services, Ordnance Services, Remount Services and Veterinary Services. The strength of the combatant troops of the Indian Army on August 1, 1914 was 155,423 men.[23]

The Indian Infantry (including the Pioneers)

At the outbreak of the First World War, the Indian Army had 118 regiments of Infantry and Pioneers.[24] Each regiment had 1 battalion, except and 39th Garhwal Rifles and ten Gurkha regiments, each of which consisted of two battalions. The single battalion regiments were chained together in groups of 2 or 3 units.[25] Each group had a permanent regimental centre, where one of the battalions was always located. A soldier of the battalion was liable to serve in any other battalion of the group. During emergency, the regimental centre was employed to reinforce the other units of the group.

Practically, these linked battalions were independent of each other. Whenever they proceeded on service, each of them left a self-contained depot, comprising 1 or 2 British Officers (BOs), some administrative clerical staff, recruits, sick men and other surplus to war establishment.[26] Each depot was responsible for enrolment and training of its new recruits. It also maintained the records of its battalion.

The Pioneers were those infantry battalions which were specially trained for road repairing and making and digging trenches. They accompanied the infantry battalions. The composition of the Pioneer battalions and the Infantry battalions was similar.

A battalion was commanded by a Colonel or Lieutenant Colenel.[27] Each battalion had as its Second in Command a Lieutenant Colonel or a Major. In 1914, there were five different strengths of battalions, varying between 600 and 912 (of 10s and 10 Rs.) but most of the battalions had the following establishment:[28]

British Officers (BOs)	-	14	
Indian Officers (IOs)	-	16 }	912
Indian Other Ranks (IORs)	-	896}	

This establishment consisted of the Commandant, the Adjutant and Quartermaster and 8 Companies.[29] A maxim gun section was also included in the battalions of field army.[30] For the purpose of training, 2 companies were linked together and known as a double company. Thus, a battalion consisted of 4 double companies. Each double company was commanded by a Lieutenant Colonel, Major or a Captain. Each double company commander was assisted by the double company officers. In 1907, a company was commanded by a Subedar, an Indian Officer.[31] It appears that no change on this score had been made before 1914 and Subedars remained commanders of companies.

The Indian Cavalry

In 1914, the Indian Army had 39 regiments of cavalry,[32] besides the Bodyguards of His Excellency the Governor-General. On August 1, 1914 the Indian Cavalry consisted of 560 British Officers and 24,476 Other Ranks.[33] There were two types of Cavalry regiments -*non-Silladar* and *Silladar*.

In the *non-Silladar* cavalry regiments the needs of the soldiers were supplied by the Government. Three of the thirty-nine regiments of the Indian cavalry were organised on the *non-Silladar* system. They were the 26th King George's Own Light Cavalry, the 27th Light Cavalry and the 28th Light Cavalry.[34]

The remaining 36 regiments of the Indian cavalry were organised on the *Silladar* system. As mentioned earlier, under this system the individual soldiers supplied and maintained his horse, clothing, equipment and arms (other than rifle) receiving in return a higher rate of pay than the *non-Silladar* soldier. The more wealthy and influential *Silladars* were also allowed to enlist fellow countrymen, who were too poor to provide their own horses and equipment. The men who were so enlisted were known as *Bargirs* and were equipped and maintained at the expense of their more fortunate patrons, who in turn drew a recognised proportion of the pay of their *Bargirs*.

Before the war, the Colonel commanding an Indian cavalry regiment used to receive an annual grant of money from the Indian Government in lump sum to maintain the regiment. The *Sowar* (soldier) paid for his horse and equipment and on his discharge from the regiment, his *Assami* as it was called, was valued and a lump sum was paid to the soldier.[35] His horse and equipment remained with the regiment.

The powers of the Colonel commanding a regiment were immense. He was free to buy horses and rations for his men. He would decide from which part of India his men would be recruited and he could actually decide how he would arm his regiment. He would decide whether they were to be lancers or light or heavy cavalry.

The sanctioned strength of each regiment was 14 British Officers and 620 Indian Other Ranks.[36] Each regiment consisted of four squadrons of identical composition, each of which had to furnish a proportion of specialists when required. Each regiment was commanded by a Lieutenant Colonel or a Major. A squadron was commanded by an officer of the rank of Lieutenant Colonel, Major or Captain.[37] As each regiment consisted of four squadrons of identical composition, the strength of each squadron would work out to 3 or 4 British Officers and 155 Indian Other Ranks.

The Indian Artillery

The strength of the Indian Artillery on August 1, 1914 was 4,160 men which included 67 British Officers.[38] The Indian Artillery had 12 Batteries [39] of Mountain Artillery. Besides these 12 batteries, the Indian Artillery had one corps of the Indian Coast Artillery consisting of 379 Indian Other Ranks.[40] The unit was immobile and was meant to defend the coast.

A mountain battery had six 10-pounder guns. The sanctioned strength of a battery was 328 men, which included 5 British Officers and 323 Indian other ranks.[41] As the establishments of Horse, Field, Heavy, Mountain and Garrison batteries were similar,[42] it appears that a Mountain battery like a field battery was commanded by a Major, who had battery staff consisting of a second in command (Captain), a Sergeant-Major, a Quarter Master Sergeant, Signallers, Trumpeteers etc,[43] but these men did not form a separate permanent battery headquarters.

A battery was composed of 3 sections. The establishment of a battery was the sum total of the establishments of its 3 sections.[44] Therefore, it appears that the strength of a section was 1 or 2 British Officers and 107 or 108 Indian Other Ranks. Each section had 2 guns (10 pounders) with limbers and four ammunition wagons.[45] A section was commanded by a Subaltern.[46]

A section of battery was composed of 2 sub-sections.[47] A sub-section was the smallest self-contained tactical unit. A sub-section consisted of a gun with limber, and two ammunition wagons.[48] To carry its gun and two ammunition wagons, a sub-section had three 6-horsed teams. The strength of the personal of the sub-section was decided by the number of gunners required to work the gun, and by the number of drivers required to manage the teams.[49] Besides, a sub-section had a few more men, who were required for the two General Service wagons allotted to the flanking sub-sections, for battery stores, for battery staff and as spare.

The Sappers and Miners

The Sappers and Miners were responsible for engineering work. The actual strength of the Sappers and Miners, on August 1, 1914 was 67 British Officers, 159 British Other Ranks and 4,792 Indian Other Ranks.[50] In 1914, there were three corps of Sappers and Miners; namely, the 1st King George's Own Sappers and Miners, the 2nd Queen Victoria's Own Sappers and Miners and the 3rd Sappers and Miners. Each of these corps was commanded by a Lieutenant colonel, who was assisted by two Majors.

Each of these corps had Headquarters and 3 Depot Companies, Field Companies, printing Section, Bridging Train Section and a Photo-litho Section. Some of them also maintained Railway Companies and a Defence Light Section. The sanctioned strength of the Headquarters and 3 Depot Companies was 6 British Officers, 8 British other ranks and 186 Indian other ranks.[51] The Headquarters' staff consisted of 4 British Officers, a Quartermaster and two officers taken from the Depot Companies.[52]

The sanctioned strength of field companies was 2 British Officers, 2 British other ranks and 101 Indian Other Ranks.[53] A company was composed of a Headquarters and 3 sections. Each section was so equipped as to undertake any work independently.

The Railway Company was meant to deal with railway work, i.e., repairing engines and railway lines etc. The sanctioned strength of a Railway Company was 3 British Officers and British other ranks and 196 Indian ranks.[54]

The Bridging Train section was meant to make floating bridges on rivers, canals etc. A section's sanctioned strength, in 1914, was 10 Indian Other Ranks.[55]

The printing section dealt with the printing work of the corps. In 1914, its sanctioned strength was 2 British other ranks and 4 Indian other ranks.[56]

Each Photo-litho section was composed of 2 British Officers and 4 Indian other ranks.[57] This section was responsible for photography and lithography work.

Each Defence Light Section consisted on 1 British Officer, 13 British other ranks, 249 Indian Other Ranks and 7 followers.[58] This section was meant for doing electric jobs.

Signal Service

In 1914, there were four divisional signal companies and one wireless section.[59] These were affiliated to the Sappers and Miners but formed a separate part. For administrative purpose, they were independent of the Sappers and Miners. The strength of the Indian Signal Service on August 1, 1914 was 22 British Officers, 207 British Other Ranks and 375 Indian Other Ranks.[60]

Each Divisional Signal Company consisted of 5 British Officers, 44 British other ranks and 88 Indian ranks and 11 followers.[61] The Wireless Signal Company consisted of 1 British Officer and 10 British Other Ranks.[62] These companies were commanded by a Major or a Captain. On the outbreak of the war, it was found that some more companies had to be raised to meet the war requirement. For this purpose, a Signal Service Depot was formed, to train new recruits, at Kirkee, in October 1914. During the war many more units were raised.

The Telegraph in India were managed by the Telegraph Branch of the Posts of Telegraphs Department assisted by 600 military telegraph operators and 100 wireless operators, who were attached from the British units in India.[63]

The Supply and Transport Corps

The supply and Transport Corps in 1914 was administered by the Quartermaster General and was one of the principal services included in the Quartermaster General's charge.

The Supply branch responsible for rations for the Indian troops in certain localities, grain and fodder for army animals (excluding the animals of the *Silladar* Cavalry Regiments), fuel for the Indian troops, bedding and certain articles of clothing for troops and hospitals, and miscellaneous supplies such as cooking utensils, lamps, basins etc. In 1914, the total strength of this branch was 3,858 men including the followers.[64]

In 1914, at each of the principal cantonments in which British troops were stationed there was a supply depot in the charge of an officer of the Supply and Transport Corps, and there were smaller depots at out stations where there were British detachments. The reserves of food and clothing were held separately in nine reserve depots at the Headquarters of the divisions. A stores officer was posted at Cawnpore (now Kanpur), who purchased textiles, boots and other leather goods from local firms. The purchase of other items was made by the Station Commander of the division.

Before the war, the Transport branch had only animals and no mechanical vehicles. The strength of this Branch in 1914 was 19,914 men including followers.[65] The Transport branch had 2 main divisions - wheeled transport and pack transport. This service was meant to convey the stores and luggage of military forces operating in the field.

(1) Wheeled transport:

(a) Mules	...4	Cavalry Brigade Corps
	...3	Cavalry Brigade Cadres[66]
(b) Bullocks	...3	72 half troops of an aggregate 3,642 bullocks

(iii) Pack Transport :

(a) Mules	...17	Pack Corps
	...15	Pack Corps
(b) Camels	...8	*Silladar* Camel Corps
	4	Grantee Camel Corps

In addition to these, a certain amount of local mule transport was also maintained on an unorganised basis by certain divisions and brigades.

The Ordnance Services

The Ordnance Department was under the charge of the Director General of Ordnance. This Department consisted of 3 sections - the factory section, the stores section and the inspection section. Each section was placed under the control of a Director. The responsibility of this department was to supply the army munitions of war, such as small arms, guns, ammunition and other equipment of technical military character.

Before the war, there were seven main arsenals and seven factories, together with four or five small depots. The 7 main arsenals were responsible for the supply to the division or divisions allotted to them. The Ordnance Officer in charge of an arsenal was attached to the divisional staff with the designation of Assistant Director of Ordnance Services. His function was to coordinate the ordnance supply with the demand of the division.

The Indian Medical Services[67]

In 1914, the Indian Medical Service was administered by the Director of Medical Services in India. The Indian Medical Service had two main corps - Army Hospital Corps and Army Bearer Corps. Both the Corps had specific duties. The former treated patients while the latter carried patients to hospitals.

The regimental hospitals were not self-contained and patients had to arrange for their own food.[68] The staff of the hospital consisted of a medical officer, a sub-assistant surgeon, ward orderlies who were drawn from the combatant personnel of the regiment, and a few followers such as *bistis*, cooks, and sweepers.[69] The patient brought his own bedding and clothing and generally subsisted on his own rations. Fans were generally not provided. On the whole, those hospitals were not properly equipped.

The Remount and Veterinary Services

Before the war, Remount Service was administered by the Director General of the Remount Department, who was assisted by a Staff Veterinary Officer and his Personal Assistant. Besides, there were 17 Superintendents, 2 Assistant Superintendents and 9 Veterinary Officers.[70] This department was meant for purchasing, rearing and issuing remounts to the British cavalry, artillery and 3 non-*silladar* regiments of the Indian Army, and the supervision of horse, mule and donkey breeding in certain selected areas.

Before the war, the Army Veterinary Service chiefly took care of the animals of the British units. The responsibility for the veterinary care of animals of the Indian Army lay with the units. Each unit was responsible for the care of its own animals. In case of emergency, the Army Veterinary Service was called upon to look after the animals of the Indian units.

This department was administered by the Director of Veterinary Services. He was assisted by the Deputy Assistant Director. India was divided into three circles - Northern, Central and Southern. Each circle was in charge of an Inspecting Veterinary Officer. A Veterinary Assistant of an Indian unit belonged to that particular unit.

The Auxiliary Force

In 1914, there were a few volunteer regiments. They consisted of Europeans only. They were employed to relieve the regular regiments of their ordinary routine work but were limited to local boundaries.[71] Each Volunteer Regiment was given an adjutant from a regular regiment.[72] The Volunteers were not properly trained.

On July 1, 1914, the strength of the Reserve Force of Indian Army was 33,677 men.[73] These were distributed in the following manner:[74]

The Indian Artillery	...	928	men
The Indian Cavalry	...	1546	men
Sappers and Miners	...	1158	men
The Indian Infantry	...	30045	men

There were only about 40 officers in the Reserve Force, before the war.[75] They were divided into two branches - Cavalry and Infantry. The men of the Reserve Force were called up annually for training. They were trained with contemporary weapons.

Imperial Service Troops

The Imperial Service Troops consisted of the military forces raised and maintained by the rulers of the different Indian States. These rulers often lent their forces to the British Indian Government to assist them in different wars. In 1889 the Indian Government decided to allot a portion of troops of the states for the defence of the motherland and to fight alongwith the Indian Army troops.[76] The principles underlying the scheme were that the maintenance of these forces would be on entirely voluntary basis, and that these troops would be officered by Indians.[77] The Government of India only provided a staff of British officers, termed as the 'Military Advisers and Assistant Military Advisers' to assist and advise the Imperial

Service Troops in organisation and training. The head of this staff was the 'Military Adviser-in-Chief' of the Government of India, a senior military officer.

In 1914, before the war, 29 States[78] maintained Imperial Service Troops. The total strength of all ranks was as follows:[79]

Cavalry	...	7,673
Infantry	...	10,298
Artillery	...	373
Sappers	...	741
Signals	...	34
Camel Corps	...	673
Transport Corps	...	2,723
	Total	22,515

The organisation of the troops of different states differed greatly. In the infantry, the platoon and company system existed in a few states only.[80] The cavalry too was not organised on any uniform basis. The strengths of units of different states differed. The working strength of each unit of sappers was two thirds that of a regular unit.[81]

The efficiency of troops differed from state to state. Some of them were better trained while others were poorly trained. Their peace and war establishments were different from those of the corresponding units of the Indian Army.

An Assessment of the Indian Army

The organisation, training and equipment of the Indian Army were defective in many ways. Though many schemes were considered for the improvement of the Indian Army, yet before the First World War they were not fully implemented.

The British Parliament controlled the Government of India through the Indian Office. The business of the British Parliament was too great and too complex to enable it to take decisions quickly on Indian military matters. Moreover, most of the members of the British Parliament were not very well aware of the Indian conditions, and so whenever any subject pertaining to the Indian Army was taken up, it became difficult for them to arrive at a balanced decision. Some of the recommendations for the improvement of the Indian Army could not be implemented because the British Parliament did not agree to them. Besides, the Commander-in-Chief of the Indian Army could communicate to the War Office only through the India Office. These practices led to delays and after the war, the Esher Committee recommended the abolition of both the above mentioned practices.

The Commander-in-Chief had to perform multifarious duties. There was no organisation to assist him in the performance of his administrative duties. This adversely affected the efficiency of the Indian Army. Of course, the Defence Committee existed but it was only a consultative body and had no administrative functions. In addition, the Commander-in-Chief had to look after the work of the Military Supply Department, which was directly under him. Hence, it was not possible for the C-in-C to dispose off even routine matters quickly.

Lord Kitchener's scheme had intended that each divisional area would include one or more definite war formations together with the garrison troops necessary for the internal security of the area. However, as it involved wholesale readjustment of accommodation at high expenditure, it was never completed. The troops allotted for internal security, were, in many cases, stationed outside their respective areas.[82] These troops could not easily be concentrated at one place for training. The result was that the troops could not be given adequate and continuous training.

The elimination of administrative responsibilities from the higher command of armies imposed an additional burden on Army Headquarters, where the administrative machine was clogged by a mass of minor detail.[83] The direct dealing of Army Headquarters with the divisions, for administrative matters, led to delays in routine work.

The Divisional Commanders were overwhelmed by large administrative responsibilities imposed on them, and their staffs were insufficient to meet the immediate requirements of administration or to provide for continuity on mobilization.[84] Therefore, they were unable to devote sufficient attention to their primary duty, the training of troops for war.

The composition of the divisions was not adequate. Two of the nine divisions had no Mountain Artillery Brigades. The divisions did not contain adequate numbers of Sappers and Miners. A division had only 2 companies of Sappers and Miners but war experience showed that at least 3 companies were required.[85]

The Indian Infantry battalions were linked in groups though in fact they were independent of each other. Each of them left behind its own depot, composed of 1 or 2 British Officers, some administrative and clerical staff, recruits and sick men and others, surplus to the war establishment.[86] Each depot enrolled and maintained its own recruits and maintained the records of its battalion. This meant that many trained officers and soldiers were unable to go on field service. As each depot trained its own recruits under its own officers, uniformity in training could not be achieved. The standard of training and efficiency differed from one depot to another. The strength of each battalion was not the same. The strength of Indian Ranks ranged between 600 and 912. On distribution of the battalions to the different theatres, and on mobilisation, this had to be kept in mind.

In 1914, there were 36 *Silladar* regiments and only 3 *non-Silladar* regiments. The *silladar* system had many drawbacks. The main drawback was lack of standardisation. Every commandant was at liberty to fix his own pattern of equipment other than firearms and the stamp of the animal. To a large extent the standard of efficiency of a unit depended on the business capacity of the Commanding Officer, which was not always par with his soldierly qualifications.[87] In this system, as every soldier had to pay for his horse at the time of enlistment, it was difficult to procure large numbers of reinforcements. The *Silladar* regiments were responsible for their pastures and breeding of their horses. The soldiers, therefore, had to devote a lot of time to the execution of these jobs.[88]

The Indian Artillery consisted of only Mountain batteries which were useful only in hilly regions, and one corps of coast artillery. It had no Field, Horse or Heavy artillery. The batteries had only one type of gun —the 10 pounders. They had no Howitzers in 1914, lacking a very important weapon of war.

The sanctioned strength of a Sapper and Miner Company was not sufficient.[89] The Headquarters of a Sapper and Miner Company was understaffed for the work they had to perform.[90] This led to delays. There were no well organised electrical and mechanical services.[91] During the war their absence was badly felt, specially on the lines of communication.

The Indian Signal Service was also not well organised. There were only 4 divisional companies and one wireless section. Before the war the total strength was only 604 men including British Officers. This number of men was quite insufficient to carry out its work.

Before the war, the Supply service was not responsible for the rations of the Indian troops, except in certain cases. The transport branch had only animals. It had no mechanical transport service. This hampered the mobility of the army.

The strength of the Reserve Force was again insufficient. The Artillery, Cavalry and Sappers and Miners branches had only a small number of men. It appears from the figures of the Reserve Force that the Signal

Branch had no reserves. The officers in the Reserve Force numbered only 40. They belonged either to Infantry or Cavalry.[92] The other branches had no officers in the Reserve Force.

The Imperial Service troops were not organised on a uniform basis. The company system had not been introduced throughout the Infantry.[93] The units were also not of one size. This was the case in every branch. Many ruling princes maintained small units, and it was difficult to amalgamate them to form a battalion of infantry or brigade of cavalry as their training differed within the units as also in respect of the Indian Army. There was also no system of reserves for the Imperial Service Troops.[94]

The soldiers of the Indian Army lacked proper training and techniques of warfare in differing geographical conditions. They were also probably not aware of the effects on weapons of different temperatures, heights etc.

Thus, in 1914, not only was the organisation of the Indian Army defective, but the training of the officers and men was also inadequate, apart from lacking weapons already in use in the European armies.

It was with this kind of organisation, in-built deficiencies and insufficient training and equipment, that the Indian Army was ordered to fight for the Allied cause in World War I.

NOTES

1. *The Army in India and its Evolution,* compiled by the Government of India, Calcutta, 1924, p.3
2. J.W.Fortesque, *A History of the British Army* (Vol.2), London, 1899, p.172
3. *The Army in India and its Evolution, op.cit.*, p.6
4. *Ibid.*, p.7
5. *Ibid.*, p.10..
6. S.D. Pradhan, 'Organisation of the Indian Army on the Eve of the Outbreak of the First World War', *U.S.I. Journal* (The Journal of the United Service Institution of India), Jan-Mar 1972, New Delhi, p.63.
7. *Ibid.*
8. Government of India, *Report. Army in India Committee,* Part III, p.1
9. *Ibid.*
10. *Ibid.*

11. *The Army in India and its Evolution, op.cit.* p.30. The detailed organisation of the Army is shown in Appendix A.
12. Lord F.S. Roberts, *Forty-one Years in India,* Vol. II, London, 1897, p.363.
13. General Sir O' Moore Creagh, *Indian Studies,* London, p.223.
14. S.P. Cohen, *The Indian Army,* London, 1971, p.42.
15. Recruiting in Indian Before and During the War of 1914-1918 Army Headquarters, India, 1919.
16. S.D. Pradhan, 'The Indian Army and the First World War' in D.C. Ellinwood and S.D. Pradhan eds.) *India and World War I,* New Delhi, 1978, p.57.
17. *Report, Army in India Committee, op.cit.,* Part I, Sec. 1, p.4.
18. *The Army in India and its Evolution, op.cit.,* p.54.
19. *Report, Army in India Committee, op.cit.,* Part I, sec. III, p.6.
20. *Ibid.,* Part II, Sec. I, p.6.
21. *The Army in India and its Evolution, op.cit.,* p.53.
22. *Ibid.*
23. *The Army in India and its Evolution, op.cit.,* p. 219
24. Government of India, *Indian Army List,* October 1914, pp. 469-605
25. *Ibid.,* pp. 469-605
26. *The Army in India and its Evolution, op.cit.,* pp.99-100.
27. *Indian Army List, op.cit.,* pp.469-605.
28. *The Army in India and its Evolution, op.cit.,* p.102.
29. *Indian Army List, op.cit.,* pp. 469-605.
30. The Army in India and its Evolution, op.cit., p.102.
31. E.Collen, *The Indian Army - A Sketch of Its History and Organisation,* London, 1907, p.50.
32. *The Army in India and its Evolution, op.cit.,* p.219.
33. *Ibid.*
34. *Ibid.,* p. 91
35. F. Guest, *The Indian Cavalryman,* London, 1959, p.90.
36. *The Army in India and Its Evolution, op.cit.,* p. 234.
37. *Indian Army List, op. cit.,* pp. 405-448.
38. *The Army in India and its Evolution, op.cit.,* p.219.
39. M.D., H.S., *Summary, Army in India,* p.2.
40. *The Army in India and its Evolution, op.cit.* p.231.
41. *Ibld.*
42. *Ibid.,* p. 70.
43. *Ibid.,* p.71.
44. *Ibid.*

45. M.D., H.S., *Proceedings, Advisory Council,* Vol.2, Annexure B.p.1.
46. *Ibid.*
47. *The Army in India and its Evolution,* op.cit., p. 71.
48. *Ibid.*, p.70.
49. *Ibid.*, p.70.
50. *Ibid.*, p. 219
51. *Ibid.*, p.232.
52. M.D., H.S., *Report, Sappers and Miners Organisation;* p. 11.
53. *The Army in India and its Evolution, op.cit.*, p.232.
54. *Ibid.*
55. *Ibid.*
56. *Ibid.*
57. *Ibid.*
58. *Ibid.*, p. 233.
59. *Ibid.*, p.109.
60. *Ibid.*, p.219.
61. *Ibid.*, p.219.
62. *Ibid.*, p.233.
63. *Report, Army in India Committe, op.cit.*, Part IV, Sec. 1, p.19
64. *The Army in India and its Evolution*, op.cit., p.128.
65. *Ibid.*, p.131.
66. *Ibid.*, p. 130. The crops were those units which were maintained in peace time at full war strength, while the cadres were those units which were maintained in the form of a nucleus capable of fairly rapid expansion to full strength on mobilisation.
67. For a fuller account see D.R. Thaper, *The Morale Builders,* Bombay, 1965.
68. In regimental hospitals there was no fooding arrangement for patients.
69. *The Army in India and its Evolution, op. cit.*, p. 121.
70. *Ibid.*, p. 143.
71. *Ibid.*, p. 151.
72. *Ibid.*
73. M.D., H.S. *Summary, Army in India,* p.4.
74. *Ibid.*
75. *Report, Army in India Committee, op.cit.* Part VIII, p.85.
76. M.D.,. H.S. *Report, Imperial Service Troops for 1919-1920,* File No. 1311/H/I, p.1.
77. *Ibid.*
78. *The Army in India and its Evolution, op.cit.*, p.156.

79. *Ibid.*
80. M.D., H.S., *Report, Imperial Service Troops*, p.13.
81. *Ibid.*, p.4
82. *Report, Army in India Committee*, *op.cit.*, p. 1.
83. *Ibid.*, p.2.
84. *Ibid.*, p.2.
85. *Ibid.*, p. 28.
86. *The Army in India and Its Evolution*, *op.cit.*, pp.99-100.
87. M.D., H.S., *Proceedings, Advisory Council*, Vol. I, p.8
88. *Ibid.*, p.19.
89. *Report, Army in India Committee*, *op.cit.*, Part IV, Sec. IV, p.28.
90. M.D., H.S., *Report, Sappers and Miners Organisation*, p.11
91. *Ibid.*, p.13.
92. *Report, Army in India Committee*, *op.cit.*, Part VIII, p. 85.
93. M.D., H.S., *Report, Imperial Service Troops*, p.13.
94. *Ibid.*, p. 14

2

Composition of the Rival Forces

Composition of the Indian Expeditionary Force

As soon as the First World War broke out, the East African problem came into the limelight. The peculiar situation of German East Africa, in the African Continent, forced the British Government to take action immediately. Four British protectorates bordered German East Africa - Uganda (1894) and British East Africa (1886) in the north, and Northern Rhodesia (1893) and Nyasaland (1891) in the south[1]. The British Government anticipated an attack from German East Africa[2], which would not only endanger the neighbouring British Protectorates but also prove detrimental to British trade with neighbouring territories. Moreover, the British Government realised that their occupation of German East Africa would not only link her Protectorates in Africa and ensure the safety of her commerce and trade but would also give her a good naval base, markets and and a territory rich in raw materials.[3]

Before the British Government could decide to attack German East Africa, it was necessary to strengthen her forces in the Protectorates. On August 4, 1914, the Governor-General of British East Africa sent a telegram to the Colonial Office, then responsible for defence matters concerning the Protectorates, explaining the weak position of British East Africa[4]. The Colonial Office found it expedient to send some troops there to strengthen its defences. In every previous emergency in East Africa, and troops required to supplement local forces were called for from India[5]. As earlier, the Colonial Office requested the Government of India to spare a brigade of Indian Infantry and other troops for service in British East Africa[6].

Simultaneously, the Offensive Sub-Committee (then formed for the consideration of combined operations in foreign territory)[7] "recommended the despatch of an expedition from India against the port of Dar-es-Salaam, a potential hostile naval base, the capture of which would facilitate the protection of commerce and the defence of neighbouring British possessions."[8] Hence, another request was made to the Government of India to spare more troops for the capture of Dar-es-Salaam.

The Government of India complied with the demand, and decided to send two forces tc East Africa - one to reinforce the troops in British East Africa, and another for operations against German East Africa. The former was known as the Indian Expeditionary Force 'C', (IEF 'C') while the latter was known as the Indian Expeditionary Force 'B' (IEF 'B').

Force 'C' was given priority because the Germans had already gone on the offensive against British East Africa[9]. Force 'C' was commanded by Colonel (later Brigadier General) J.M. Stewart.[10] This force consisted of the Brigade Headquarters, the 29th Punjabis and 2 battalions of the Imperial Service Troops composed of Jind, Rampur, Bharatpur and Kapurthala Infantry Troops (4 companies each)[11].

After reaching Mombasa, Stewart found that some artillery units were also required and a request for them was made to India[13]. To meet this requirement, two voluntary units were raised - the Calcutta battery and the Maxim Gun Company[14]. These two, along with the 17th Mountain Battery, two battalions of the Imperial Service Infantry and a detachment of the 29th Punjabis sailed from Bombay to British East Africa on September, 20, 1914 and became part of IEF 'C'[15]. The total strength of these units was 2, 165 men excluding followers[16]. Whenever the effective strength of these units went down, more men were sent to reinforce the army.

When it received a demand for a force to be sent to German East Africa for capturing it, the Government of India hastened to form such a force. The Army Department under the Viceroy was informed on August 8, 1914 by telegram from the Secretary of State for India, about the mode of formation of the force. It read: "Such a force will be managed by India entirely, in communication with the War Office in a similar manner to the China Expedition."[17] On August 9, 1914, the Secretary of State sent another telegram to the Viceroy stating the number of troops required for German East Africa, *i.e.* seven battalions of Indian troops including the Imperial Service, one Mountain Battery, one Company of Sappers, a Howitzer Battery and a Cavalry detachment.[18]

On August 18, 1914 it was decided that Force 'B' would consist of the 16th Infantry Brigade complete, one Pioneer Battalion of Faridkot Sappers, three Imperial Service Battalions, one Mountain Battery and possibly some heavy guns[19]. Brigadier General A.E. Aitken was appointed Commander of this force.[20] Later, two Railway companies (25th and 26th) were also allotted to this force.[21]

While the preparations were going on for the despatch of Force 'B', the situation in Europe had deteriorated for the Allies. Therefore, the despatch of the force was postponed because it was found unjustifiable at a moment when other theatres, regarded as vital, needed every able man and gun.[23] The expedition, however, was not cancelled and by the beginning of September 1914 when the situation in the Western theatre improved and in the Eastern waters it appeared more threatening with the German cruiser *Königsberg* (fitted with 4.1" machine guns) unlocated and six other German cruisers which had been in the Pacific or South Atlantic expected to appear in the Indian Ocean,[24] threatening the line of communications from England to the East, it became essential to deprive the Germans of their naval base in the Indian Ocean. The British resumed the German East African project.

The Secretary of State for India asked the Viceroy on September 9, to retain Force 'B' intact.[25] Meanwhile, the 16th Infantry Brigade had been assigned to the Persian Gulf.[26] On September 10, 1914 the Viceroy informed the Secretary of State about the probable new composition of Force 'B'. According to him the Force 'B' was to be composed of the Bangalore Brigade comprising the 63rd Carnatics raised to field service strength, the Royal North Lancaster regiment, the 98th Infantry, the 101st Grenadiers, the 28th Mountain Battery, the 61st Pioneers, a Kashmir battalion (Imperial Service Troops), the Faridkot Sappers, a composite battalion of Gwalior and Nabha Infantry and the 13th Rajputs.[27] The telegram also asked the of State to confirm if the force also required the services of two Railway Companies. The Secretary of State informed him on September 16, 1914 that the addition of Railway Companies was advisable.[28] Consequently, the Viceroy allotted the 25th and 26th Railway Companies to the force.[29] It was also decided that Brigadier-General Aitken would command the force and Brigadier-General Wapshare and Colonel Tighe would accompany him.[30] Brigadier General Wapshare was given command of the Bangalore Brigade[31] while Colonel Tighe was given command of the Imperial Service Brigade.[32]

On September 22, 1914 the Viceroy intimated the Secretary of State that he hoped to despatch Force 'B' in October. It was composed of the following units:

(i) Bangalore Brigade comprising:
   2nd Battalion, Loyal North Lancashire Regiment
   63rd Carnatics
   98 Infantry
   101st Grenadiers
   61st Pioneers

(ii) Imperial Service Brigade comprising:
   2nd Kashmir Rifles
   13th Rajputs

(iii) Composite battalions of 4 companies of the 3rd Gwalior infantry and 4 companies of the 3rd Kashmir Rifles

(iv) Other units of the Force:
   Gun detachment for Armoured Train
   28th Mountain Battery
   Faridkot Sappers
   The 25th and 26th Railway Companies
   Two Brigade Sections Signal Company
   Bridging Train
   Ambulance and Supply details
   Printing and Litho Sections
   Punjab Coolie Corps
   and some other det
   achments for administrative purposes.

The units of Force 'B' were despatched to East Africa from Bombay and Karachi on October 16 and 17, 1914, respectively.[34] This force arrived off Mombasa on October 31, 1914 and from there proceeded towards Tanga on November 1, 1914.[35] The total strength of Force 'B' was 7,972 men excluding followers[36].

After operations in East Africa had begun, owing to the administrative and tactical difficulties, it was found inexpedient to keep Forces 'B' and 'C' separate and so these forces were combined. The combined force came to be known as Force 'B' in early December 1914.[37]

The Force 'B' received occasionally new units during course of the war. In January 1915, one squadron 17th Canatry and 130th Baluchis (Jacob Rifles) were sent from India.[38] One company of the 130th Baluchis having beend disbanded for insubordination at Rangoon, the battalion was brought upto the strength by attaching one company from the 46th

Punjabis.[39] The strengths of the 17th Canatry and the 130th Baluchis was 127 and 447 men respectively.[40] Another unit was sent to East Africa in December 1915. This was the 17th Infantry, then stationed at Mauritius. It was ordered to go to East Africa and join Force 'B' there. It reached Kilindini on December 16, 1915. Its strength was 747 men.[41]

In January 1916, it was decided to make an attack on the Kilimanjaro area. For this attack, more units were required. At this juncture, most of the units to reinforce the British troops in East Africa came from the Union of South Africa. However, two units were also sent from India. They were the 40th Pathans and the 129th Baluchis. The 40th Pathans reached East Africa (Kilindini) on January 6, 1916[42] and the 129th Baluchis reached there on January 8.[49] The 129th Baluchis were at that time in France and had to be withdrawn from there. The strengths of the 40th Pathans and the 129th Baluchis were 853 and 844 men, respectively.[44]

In the same month one more unit - the 5th Light Infantry - was sanctioned for East Africa. The Commander-in-Chief in India was informed by the Secretary, War Office, London, about the itinerary of the 5th Light Infantry on February 1, 1916. According to the depatch, the unit was to reach Mombasa on March 6.[46] However landed there two days earlier on March 4, 1916.[46] It was composed of seasoned soldiers with recent battle experience.[47] The strength of the 5th Light Infantry was 525 men excluding followers.[48]

Two Railway Companies were raised in March 1915 in Indian to meet the additional demand for Railway Companies in East Africa. The 27th and the 28th Railway Companies were raised and sent to East Africa by April of 1916.[49] The effective strengths of the 27th and the 28th Railway Companies were 211 and 233 men, respectively.[50]

By June 1916, the 29th Punjabis were exhausted. Most of the soldiers were sick and unable to fight. Therefore, it was decided to withdraw this unit. In exchange for the 29th Punjabis, a new unit - the 57th Wilde's Rifles (Frontier Force) - was sent to East Africa. The 57th Wilde Rifles (or the 57th Rifles) landed at Mombasa on July 12, 1916.[51] The strength of this unit was 886 men excluding followers.[52] Another battalion, the 30th Punjabis (about 1040 men) reached East Africa in October 1916.[53]

At the end of 1916, two more Mountain batteries reached East Africa from India. They were the 1st Kashmir Mountain Battery, which disembarked at Dar-es-Salaam on December 5, and the 22nd Mountain Battery which reached Kilwa on December 18.[54] Their strengths were about 191 and 243 men, respectively, excluding followers.[55]

In 1917, one more Mountain Battery - the 24th Mountain Battery - was sent to East Africa. It disembarked at Dar-es-Salaam on April 26, 1917.[56] The strength of this unit was about 275 men excluding followers[57]

All the units sent to East Africa from India were regarded unsuitable for service in the European theatre because they were either ill-equipped or ill-trained or had been exhausted in recent combat. Therefore, these units forming a major part of the British Force in East African Campaign were not the best units of India. Altogether, the units sent to East Africa were the 29th Punjabis, the 30th Punjabis, the 63rd Carnatics, the 98th Infantry, the 61st Pioneers, the 129th Baluchis, the 130th Baluchis, the 17th Infantry, the 40th Pathans, the 57th Rifles, the Calcutta Battery, the Maxim Gun company, the 27th Mountain Battery, the 28th Mountain Battery, the 25th, 26th, 27th and 28th Railway Companies, one composite battalion of the Jind and Rampur Infantries (four companies each), one composite battalion of the Bharatpur and Kapurthala Infantries (four companies each), one composite battalion of the 3rd Gwalior and the 3rd Kashmir (four companies each), the 13th Rajputs, the Faridkot Sappers, the 1st Kashmir Mountain battery, and the 22nd the 25th Mountain batteries. Besides these, some Signals sections and Bridging Train sections, were also sent to East Africa from India. The total number of soldiers, sent from India was 17, 525 men.[58]

In addition to these units, there were many other units on the British side. There were two local battalions, known as the King's African Rifles and a few British units[60]. Moreover, within British Africa, the settlers had formed a Corps known as the East African Mounted Rifles, and another Mounted Corps, the Belfield's Scouts[61]. But the largest number of units which poured into this theatre of war later, came from the Union of South Africa - two infantry brigades, one mounted brigade, and 5 batteries of Field Artillery, totalling about 18,700 men by March 1916.[62] The British force received reinforcements from time to time and by December 1916 its total strength had risen 98,580 men.[63]

Weapons used by the Indian Units

The rifles used by the Indian soldiers were of two types - M.L.E. (Martini Le Enfield) Mark I and S.M.L.E. (Short Magazine Le Enfield). Force 'C' was armed with M.L.E. Rifles[64] while Force 'B' was given S.M.L.E. Rifles.[65] Most of the units in southern India were armed with the obsolete converted long M.L.E. Rifles before mobilisation. Just before mobilisation, the units of the IEF 'B' were re-armed with the S.M.L.E.

Rifles. Besides rifles, the Indian units used Lewis guns, Machine Guns, 10-pounders, 12-pounders, 2.75 inch guns and 3.7 inch Howitzers.

The Martini Le Enfield (MLE) Rifle was longer than the SMLE type of rifle, and was supposed to be inferior to the latter. It could fire up to 40 rounds per minute without taking aim.[66] These rifles were called 1914 pattern rifles. The length of a rifle of the 1914 pattern without bayonet was 3 feet 101/4 inches and with bayonet it was 5 feet 31/4 inches. The weight of the rifle with bayonet was 10 lbs. 8 oz. Its calibre was .303 inch. It had a vertical fixed box type magazine which could accommodate 5 cartridges at the maximum. The cartridge used in it was 3.05 inch long and weighed 415 grains. Its barrel was rifled.[67]

The Short Magazine Le Enfield (SMLE) Rifle was 3 feet 81/2 inches long without bayonet and 5 feet 2 inches long with bayonet and it weighed 9lbs. 101/2 oz. with bayonet. Its calibre was .303 inch. It had a detachable verticle box type magazine which could accommodate 10 cartridges at the maximum. The cartridges used in it were of two types - Mark VI and Mark VII, both 3.05 inch long. The Mark VI weighed 415 grains and the Mark VII weighed 381 grains. Its barrel too was rifled.[68]

The Lewis gun was an infantry weapon which can be placed between rifles and Machine guns. A Lewis gun was lighter than a Machine gun, weighing 26 lbs. Its biped (stand) weighed an additional 3 lbs. Its barrel was cooled by an air cooling system. A Lewis gun could fire 400 to 600 rounds per minute. It could fire up to 800 yards accurately, but could not keep firing continuously like a Machine Gun as its barrel grew too hot after a few seconds.[69]

The Machine Guns used in World War I were of two types - Maxim guns and Vickers guns.[70] The Maxim gun weighed 60 lbs. And its calibre was .303 inch. A Maxim could fire up to 500 rounds per minute. The cooling arrangement of Maxim guns was based on a water system.[71] The Vickers gun weighed 28 lbs. And its calibre, too, was .303 inch. A Vickers gun could fire upto 500 rounds per minute. The cooling arrangement of Vickers guns was also based on a water system.[72]

Unfortunately, of the Indian battalions which embarked for East Africa, only the 101st Grenadiers and the 61st KGO. Pioneers were trained in the use of Machine guns before 1914.[73] The other battalions were given

Machine guns at the time of embarkation. As such most of the soldiers at the time of embarkation, were not acquainted with the use of Machine guns.

The Indian artillery batteries were equipped with 10-pounder guns at the time of outbreak of the First World War.[74] In the beginning, the guns were carried on mules. In 1915, one section of each battery was given a carrier transport.[75] From the official range table it is evident that these guns used sharpnel type projectiles, each weighing 10 lbs.[76] Its maximum range was 6,000 yards.

The Calcutta Battery was armed with 12-pounder guns.[77] Its projectile also was of sharpnel type, weighing 12 lbs. Its maximum range was about 6,000 yards[78]. These guns performed excellently in the Campaign.

The 22nd Mountain Battery, which had reached East Africa on December 18, 1916, was given four 2.75 inch guns at the end of August 1917.[79] According to the official Range Table of 2.75 inch gun, the projectile of the gun was of sharpnel type weighing 121/2 lbs and its maximum range was 5,800 yards.[80]

The 22nd Mountain Battery got 3.7 inch Howitzers in January 1918 in exchange for its 2.75 inch guns.[81] According to the official Range Table the projectiles of the Howitzer were of two types - shrapnel and star shell - each weighing 191/2 lbs. The same table shows that its maximum range was 6,000 yards.[82]

Composition of the German Force

According to Vorbeck, German East Africa had, at the time of the outbreak of the First World War, 216 Europeans and 2,540 Askaris[83] (native soldiers), who formed the Protective Force. However, according to British intelligence sources, there were 261 Europeans and 2,478 Askaris.[84] Crowe wrote that the number of Askaris was about 2,500.[85] Vorbeck wrote later that there were only 218 whites and 2,542 Askaris.[86] The figures of Vorbeck appear more accurate than the other's. The Protective Force was known as the German Schutztruppe.

The German Schutztruppe consisted of fourteen companies.[87] According to British intelligence sources, each company consisted of 3 or 4 European Officers and 162 Native soldiers, and had 2 light field guns and 3 Machnie guns, before the outbreak of the war.[88] According to Crowe, each company consisted of 162 men (it appears that he gave the number of Askaris only) and had 2 to 4 Machine guns[89]. According to the German

Commander's statement, just before the war, each company was brought upto an establishment of about 16 Europeans, 160 Askaris and 2 Machine Guns.[90] The above figures show more or less the same number of Askaris but the numbers of Europeans differ.

Each company was organised in 3 platoons, each of which consisted of 50 men. In each company there was a section of 2 to 4 Machine guns. The company was a self-contained unit with its transport consisting entirely of porters, of whom some 15 per cent were armed with rifles as a reserve on which to draw in case of necessity. There were 322 porters to a company. In addition to ammunition and supplies, they carried a collapsible boat for crossing rivers, reserves of clothing and boots, the Machine guns and the equipment connected with them and medical stores. Besides the porters, there were the Askari boys, who were the batman of the Askaris. They were employed in the proportion of one to every two Askaris.[91] However, according Vorbeck and a British Officer, Brigadier General Collyer, the number of carriers (porters) allotted to each Company was about 250.[92]

In addition to these 14 companies, there was one signalling detachment consisting of 30 men.[93] For training and recruiting purposes, there was a recruiting depot, which was situated at Dar-es-Salaam and consisted of 160 men.[94]

German East Africa had an armed Police Force which consisted of 45 Europeans and 2,154 Askaris.[95] Shortly after the outbreak of War, the Protectorate Police Force was placed under the military authority.

Before the war, the Volunteer Rifle Corps was being formed in Ushambara country around the Kilimanjaro, near the Meru Mountainst.[96] The Corps was intended to include all the Germans capable of bearing arms in this area. The Corps trained people in handling weapons and acquainted them with the basic essentials of warfare. The bulk of the three thousand Europeans who were enrolled during the course of the war, was furnished from these territories.[97] In German East Africa, almost every European possessed a useful sporting rifle.[98] They formed an important source of reinforcement for the Protective Force (Schutz-truppe), during the war. But as their rifles' pattern and calibre were different from those of the Protective Forces, they did, however, face considerable difficulty in the handling rifles of the Protective Force.

Beside the above-mentioned sources of reinforcement, there was one other important source. That was the crew of those ships which were either destroyed or sunk during the campaign. The Protective Force received 322 men from the *Königsberg* and 102 men from the *Möve* during the Campaign.[99]

Shortly after the outbreak of the war, four new companies were raised out of the Police Force and the German Reservists who had been recalled.[100] The total number of companies rose to 18. The white personnel not needed for the field companies were formed into the Schutzen (Sharpshooter or Rifle) Companies.[101]

During the course of the campaign, the number of companies was increased. In 1915, the number of Field Companies rose to 30, that of the Schutzen (Rifle) Companies to 10, and that of other units of company strength to about 20.[102] The number of combatants in each company was raised to 200 during the course of the campaign and the companies were allowed to enrol supernumery Askari.[103] By the end of 1915, the maximum strength attained was 2,998 Europeans and 11,300 Askari, including Naval personnel, administrative staff and hospital service.[104] The strength of the Pretective Force attained its highest level of 3,007 whites and 12,100 Askaris in March 1916.[105]

The uniform of the soldiers of the Protective Force was khaki drill; the natives had khaki putties and boots and red tarbooshes with khaki covers, and the number of the company in brass on it. The Europeans wore cork helmets, yellow boots and leggings. In marching order, the troops carried valises and blankets as well as water bottles, haversacks and pouches. The police had the same uniform, with a red cross-belt, a 'P' in white on the sleeve and an Imperial eagle in front of the tarboosh.[106]

In 1914, German East Africa was not without a navy. There were two ships - the *Königsberg* and the *Möve*. The *Königsberg's* crew consisted of 322 men and the *Möve's* crew consisted of 102 men.[107] These men were trained in handling the weapons of ships. They proved very useful not only on board but also on land, when they joined land forces. They very ably handled the salvaged guns of their ships.

The remarkable and forceful personality of Vorbeck, the leader of the German troops, influenced the whole Campaign in German East Africa. He had been given appointment as the Commandant of the Protective Force in January 1914.[108] About 40 years of age, he had had a distinguished career and was an energetic, good disciplinarian and extremely careful and precise though not very sociable; stubborn rathern than dashing. He took his profession seriously and was unmarried.[109]

He had had experience of native and bush warfare gained in the Herero and Hottentot Campaigns of 1904-6 in which he was wounded. He served during the above mentioned campaign as a Company and Detachment Commander. There, he formed a high opinion of the fighting capacity of certain of the native tribes of Africa which proved very useful to him ten years later.[110]

He had qualified at the German Staff College, had seen service also in China in the Boxer Rebellion. His peace time service had alternated between regimental duty and the General Staff.[111]

Vorbeck had the knack of tackling the Askaris. He knew how to lead them in war. This is evident by the fact that during the whole campaign he could maintain his army in order though he had lost almost the whole German Colony. It seems that his guidance and presence were sources of great strength to his soldiers.

The German Native Soldiers (Askaris) had a great advantage over the Indian soldiers. The Askaris belonged to German East Africa and knew the coutry very well. Moreover, they were immune to many of the deadly diseases that were then prevalent in German East Africa. The Askaris were recruited from the various declared martial tribes.

There were then four main declared martial tribes — the Bantu, Wahuma, Masai and Zulu.[112] The German Protectorate Force enrolled the Askaris mainly from these tribes and their offshoots. The Germans believed there was a vast difference between the Askari class and the ordinary native of the country. They considered only the natives from the Askari classes fit for recruitment as the latter were receptive to military ideas as a consequence of their life spent in the exercise of force. The non-Askari class natives were regarded inferior and timid unsuitable for the German force. The Askari class theory of the Germans in German East Africa was similar to that of the Martial Race theory of the British in India.

The Bantu people were tall and dark skinned. They were mainly found in the coastal region and the mountainous country adjacent to it — Wilhelmstal, Pangani, Tanga, Bagamoyo, Dar-es-Salaam, Lindi, Kilwa, Rupiji, Killimanjaro and the districts of Moshi and Arusha.[113] This tribe was famous for its martial qualities. They were easily trained and became first class fighting soldiers. This tribe, in German East Africa had split up into many branch-tribes, which were known by different names.[114]

The Wahuma people were tall with fine physiques, high foreheads and oval-shaped faces. They were lighter in colour than the other natives of German East Africa. They had settled in the north-west part of the Protectorate, where they were known by different tribal names. Probably the best known of them was the Watussi in Ruanda. By virtue of their far superior intelligence and knowledge of warfare, they had always dominated all other tribes within their sphere of influence.[115]

The Masai were also very different to the other natives and like the Wahuma they represented the same sort of feature. They were found in the Masai steppe lying in the north-eastern corner of the German Protectorate in the districts of Nwanza, Arusha and Kondoa-Irangi. Until the introduction of European administration, the Masai were the terror of all who were within their striking distance. They were found to be good irregular soldiers of the guerilla type but it was a difficult task to keep them in constant discipline.[116]

The Zulu tribe was one of the most important tribes, famous for its warlike qualities. In 1889, the German Protectorate Force was composed chiefly of Zulus. They were found largely in the southern part of the Protectorate. There, they reared cattle and engaged in slave hunting. Their profession required fighting and so they retained their quality of fighting. In 1914, they were known under different local tribal names and among them most famous were the Wangoni and the Wayao.[117]

Besides these tribes, a few other tribes provided porters to the Protective Force. Among them the important tribe was the 'Ruga-Ruga'. The members of this tribe were enlisted in the beginning of the war as porters but later they were trained as soldiers. They were armed originally with muzzle loaders, but later received rifles as they became available from casualities among the Askaris.[118]

The Askaris were enlisted for five years' service with the colours, but were allowed to re-engage if they were satisfactory. The native Non-Commissioned Officers were allowed to remain as long as they were physically fit.[119]

Many of the Askaris enrolled during the war were fully or partially trained. German East Africa had received a considerable addition of recruits (Askaris) from British East Africa when some battalions of the King's African Rifles were disbanded a few years before the outbreak of the war, on the recommendation of the Governor at that time.[120] In addition to this, there were the partially trained porters and the Askari batman with the companies. During the course of the war, whenever need arose they were enrolled and within a very short period of training, they became efficient soldiers.

Weapons of the German Force (Schutztruppe)

At the outbreak of the war, the Protective Force (Schutztruppe) had two types of rifles - the Mauser rifles[121] and the 1871 pattern Mauser rifles firing smoky (black) powder.[122] Of the original 14 companies, 8 were armed with the 1871 pattern rifles.[123] During the campaign, the German Force mainly used the above mentioned two types of rifles. According to British intelligence, the German East Africa's artillery consisted of about 60 guns most of which were about 3 inch calibre with a few of larger calibre.[124] The same number is given by Maj F.S. Keen, a British Officer[125], while Crowe states that there were 64 guns.[126] These number of guns included the guns of the *Königsberg*. The Schutztruppe had in the beginning of war, 100 Machine Guns.[127] Major F.S. Keen puts the number of Machine Guns at 80.[128] According to Crowe, there were 84 Machine guns.[129] The numbers of guns and Machine Guns given by the British Officers seems correct for two reasons. First, their numbers do not vary much; and secondly, they gave these numbers after the war when the possibility of learning the facts was greater.

After the blockade of German East Africa by the British, it became extremely difficult for the Protective Force (Schutztruppe) to get arms and ammunition from Germany. Therefore, it was not possible for the Schutztruppe to equip her units with contemporary or more arms. The Schutztruppe occasionally received modern and more weapons by capturing them from the British forces[130] or through blockade runners. At Tanga in November 1914, for instance, 16 Machine Guns, 455 rifles and 600,000 rounds of ammunition fell into the Schutztruppe's hands on the occasion of the landing of Force 'B'. In February 1915, some small guns and Machine Guns were captured on board the *Adjutant*.[132] This ship had originally belonged to the Germans. In 1914 it was taken by the British but was retaken by the Germans in February 1915. The German ship *Rubens* reached Mansa Bay in April 1915 defying the British blockade. The British ship *H.M.S. Hyacinth* chased the *Rubens* and fired on the latter. The *H.M.S. Hyacinth* returned believing that the *Rubens* had been destroyed. The Germans, however, salvaged the arms and ammunition on the board.[133] The *Rubens* cargo included 1800 rifles, two 6 cm. guns, $4\frac{1}{2}$ million rounds of small arm ammunition, 1,000 rounds of 10.5 cm.

(1.4 inch), 500 rounds of 8.8 cm, 4,000 rounds of 6 cm, 3,000 rounds of 3.7 cm, and one ton of explosives (Trinintronysol).[134] Crowe states that the German Force obtained from the *Rubens* some thousands of Mauser rifles, Machine Guns, bayonets, some millions of small arms ammunition and 500 rounds of 10.5 cm shells.[135] In March 1916, another German blockade runner, the *Maria* had on board four 10.5 cm Howitzers, two 7.5 cm Mountain Guns, several Machine Guns, a considerable quantity of small arms ammunition and ammunition for the *Königsber's* guns.[136] Crowe states that the *Maria* brought a battery of 4.1 inch Howitzers, two batteries of Mountain Guns, 50,00,000, 12 Machine Guns, rounds of Mauser Rifles and a quantity of ammunition for 1871 pattern rifles.[137] Whatever the truth, it is certain that this ship brought in considerable war material.

Before the outbreak of the war, German East Africa had only one important warship - the *Königsberg* - which carried ten 4.1 inch and two 3.5 inch guns which were salvaged after her destruction in July 1916.[138] and employed by the German Force against its enemy. These guns proved very troublesome to the British.

During the campaign, the Schutztruppe's main problem was to acquire sufficient quantity of ammunition to carry on the war. Due to the blockade it was difficult to obtain anything from Germany. The Germans replenished their depleting stock of ammunition not only by capturing from their enemy or receiving them from successful blockade runners but by manufacturing ammunition in local workshops.[139]

Details of the German Weapons

As mentioned earlier, the Schutztruppe used mainly two types of rifles — the 1871 pattern Mauser rifles and contemporary Mauser rifles. Its artillery consisted of guns most of which were about 3 inch calibre and a few of larger calibre. In addition to the guns which the Schutztruppe had at the time of outbreak of the war, more guns were acquired during the course of the Campaign. The *Rubens* brought 6 cm guns along with ammunition for 8.8 cm guns, 3.7 cm guns and 10.5 cm guns, which proves that the Schutztruppe had guns of the calibres mentioned above. In addition, the *Maria*, another blockade runner brought 4.1 inch Howitzers and 7.5 cm Mountain Guns. From the *Königsberg* ten 4.1 inch guns and two 3.5 inch guns were obtained. Besides these the German Force had Machine Guns and pom-poms.[140]

The 1871 pattern Mauser rifle used black powder and lead bullets.[141] The calibre of the rifle was 0.42 inch.[142] The value of this rifle was equivalent to the Martini Henry.[143] On firing, the black powder used in the rifle erupted from the rifle in a thick cloud.

The contemporary Mauser rifles were an improved model. In this rifle black powder was not used and so it was smokeless.[144] It was 4 feet $1\frac{1}{2}$inches long without bayonet, and 5 feet $9\frac{1}{4}$ inches long with bayonet, weighing 9 lbs. and 19 oz. with a byonet. Its calibre was 0.42 inch. It had a fixed verticle type magazine which could accommodate 5 cartridges at the maximum. The cartridge used in it was 3.18 inches long and weighed 369 grains.[145]

The Germans had 3 types of Machine Guns: (a) a Model type which weighed 21 lbs; (b) an Experimental type which weighed 23 lbs, its cooling arrangement based on an air system and it could fire up to 400 rounds per minute; (c) The service type, which weighed 25 lbs, its cooling arrangement based on a water system and it could fire upto 700 rounds per minute.[146]

The effective range of the German Machine guns was 2187 years.[147] The German guns carried 20 per cent more ammunition than the British Machnie guns which carried 250 rounds.[148]

The details of most of the German guns are not available. The pom-pom was a one-pounder quick firing gun. The 4.1 inch *Königsberg* naval guns had an effective range (on land) of about 14,000 yards; and in addition to its ordinary shell it could fire High Explosive Shells with a time fuse. The German 4.1 inch Howitzer was a very light and handy weapon. Its range was upto 6,500 yards. It could fire shrapnel as well as High Explosive Shells.[149]

A comparison between the armies and arms of the Germans and the Indians would prove that the odds were against the former. The Indians had superiority in numbers and were reinforced from time to time during the course of the campaign. Besides, the Indian force had the support of other British units and the native troops of British East Africa. The German Force in the beginning of the war was only about one third of the Indian Force (excluding the British units and the native troops of British East Africa). Later, in 1916, when the South African units joined it, the German Force became one fifteenth the British Force. In matters of weapons also, the Indian Force had superiority in both numbers and quality. The German Force was equipped with old pattern artillery. Most of their rifles and light machine guns, which could be carried easily by the soldiers over the difficult terrain of German East Africa discharged black smoke on firing that disclosed their position, leaving the Indians little difficulty in locating their targets. Besides, it was not possible for them to easily get more arms and ammunition as the British had imposed a blockade around German East Africa.

This superiority of the Indians was, however, counter-balanced by other factors. The German Force was mainly composed of native who were immune to the deadly diseases prevalent in German East Africa and they were able to fight till the end of the war. The Indians, on the other hand, easily fell victim to these deadly diseases. Besides, the Askaris knew the country very well and their mobility was much greater than that of the Indian soldiers. In addition to these advantages, the German Force had one more advantage over the Indian Force which counted for more than any other factor in the campaign. The German Force was commanded by a very able leader, von Lettow Vorbeck who knew how to handle his force and utilize his resources to gain the advantage over his enemy. His very presence was a source of inspiration to his soldiers. The commanders of the Indian force before the coming of General Smuts were no match for von Lettow Vorbeck.

NOTES

1. See Map at the end.
2. *History of the Great War,* Military Operations, East Africa, Vol. 1, London, 1941, p. 17
3. *Ibid.*, p.30.
4. *Ibid.*, p.29.
5. *Ibid.*
6. *Ibid.*
7. *Ibid.*, p.30.
8. *Ibid.*
9. *Ibid.*, p.31.
10. M.D., H.S., War Diary, IEF 'C', Vol. 1, p. 14.
11. *Ibid.*, p. 14.
12. M.D., H.S., G.S.B., The European Crisis, Vol. 3, p. 492.
13. M.D., H.S., War Diary, IEF 'C', Vol. 2, pp. 68-52.
14. *Ibid.*, pp. 48-52.
15. *Ibid.*, pp. 61-62.
16. M.D., H.S., War Diary, IEF 'B', Vol. 2, p. 51.
17. *Ibid.*, Vol. 1, p. 2.
18. *Ibid.*, p. 6.

19. *Ibid.*, pp. 38-39.
20. *Ibid.*, p. 53.
21. *Ibid.*, p. 42.
22. *Ibid.*, p. 72.
23. *History of the Great War, op.cit.*, p. 62.
24. *Ibid.*
25. M.D., H.S., War Diary, IEF 'B', Vol. 2, p. 14.
26. *History of the Great War, op.cit.*, p. 62.
27. M.D., H.S., War Diary, IEF 'B', Vol. 2, pp. 14-15.
28. *Ibid.*, p. 34.
29. *Ibid.*, p. 37
30. *Ibid.*, p. 24
31. *Ibid.*, p. 35
32. M.D., H.S., G.S.B., The European Crisis, Vol. 3, p. 1185.
33. M.D., H.S., War Diary, IEF 'B', Vol. 3, pp. 43-45.
34. *Ibid.*
35. *Ibid.*, p. 68.
36. *History of the Great War, op.cit.*, p.530 b.
37. M.D., H.S., War Diary, IEF 'B' Vol. 5, p. 4.
38. The Tsetse was a deadly fly.
39. *History of the Great War, op.cit.*, p. 119 fn.
40. M.D., H.S., War Diary, IEF 'B', Vol. 7, p. 38.
41. *Ibid.*, Vol. 17, p. 20.
42. *Ibid.*, Vol. 18, p. 22.
43. *Ibid.*, p. 21.
44. *Ibid.*, Vol. 20, pp. 24-26.
45. *Ibid.*, Vol. 19, p. 6.
46. *History of the Great War, op.cit.*, p. 312 fn.
47. *Ibid.*
48. M.D., H.S., War Diary, IEF 'B', Vol. 22, p. 27.
49. *Ibid.*, Vol. 23, pp. 72-73.
50. *Ibid.*
51. *History of the Great War, Op.cit.*, p. 312 fn.
52. M.D., H.S., War Diary, IEF 'B', Vol. 24, p. 29.
53. *Ibid.*, Vol. 28, p. 183.
54. C.A.L. Graham, *The History of the Indian Mountain Artillery*, Aldershot, 1957, p. 149.
55. M.D., H.S., War Diary, IEF 'B', Vol. 28, p. 9.
56. C.A.L. Graham, *op.cit.*, p. 150.
57. M.D., H.S., War Diary, IEF 'B', Vol. 28, p. 9.

58. The figure is obtained by summing up the strengths of all the units of Forces 'B' and 'C'
59. J.H.V. Crowe, *General Smuts' Campaign in East Africa,* London, 1918, p. 41. (Brigadier General J.H.V. Crowe commanded the Royal Artillery in East Africa during the Campaign).
60. *Ibid.*, pp. 40-41.
61. *Ibid.*, p. 41.
62. J.J. Collyer, *The South Africans with General Smuts in German East Africa,* Pretoria, 1939, p. 50. (Brigadier General J.J. Collyer served as the Chief of General Staff of the British forces in east Africa during the Campaign)
63. *Ibid.*
64. M.D., H.S., War Diary, IEF 'C', Vol. 2, p. 28.
65. *History of the Great War, op.cit.*, p. 69.
66. W.W. Greener, *The Gun and its Development,* London, 1884, p. 137.
67. H.P. Dela-Bere, 'Modern Military Rifles', *U.S.I. Journal, July 1919,* p. 319.
68. *Ibid.*
69. J.G. Leckey, 'Notes on Tactical Use of Lewis Guns in Mountain Warfare', *U.S.I. Journal, July 1920,* pp. 178-180.
70. J.C. Deck Bruce-Kingsmill, 'Machine Guns', *U.S.I. Journal, January 1916,* p. 49.
71. H.P. Dela-Bere, 'Automatic Weapons', *U.S.I. Journal, July 1918,* p. 309.
72. *Ibid.*
73. *History of the Great War, op.cit.*, p. 70.
74. C.A.L. Graham, *op.cit.*, pp. 135-137.
75. *History of the Great War, op.cit.*, p. 219 fn.
76. C.A.L. Graham, *op.cit.*, pp. 444.
77. *History of the Great War, op.cit.*, p. 220.
78. C.A.L. Graham, *op.cit.*, p. 444.
79. *Ibid.*, p. 152.
80. *Ibid.*, p. 445.
81. *Ibid.*, p. 154.
82. *Ibid.*
83. Von L. Vorbeck, *My Reminiscences of East Africa,* London, 1920, p. 19. He was Commander of the German forces in German East Africa during World War I.

84. M.D., H.S., G.S.B., Plan, Operations Against German East Africa, p. 7.
85. J.H.V. Crowe, *op.cit.*, p. 26
86. Von L Vorbeck, 'The Germans in Africa', *The Times*. December 10, 1952.
87. Von L Vorbeck, *op.cit.*, p. 22.
88. M.D., H.S., Plan, Operations Against German East Africa, p. 8.
89. J.H.V. Crowe, *op.cit.*, p. 25.
90. Von L. Vorbeck, *op.cit.*, p. 22.
91. J.H.V. Crowe *op.cit.*, p. 25
92. Von L. Vorbeck, J.J. Collyer, *op.cit.*, p. 22, op.cit., p. 23
93. M.D., H.S., Plans, Operations Against German East Africa, p. 8.
94. *Ibid.*
95. Von L. Vorbeck, *op.cit.*, p. 22.
96. *Ibid.*, p. 4.
97. *Ibid.*, pp. 5-6.
98. *Ibid.*, p. 6.
99. *Ibid.*, p. 19.
100. *Ibid.*, p. 22.
101. A Buchanan, *Three Years of War in East Africa*, London, 1919, p. 23.
102. Von L. Vorbeck, *op.cit.*, p. 71.
103. *Ibid.*, p. 72
104. *Ibid.*
105. Von L. Vorbeck, 'The Germans in Africa', *The Times*, December 10, 1952.
106. M.D., H.S., Plan, Operations Against German East Africa, p. 8.
107. Von L. Vorbeck *op.cit.*, p. 19.
108. M.D., H.S., Plan, Operations Against German East Africa, p. 9.
109. *Ibid.*
110. J.J. Collyer, *op.cit.*, p. 26.
111. *Ibid.*, p. 26.
112. *Ibid.*, pp. 16-20.
113. *Ibid.*, pp. 16-17.
114. *Ibid.*
115. *Ibid.*, p. 17.
116. *Ibid.*
117. *Ibid.*, pp. 17-19.
118 J.H.V. Crowe, *op.cit.*, p. 33.
119. *Ibid.*, p. 25.

120. *Ibid.*, p. 27.
121. F.S. Keen, Lecture on 'The Campaign in East Africa', *U.S.I. Journal, January 1917*, p. 74.
122. Von L. Vorbeck, *op.cit.*, p. 23.
123. *Ibid.*
124. M.D., H.S., G.S.B., The European Crisis, Vol. 6, Case No. 9579, p. 1.
125. F.S. Keen, *op.cit.*, p. 74.
126. J.H.V. Crowe, *op.cit.*, p. 25.
127. M.D., H.S., G.S.B., The European Crisis, Vol. 6, p. 1.
128. F.S. Keen, *op.cit.*, p. 74.
129. J.H.V. Crowe, *op.cit.*, p. 25.
130. The term 'British forces' includes all the units which fought for Britain.
131. R. Meinertzhagen, *Army Diary*, London, 1926, p. 104. He was the Intelligence Officer of Force 'B'.
132. J.H.V. Crowe, *op.cit.*, p. 35.
133. *Ibid.*
134. *History of the Great War, op.cit.*, p. 154.
135. J.H.V. Crowe, *op.cit.*, p. 35.
136. *History of the Great War, op.cit.*, p. 287.
137. J.H.V. Corwe, *op.cit.*, p. 287.
138. *History of the Great War, op.cit.*, p. 152.
139. J. Buchan, *Nelson's History of the War*, Vol. 10, London, p. 130.
140. J.H.V. Crowe, *op.cit.*, p. 102.
141. A. Buchanan, *op.cit.*, p. 22.
142. W.W. Greener, *op.cit.*, p. 140.
143. G.S. Keen, *op.cit.*, p. 74.
144. Von L. Vorbeck, *My Reminiscences of East Africa, op.cit.*, p. 8.
145. H.P. Dela-Bere, *op.cit.*, p. 319.
146. J.C. Deck Bruce-Kingsmill, *op.cit.*, pp. 55-56.
147. Machine Gun Fire: Truncation from General Official Text Book for Instruction in War School *R.U.S.I. Journal, July 1911*, p. 911. (The Journal of the Royal United Service Institution of England).
148. J.C. Deck Bruce-Kingsmill, *op.cit.*, p. 56.
149. S.H. Sheppard, 'East African Campaign', *U.S.I. Journal, April 1919*, p. 154.

3

Topography of German East Africa

Physical Description

In the nineteenth century, the whole of Africa was known as the 'Dark Continent'. It was only at the end of the 19th century that some efforts were being made to penetrate into the continent and open it to European domination. Later, the Europeans learned the worth of Africa when it was discovered that the whole continent was full of precious minerals and other valuable commodities like ivory and rare woods apart form vast areas of fertile land. They realised that this continent would provide them with raw materials as well as a good market for their products. As a result, all the big European powers tried to occupy as much territory as they could. Germany, which had only recently taken birth as a nation, was naturally interested in enhancing its prestige with 'a place in the sun.' Germany sent expeditions to Africa - in the South-west and the East. In November 1884, Dr. Karl Peters established the German Colonial Society in East Africa. Gradually, this Society procured rights over the territory which was later known as German East Africa. On February 17, 1885, the German Emperor granted a charter of protection for the German Colonial Society in respect of the territory acquired. The boundaries of German East Africa were established by the Anglo-German Agreement of 1890.

German East Africa covered an area of over 380,000 square miles[1] - that is, it was nearly twice as large as Germany in 1914.[2] It had an eastern seaboard of about 500 miles. Northwards, it had some 600 miles of land frontier and 400 miles of the coast of Lake Victoria. Westwards there was 700 miles of lake edge and 200 miles of land frontier. Southwards there was about 450 miles of land frontier most of which followed the Ruvuma river.[3]

The German Protectorate was bounded in the north by British East Africa. In the north-west lay Uganda, which too was a British Protectorate. Between the conjunction of German East Africa, British East Africa and Uganda lay a great Lake, Victoria-Nyanza. German East Africa's boundaries included nearly half the lake. In the west, a Belgian protectorate — Belgian Congo bordered the German colony. Between German East Africa and Belgian Congo lay another great lake, Tanganyika. The German colony included some part of the lake. The land frontier was smaller than the water frontier between these two states. In the south-west it was flanked by two states, Rhodesia and Nyasaland, which were also British Protectorates. The frontier line between Rhodesia and German East Africa was mainly on land; only a small portion was on Lake Tanganyika. Between Nyasaland and German East Africa lay another lake, Nyanza. German East Africa included some part of this lake and the frontier line between these two states was mainly on this lake. In the south, the neighbour was Portuguese East Africa, a Portuguese Protectorate. Between these two states the boundary line ran along the Ruvuma river. To the east lay the Indian Ocean. The coastline is bordered by a maritime plain 10 to 30 miles broad.[4] The island of Zanzibar was in British possession, lying opposite Dar-es-Salaam and the island of Mafia opposite the delta of the Rufiji was under the Germans.

Geographically, this area may be divided into four regions. From the interior edge of the coastline, the country rises gradually to the great plateau about 4.000' high, which covers most of the hinterland.[5] The plateau is bordered on the east by the Pare, Nuguru, Uluguru and Mahenge mountains. The plateau falls sharply to the west to the level of Lake Tanganyika (2,590 feet) and Lake Nyasa (1,607 feet).[6] The plateau is composed of ancient crystalline rocks, mostly gneisses of the basement complex, mantled by great lava and other deposits.[7]

The eastern part of the plateau has an altitude of from 1000 to 3000 feet. The northern portion of this part is composed largely of volcanic rocks and consists of semi-desert and desert. The southern portion is better watered and consists of fertile land.[8]

The coastal plain and the islands are generally below 1,000 feet in altitude. They consist of sand and coral limestone. The costal plain too is fairly well watered.[9] It has some good ports like Tanga, Dar-es-Salaam, Kilwa Kisiwani and Kilindini. The coastal area has had contact with outside world since pre-Christian days and had many trading settlements. Kilwa probably dates from the 10th century A.D. and became the most important port on the East African coast until the sixteenth century.[10]

The fourth sub-region of German East Africa is composed of a number of separate blocks of highland that rise above the plateau level to an average altitude of over 6,000 feet, individual peaks such as Mount Kilimanjaro rising above the snowline.[11] The most important highland areas are the Kilimanjaro, Meru and Uṣhambara mountains in the north and from Mbeya to Iringa in the south.

From the topographical point of view, German East Africa, when converted into a theatre of war, proved a great obstacle in the way of the Allied operations because of its irregular terrain. At the same time, the Germans had the advantage for they could erect defensive barriers. This became a vital factor during the military operations in this area.

Owing to the different altitudes of different parts of the country, it has considerable diversity in climate. Along the coast and inland at low elevations, it is hot all the year round. At higher elevations the temperature of days and nights varies greatly.[12] The rainfall also varies; at some places it is more or less nil while at other places it is more than 100 inches per year.

The plateau has a variety of climates, ranging from the equatorial type in the northern part to an almost temperate climate in the southern part. The plateau is situated south of the equator and therefore affected by the south-east trade winds in summer and the north-east trade winds in winter.[13] It has seasonal rainfall from October-November to April-May.[14] According to a weather survey, it is found that the rain bearing south-easterly winds cause heavy precipitation on the south-eastern fringe of the plateau and highland masses and peaks such as the Rungwe and Uluguru Mountains and Mount Kilimanjaro. The Rungwe Mountains, for example, receive over 100 inches a year. There is a marked rain shadow on the eastern half of the plateau which has less than 30 inches of rainfall. Partly because of its location on the eastern leeward side of the continent, the plateau's rainfall, which is largely convectional, is extremely variable and in areas with less than 30 inches of rainfall a year cultivation may be hazardous. Dodoma, with an average annual rainfall of 22.24 inches, had annual totals varying from less than 13 inches to 26 inches in the period 1953-56.[15] According to the imformation available to the army in 1914, the annual rainpall at Tabora was 13 inches per annum.[16] Later survey reports calculate that Manyoni, on the Central Railway and within 100 miles of Dodoma has an annual rainfall of 27 inches; while to the north-east of Dodoma the average totals not more than 20 inches.[17] However, it has been found that in this region there is a high variability of rainfall from year to year.[18]

Two types of winds blow in the coastal the north-east monsoon from December to March and the south-east monsoon from May to October. Much of the area has two rainy seasons. The average annual rainfall varies from 60 inches in the northern part to 35 inches in the southern part.[19] According to the information available to the army in 1914, the rainfall of Dara-es-Salaam was about 50 inches per annum, of Moshi about the same and of Tanga about 60 inches.[20] This area may be described as pleasant in the dry season but somewhat unhealthy during the rains. Mangrove swamps occupy much of the coast, especially around the estuaries.[21]

The north-east highlands of German East Africa, which include the mighty Kilimanjaro (19,340 feet), the highest mountain in Africa, Meru (14,979 feet) and the Pare-Ushambara Mountains receive heavy rainfall. Recent meteorological reports show that the upper parts of the Ushambara, Kilimanjaro and Meru receive over 60 inches of rain annually while on their north-west sides are areas which receive only a little more than 20 inches.[22] The southern highlands (Mbeya and Iringa) receive over 30 inches of rain annually.[23] The temperature varies greatly in the plateau from frost at night to boiling temperatures by day.[24]

The coastal area is hot and steamy.[25] On the coast the thermometer does not rise very high, but it does not drop very much either. For most of the year in Dar-es-Salaam, for instance, no covering is required at night, even when sleeping practically in the open.[26] The average coastal temperature is about 80° Fahrenheit and varies hardly 10° Fahrenheit throughout the year.[27]

The climatic conditions varied much in the different part of the war theatre. During the rainy seasons, most of the parts where the rains were heavy became impassable and so the movement of troops was delayed. The temperature also varied from place to place and the soldiers were required to carry clothing. At some places, the temperature fell below freezing point at night while the temperature rose to 110° Fahrenheit by day. At such places, it was difficult for the troops to march during the daytime and sleep at night without proper clothing. Many soldiers could not bear this difference in temperature and fell ill.

Everywhere the soil is of a nature that cracks up badly in the dry weather and quickly became soggy and impassable for stretches after rain.[28] There are streaks of the black cotton soil scattered throughout the area. In the dry weather this soil stands up fairly well to wheeled traffic; a moderate fall of rain makes it impassable for motorised vehicles; a little more and no wheeled transport can be used. A heavy fall makes it impassable for any transport except porters, and often it attains a condition that renders it impassable even for them.[29] The soil of the plateau in German East Africa is nearly everywhere rich and abundantly repays cultivation. The eastern escarpment of the tableland is much broken, forming ranges of mountains which run parallel to the sea. The coastal plain is sometimes sandy, but mostly mangrove swamp.[30]

The largest part of this area in 1914-1918 was steppe covered with grass, which sprang up to a man's height during the rains and quickly died down afterwards, or parkland grass, steppe covered with bushes or trees - isolated or in groups - affording a good measure of visibility, or dense bush in which only objects at hand may be discerned.[31] The bush, there, is in varying degrees of density, extending throughout the whole theatre of operations and exercised a considerable influence on the movements and tactics of large forces. In many places for miles at a stretch the bush is so dense that it is virtually impenetrable for anything except elephants and the rhinoceros - man could only make his way through it by cutting.[32] Some parts of the plateau are covered with forests of elephant grass.[33] The elephant grass, long and tough, grows in profusion by the rivers and in moist places.

The north-eastern part of German East Africa was used for plantation by the Germans because it is fairly well watered and the climate is cooler owing to highlands like Kilimanjaro, Meru and Ushambara. Many Europeans had settled in German East Africa and were farming, mostly in the north-eastern part before 1914.[34] Coffee, tea, groundnuts, bananas and sisal were among the major crops.

The Rivers

There are important rivers like the Pangani, Wami, Kangani, Rufiji and Ruvuma in the eastern region, and the Kangera and Malagarasi in the western region.[35] These rivers have many tributaries. In addition to these rivers there are other small rivers though only a few of them are perennial.[36] From the writings of men of both the forces it is evident that most of the rivers were not navigable in 1914 and were infested with dangerous animals like the hippopotamus, crocodile and deadly fish. In rainy seasons, the currents of rivers were too strong to be easily crossed. There were only a few bridges in 1914 on important rivers and most of them required some sort of improvement to make them capable of taking vehicular traffic. Rivers played an important role in the East Africa Campaign. It was difficult for the troops to cross rivers and so their movement was delayed. They proved greater obstacles for Force 'B' than for the German Force because the former carried no boats with them while the latter had a boat with each company.

The eastern rivers influenced the operations more greatly as most of the major operations took place near them. The delta of the Rufiji was important as it proved a good shelter for the German warships. The German warship *Königsberg* remained unlocated there for a considerable time.

The Lakes

There are many lakes in this region. The official map shows big lakes bordering German East Africa. In the north is the biggest lake, the Victoria-Nyanza. The boundary of German East Africa includes the southern half of the lake. In the west, there is Lake Tanganyika and to the south Lake Nyasa. Besides, there are many small lakes inside the territory, such as the Natron, Lgarrya, Kyassi, Hohenlohe, Irema and Djipe in the north, and the Rikwa and Mkoe in the south. Boats and steamers were maintained in the bordering lakes in 1914 to provide lines of communication with the adjoining countries.

The Waterless Tracts

One of the important features of the area is its numerous waterless tracts.[37] Various sources show that during the campaign both the forces had to face difficulties in crossing long waterless tracts.

The Population

The population of the German Protectorate was estimated in 1913 at over 7,600,000 natives and about 14,000 Indians, Arabs and others.[38] According to Crowe, prior to the war, their were 4,200 whites in German East Africa, Among the 4,200 there were 450 missionaries and about 1,000 women. The number in Government employees were 436 civil officials and about 200 military officials with the Protectorate troops. The remaining 2,000 were engaged in business and developing the country.[39]

The natives in German East Africa in 1914 could be divided into about 150 tribes having different characterisitcs.[40] The aboriginal inhabitatnts were, akin to some extent, to the Bushmen and the Hottentots, being comperatively of light colour and small in stature. The traces of this type remained in the pygmy tribes and in others whose language bore a resemblance to that of the Bushmen.[41] The tribes of Bantu stock, who

Sketch 1

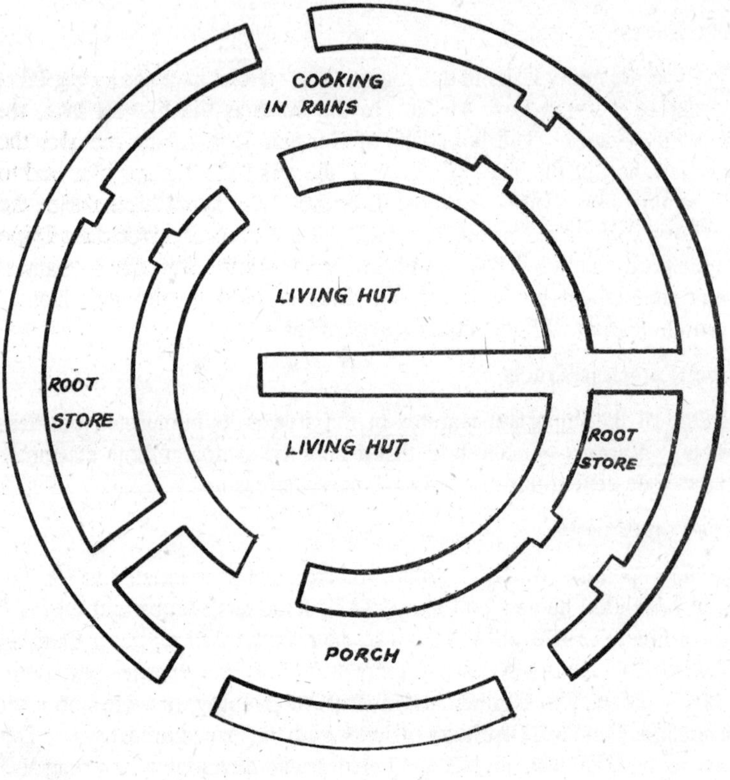

NATIVE KRAAL

had come from South Asia were principally found in the coastal region and mountainous country adjacent to it, Wilhelmstal, Pangani, Tanga, Bagamoyo, Dar-es-Salaam, Lindi, Kilwa, Rufiji and Morogoro, and in the Nguru, Uluguru, Pare, Ushambara, Kilimanjaro, Moshi and Arusha ranges. There are two groups of Hamitic natives - the Wahuma and the Masai. The Wahumas are believed to have come from Arabia. They are lighter in colour than the other natives of the country and were settled in the north-west where they were known in 1914 by different tribal names, the best known among them being the Watusai in Runada, a tall, well made people of fine physique, with high foreheads and oval-shaped faces. Owing to their superior intelligence they had always dominated over all the other tribes within their sphere of influence. The Masais are also quite different from the other tribes and are in some ways similar to the Wahumas. In 1914, they were located in the Masai steppe lying in the north-eastern corner of the Protectorate in the districts of Mwanza, Arusha and Kondoa-Irangi. Until the introduction of the European administration, the Masais were the terror of all who were within the striking distance of them. The Zulus in the southern part of the area were known by different tribe names.

All the tribes in German East Africa were not regarded fit to be enrolled as soldier by the Germans.[42] Only the more virile natives of Wahuma, Masai, Bantu and Zulu descent were considered fit for army recruitment. Before the war these tribes were led by their chiefs. The natives lived in huts. According to a contemporary writer, the native huts called Kraals had steep roofs of weather-darkened grass and low squat walls of baked mud[43] (See Sketch 1). The native huts were round in shape and well-planned. There were proper arrangements for storing water and food.

The natives showed no preference either for the British or for the Germans.[44] Collyer states that the natives reacted sensitively to the personality of any white man who aspired to lead them and Vorbeck, who knew do to deal with them, had considerable influence over them.[45] This is also evident from the fact that the native soldiers remained with him till the end of the campaign.

The native knew the country well and had an ingenious system of communication. Even in the interier it was difficult to remain unlocated from them which is clear from Vorbeck's experience. He says: *I had marched off without leaving word what road I intended to take. Suddenly in the heart of the bush, a native met us on the march, and handed me the overseas mail. The fact is that in their interchange of information the* inhabitants tell each other *everything that happens in their vicinity. Calls, fire signals, and the signal drums serve to exchange and quickly spread all news.*[46]

Important Town

In 1914, there were few important towns. These towns were situated either on the shore of the sea or in the interior, where they were connected by railway lines or roads.

Dara-es-Salaam was the seat of the Government.[47] It was a magnificent large town. It possessed an almost land-locked harbour with a narrow entrance.[48] In 1914, it was one of the most important centres for external trade. It had an old fort, which was then the headquarters of the police.[49]

Tanga was second in importance to Dar-es-Salaam and was the terminus of the Ushambara Railway. The town was half concealed by mango and coconut groves. The town had 900 houses, of which 80 were of stone. It also had an old rectangular fort which was then used as a court house and residence for the officials.[50]

Among the other important towns on the coast were Bagamoyo, Pangani, Lindi and Kilwa. In the interior, the important places were Ujiji on Lake Tanganyika, connected with Dar-es-Salaam by railway; Tabora through which this railway line ran and which was the converging point of many routes; Mwanza on Lake Victoria; Shirati and Bukoba on the east and west shores of Lake Victoria, respectively; and Moshi in the Kilimanjaro district.

Railway Lines

In 1914, there were two railway lines in German East Africa - the Ushambara Railway, which ran from Tanga to Moshi for about 220 miles and the Central Railway from Dar-es-Salaam to Ujiji on Lake Tanganyika about 743 miles. Both were of meter gauge lines.[51] The Ushambara Railway from Tanga ran through the Ushambara hills via Korogwe and reached Moshi in the Kilimanjaro range. The Central Railway ran from Dar-es-Salaam to Ujiji via Morogoro, Kilosa, Dodoma, Kilimantinde and Tabora.

Roads

In 1914, there were a few wide and well kept roads in German East Africa. There was only one metalled road connecting Dar-es-Salaam to Bagamoyo. The roads connecting the larger places were fit for motor cars, except for the fact that the bridges were not strong enough.[52] But, generally speaking, the roads were few in number and in very bad condition.[53] According to Collyer, the roads were to all intents and purposes non-existent.[54] Most of the roads had mud surfaces and had to be rebuilt after the rains every year. Collyer gives the following account about the condition of the roads :

At best they were broad tracks cut in the bush which in the fine weather allowed of the passage of motor transport. The soil was black and red cotton soil, and in no instance was a road metalled, and, as a consequence, the rainy season converted these roads into their worst condition. In the case of black soil the tracks became stretches of liquid mud rendering any movement of transport impossible. The red soil, if on high ground, would occasionally allow of the passage of light vehicles. Heavy transport, and indeed any continuous flow of transport, would reduce the soil in dry weather to powder, and all kinds of devices had to be resorted to get vehicles along.[55]

About the routes,[56] *he writes:*

A month or so, however, if the route were abandoned would see the work all undone by the rapid growth of the bush, and sometimes an effort to find a track along which hundreds of troops and wagons had passed was futile.[57]

Telegraph and Telephone Lines

In 1914, Dar-es-Salaam was connected with most of the inland towns, including Mombo, Moshi, Tabora, Mwanza and Ujiji. Ujiji was on the Cape to Cairo telegraph line. Dar-es-Salaam was also linked with the ports of Bagamoyo, Tanga, Lindi and most of the other ports. There were wireless installations at Dar-es-Salaam mwanza and Bukoba. The one at Dar-es-Salaam was destroyed at the outbreak of the war. Telephones were in use at Dar-es-Salaam, Tanga, Bagamoyo and Pangani.[58]

Economy

In 1914, German East Africa was one of the richest German Colonies. Most of its natural resources remained untapped before the outbreak of the war. Neither was all the fertile land cultivated nor were the raw materials explored and exploited. Vorbeck writes in his war memoirs: "If the country, capable of cultivation were fully utilized, it would probably be possible to support in German East Africa, which has hitherto been inhabited by about eight millions only, a population barely less than that of Germany. An Englishman captured during the war at Mahenge remarked that it would be possible to make East Africa into a second

India, and I think he was right. My experience in the war has confirmed my opinion that there exist many possibilities of economic development, of which we had hardly an inkling before the war.[59]

The chief agricultural products of German East Africa in 1914 were coconuts, rice, sesame, millets, maize, manioc and coffee. Tobacco and sugarcane were also grown.[60]

Cattle, sheep, horses, goats and pigs were reared in great abundance in the region. Vorbeck found that the cattle in the single district of Arusha were more numerous than in the whole of South-West Africa.[61] In 1914 there were said to be 400,000 cattle in the Protectorate, about six and a half million sheep and goats and 28,000 swine.[62] In addition to these, the elephant rhinoceros and hippopotamus were also found. In the later period of the campaign, the fat of these animals was used by the German soldiers to build up their energy.

Before 1914 only scant mineral wealth had been discovered.[63] In 1911 gold ore of the value of £ 46,000 was extracted, and in March 1914 it was reported that an important and rich gold seam had been discovered in the northern part of the colony near Lake Victoria.[64]

Trade in German East Africa was of considerable significance and in 1913 the total value of imports and exports amounted to over 4 million Pounds sterling. Trade was carried on mostly with Germany and Zanzibar.[55]

Wild Animals

In 1914, there were many kinds of animals and insects like lions, leopards, buffaloes, giraffes, zebras, ostriches, crocodiles, snakes, mosquitoes, tick, jiggers and tse-tse flies. They made their own impact on the campaign. Buffaloes were often killed and their flesh was eaten by soldiers whenever there was scarcity of food. Giraffes often damaged telephone lines, disrupting communication. Snakes, mosquitoes, ticks, jiggers and tsetse flies were a terror to the soldiers who were frequently disabled by their stings.

Diseases

The tropical diseases played havoc in German East Africa during the war. Malaria was endemic in the country except in the higher altitudes.[66] In addition to this, there was the African Relapsing Fever caused by ticks.[67] This fever generally made its victim physically disabled. Dysentery of a grave nature was also prevalent.[68] The jigger flea, sometimes lamed men for life.[69] The cases of sleeping sicknes were often detected.[70] The tsetse fly proved deadly to the animals and harmful to men.[71]

Such then was the theatre of the war. Its various features played a vital role in the military operations. The bush was so dense at many places that it was very difficult for the rival forces to locate each other. Because of this factor, often it was not possible for the Artillery units to give support to the advancing Infantry units. The lack of roads and rivers infested with deadly fish and crocodiles hampered the movement of the forces. The rains too, affected the campaign. Very often heavy rains compelled the forces to suspend military operations. The difference in temperature often caused sickness. Diseases played havoc. About the thirds of the total deaths during the campaign were due to various diseases.

NOTES

1. See map at the end.
2. *The Times History of the War,* Vol. 10, p. 123.
3. G.M. Orr, '1914-1915 in East Africa', *U.S.I. Journal,* October 1926, p. 60.
4. M.D., H.S., Plans, Operations Against German East Africa, p. 1.
5. *Ibid.*
6. J. Buchanan, *Nelson's History of the War,* Vol. 10, London, pp. 7-8.
7. N.C. Pollock, *A systematic Regional Geography,* Vol. 9, London, 1968, pp. 318-319.
8. *Ibid.*, p. 324.
9. *Ibid.*, pp. 324-325.
10. *Ibid.*, p. 325.
11. *Ibid.*, p. 328.
12. C.P. Fendall, *The East African Field Force, 1915-19,* London, 1921, p. 187.
13. N.C. Pollock, *op.cit.*, Vol. 9, p. 320.
14. *Ibid.*, p. 320.
15. *Ibid.*
16. M.D., H.S., Plans, Operations Against German East Africa, p.2.
17. W. Fitzgerald, *Africa,* London, 1934, p. 238.
18. A.B. Mountjoy and C. Embelton, Africa - A *Geographical Study,* London, 1965, p. 376.
19. W.A. Hance, *The Geography of Modern Africa,* New York, 1964, p. 379.
20. M.D., H.S., Plans, Operations Against German East Africa, p.2.

21. L.D. Stamp, *Africa - A Study in Tropical Development*, New York, 1953, p. 414.
22. A.B. Mountjoy and C. Embelton, *op.cit.*, p. 375.
23. *Ibid.*
24. M.D., H.S. Plans, Operations Against German East Africa, p.2.
25. G.M. Orr, *op.cit.*, p. 60.
26. C.P. Fendall, *op.cit.*, p. 187.
27. M.D., H.S., Plans, Operations Against German East Africa, p.2.
28. G.M. Orr, *op.cit.*, p. 60.
29. C.P. Fendall, *op.cit.*, p. 194.
30. *The Times History of the War, Vol. 10*, op.cit., p. 124
31. J.J. Collyer, *op.cit.*, p.8.
32. F.S. Keen, Lecture on 'The Campaign in East Africa', *U.S.L. Journal*, January 1917, p.72.
33. *The Times History of the War*, Vol. 10, *op.cit.*, p.124.
34. A.B. Mountjoy and C. Embleton, *op.cit.*, p. 375.
35. M.D., H.S., War Diary, IEF 'B', Col. I, Map I (In the pocket of the War Diary).
36. G.M. Orr, *op.cit.*, p. 60.
37. F.S. Keen, *Op.cit.*, p. 72.
38. M.D., H.S., Plans, Operations Against German East Africa, p. 7.
39. J.H.V. Crowe, *op.cit.*, p. 23.
40. M.D., H.S., Plans, Operations Against German East Africa, p.18.
41. J.J. Collyer, *op.cit.*, p. 16.
42. Please see Chapter II.
43. J. Buchanan, *op.cit.*, p. 146.
44. M.D., H.S., Plans, Operations Against German East Africa, p. 18.
45. J.J. Collyer, *op.cit.*, p. 26.
46. Von. L. Vorbeck, *My Reminiscences of East Africa,* London, 1920, p. 13.
47. M.D. H.S., Plans, Operations Against German East Africa, p.1.
48. H.L. Woodhouse, 'East Africa', *U.S.I. Journal, July* 1917, p. 334.
49. M.D. H.S., Plans, Operations Against German East Africa, p.1.
50. *Ibid.*
51. *Ibid.*, p.6.
52. *Ibid.*
53. F.S. Keen, *op.cit.*, p.71
54. J.J. Collyer, *op.cit.*, p.12.
55. *Ibid.*, p. 12.

56. Routes were often tracks made by advancing troops in and out of tree trunks and bushes and were at first merely winding tracks.
57. J.J. Collyer, *op.cit.*, p.13.
58. M.D., H.S., Plans, Operations Against German East Africa, p.6
59. Von L. Vorbeck, op.cit., p. 13
60. M.D., H.S., Plans, Operations Against German East Africa, p. 5.
61. Von L. Vorbeck, op.cit., p. 11.
62. M.D., H.S., Plans, Operations Against German East Africa, p. 6.
63. The Times History of the War, Vol. 10. op.cit., p. 123.
64. M.D., H.S., Plans, Operations Against German East Africa, p.6.
65. *Ibid.*
66. J.J. Collyer, *op.cit.*, p.9
67. *Ibid.*
68. *Ibid.*
69. M.D., H.S., Plans, Operations Against German East Africa, p. 2.
70. C.P. Fendall, *op.cit.*, p. 187.
71. J.J. Collyer, *op.cit.*, p.9.

4

The Tanga Episode

Disaster at Tanga

Before the outbreak of the First World War neither the British nor the Germans were anticipating hostilities in East Africa. The British forces were unprepared for a war and were busy suppressing the local uprisings in British East Africa.[1] Similarly, the Germans in German East Africa, were also not prepared for war.[2] Actually, the Governor of German East Africa, Dr. Heinrich Schnee, unlike Vorbeck, was opposed to war.[3] He also disliked Vorbeck's proposals for the enhancement and improvement of the German forces. Vorbeck consequently, was unable to introduce his proposed measures for the improvement of the German forces before the First World War.

On the declaration of war between Germany and England, the question arose whether there should be a campaign in East Africa or not. Vorbeck favoured a regular war in East Africa. He was of the opinion that the German forces in German East Africa, though small, might engage the Allied armies and thus prevent them from intervening in Europe or in other more important theatres.[4] This could be achieved by attacking or threatening to attack the British forces at some sensitive point.[5] His plan was to grip the enemy by throat and compel him to employ his forces in self defence.[6] He found the sensitive place for attack in British East Africa-the Uganda Railway. The British Government had not only anticipated an attack on the Uganda Railway in British East Africa[7] but also realised that the possession of German East Africa would be of great value. Therefore, it decided to attack German East Africa with the object of overthrowing German power there.[8] As in earlier wars, the help of the Indian Government was sought. India was "asked to provide two forces: one to capture and hold the principal German port, and another to reinforce the local formations in British East Africa."[9] As has been mentioned, the former force was known as Indian Expeditionary Force 'B' while the latter was known as Indian Expeditionary Force 'C'. The order for the despatch of Indian Expeditionary Force 'C' was immediately issued, while the despatch of Indian Expeditionary Force 'B' was delayed due to the various reasons explained earlier.[10]

The East African Campaign began four days after the declaration of war by England upon Germany, i.e., on August 8, 1914 when the British warship *Astrea* shelled the important wireless tower of Dar-es-Salaam.[11] The tower was not hit by the British ship but was blown up by the Germans from a rather excessive fear of its falling into British hands.[12] The British Commander of the *Astrea* made a truce with the German authorities there on the condition that they would refrain from hostile acts during the war.[13] On August 9, the Germans blew up their Survey vessel the *Möve* and its crew joined the land forces.[14] The Germans had also sunk the floating dock at the Dar-es-Salaam harbour to obstruct the entrance of British ships.[15] On August 15, Taveta, a place situated at the south-eastern foot of Kilimanjaro, in British East Africa, which was weakly held by the British, was taken by German force under Captain von Prince.[16] On August 17, 1914 the *Pegasus,* another British worship raided Tanga, thes made a truce fibe that of Dar-es-Salam.[17] Six days later, on August 23, a landing party was send off by the *Pegasus* to dismantle the telegraph station at Bagamoyo which was turned back by the Germans.[18] Some other minor encounters took place early in September, before the arrival of the first contingent from India, on both sides of the eastern part of the boundary between German East Africa and British East Africa. In Lake Tanganyika, the German steamer *Hedwig von Wismann* had destroyed the Belgian steamer *Delcommune*[19] and thereby secured command of the lake.

On September 1, 1914, the 29th Punjabi Battalion, the first contingent of IEF 'C', disembarked at Mombasa and was at once sent up the country by rail. Half of the 29th Punjabi battalion was left in the Voi Tsavo area and the remainder was sent to Nairobi, where Brigadier General Stewart had established his headquarters.[20] On September 4, the British force received information that a German force was advancing on Tsavo[21]. This German force had compelled a small British detachment on the upper Tsavo to withdraw, after an encounter near Mzima[22]. The bulk of the 29th Punjabis was concentrated at Tsavo under Major A.A. James, leaving a detachment (half a company[23]) at Voi.[24] The two companies of the 29th Punjabis with some troops of the King's African Rifles were sent up the

Tsavo valley on Setpember 5. This force failed to make contact with the German force and presumed that the German force had slipped past it in the bush.[25] The two companies of the 29th Punjabis and the soldiers of the King's African Rifles, under Captain H.T. Skinner, were ordered to turn and attack the German force in the flank and rear, driving it into Major James's troops, who by about 7 a.m. on September 6 were in position astride the Tsavo river five miles west of Tsavo.[26] However, the German force of 300 men with 2 Pompoms and 3 Maxim Guns[27], took rear guard unaware with heavy fire.[28] After the encounter, the German force retired, receiving a severe mauling.[29] In this encounter 2 soldiers were killed and 9 wounded of the 29th Punjabis[30].

During the remainder of the month, skirmishes took place between the German forces and the British forces at Kissu (12th), Campi Ya Marabu (19th), Marjareni (22nd), Ingito Hill (26th) and Mzima Camp (27th)[31] By the beginning of October 1914, the Uganda force had occupied the north-western territory of German East Africa as far as the Kagera river.[32]

Meanwhile, the remainder of Indian Expeditionary Force 'C'[33] had reached Mombasa. The total strength of the force was 27 British Officers, 200 British other ranks, 2000 Indian all ranks and 400 followers.[34]

On October 7, a German force about 300 strong[35] entered the Gazi area and started firing on the British force there.[36] In the counter-attack, one company of the 29th Punjabis hit the Germn force's right flank while one company of the Jind Imperial Service Troops attacked the left flank successfully and 2 companies of the Jind Imperial Service Troops attacked the front of the German force. This double enveloping movement combined with the frontal attack by the Indian units compelled the German force to retreat.[37]

By October 1914, the Allies' situation had improved in Europe. The Battle of Marne (1914), though indecisive, had checked the advance of the German right flank towards Paris. On October 1, began the move of the British Expeditionary Force to the north and after a march of a few days it reached close to Ypres. The British felt a bit relieved in the European theatre and decided to take up the German East African Campaign seriously, a campaign which had assumed greater importance by this time. In October 1914, many German warships, besides the *Königsberg*, were located in the Indian Ocean and it was supposed that they might be using many convenient anchorages along the German East African littoral area. These German warships posed a great danger to the British position in the east. It was considered essential by the British

Government to deprive them of their shelters in order to bring these German warships to battle or to seize them. So, a plan to capture German East Africa was immediately chalked out.

It was decided to wrest Tanga port in German East Africa as the first step of the Campaign. Tanga was situated at one of the terminal ends of the Ushambara Railway line. The Ushambara Railway line ran from New Moshi to Tanga in the northern portion of German East Africa and this region was regarded as the richest portion of the German colony. After occupying Tanga, it would have been easier for the Indian Expeditionary Force to advance to Kilimanjaro Hill along the Ushambara Railway line as New Moshi was situated on the southern slopes of Kilimanjaro. It was decided that an advance would be made in that direction after capturing Tanga, coordinated with a convergent thrust from British East Africa, thereby not only securing possession of the richest and healthiest area of the German territory but paving the way for subsequent operations farther south.[38] Accordingly, the following orders were issued to Major General Aitken, Commander of Indian Expeditionary Force 'B':

" 1 The object of the expedition under your command is to bring the whole of German East Africa under British authority . . .

" 3 His Majesty's Government desires that you should in first instance secure the safety of British East Africa by occupying the north-eastern portion of the German colony, viz., the country between Tanga and Kilimanjaro. For this purpose it is suggested that you should first occupy Tanga with 'B' Force and that, when this move has had its due moral effect on the Germans, occupying the hinterland of Tanga, Force 'C' should, if feasible, advance from Tasavo and threaten Moshi . . .

" 5 After the effective control of this region has been secured, it will be for you to consider and report your plans for the occupation of the Dar-es-Salaam-Tabora line, which should be the next object of attack[39]."

Force 'B', which consisted of 7,972 men, reached Tanga on November 2, 1914.[40]. According to the treaty made at Tanga earlier, it was agreed that Tanga would not be attacked by the British. Therefore, the Commander of Force 'B' decided to ask the German authorities to surrender the port of Tanga and in case of refusal, it was to be attacked. The British ship H.M.S. *Fox* went to the port to demand surrender on the 2nd of November, at 6 a.m., leaving the convoy a few miles[41] out at sea.[42] The German authorities refused to surrener the port and H.M.S. *Fox* returned to the convey at about 11.30 a.m.[43] Soon after, the Commander for Force 'B' began planning an attack on Tanga. According to the Intelligence Office of Force 'B' Meinertzhagen, the act of asking to the Germans to surrender the port by *H.M.S.* Fox gave sufficient notice of attack to the German and removed all the elements of surprise, which was to a great extent responsible for the disaster that took place at Tanga[44].

From the records it appears that the Germans had anticipated an attack on Tanga even before the surrender demand. Vorbeck writes that from captured English mail he had gathered informaiton about an impending attack by an Indian Expeditionary Force of 10,000 men on German East Africa and from general considerations he always expected a hostile attack on a large scale in the neighbourhood of Tanga.[45] In the month of October, he had discussed the defence of the place with the District Commissioner of Tanga.[46] However, on November 1, the only German unit in Tanga was the 17th Company.[47] Two German companies were in the frontier district north of Tanga under Baumstark.[48] Some other German units were in the Kilimanjāro area[49]. These could be sent to Tanga, by the Ushambara Railway from New Moshi.

On November 2, Vorbeck received a telegram at Moshi from Tanga informing him of the arrival of the Indian Force off Tanga.[50] Vorbeck at once decided to concentrate all the easily available German units at Tanga to meet the impending attack. The two German companies under Baumstark (15 and 16 F.K.), in the frontier district north of Tanga, were moved to Tanga.[51] On November 2, Vorbeck sent one and half companies from Moshi towards Tanga by train, followed on the 3rd morning by the Headquarters and another company. Three other companies were sent later. Beside these, all the smaller detachments employed on Railway protection duty were also pushed towards Tanga.[52] In total, the Germans had six and a half companies besides a few smaller detachments, totalling about 1,200 rifles.[53]

Meanwhile, the Commander of Force 'B' decided to disembark some of the Indian troops at Tanga to launch an attack there. Three places were regarded suitable for landing, the first shown in the Sketch 2 as Beach A, about a mile south of Ras—Kasone; the second shown as Beach B, near the Signal Tower at the north-western tip of the peninsula; and the third shown as Beach C, in the south-western area of the peninsula. As the Commander of Force 'B' feared mines, he decided not to land at the latter two places which had not been searched. The landing hence 'A' had been reconnoitered through telescope by the *Fox* in the early morning from her position just off it[54] and was decided to land there. This choice proved unfavourable for landing. The edge of a coral reef was about 500 yards

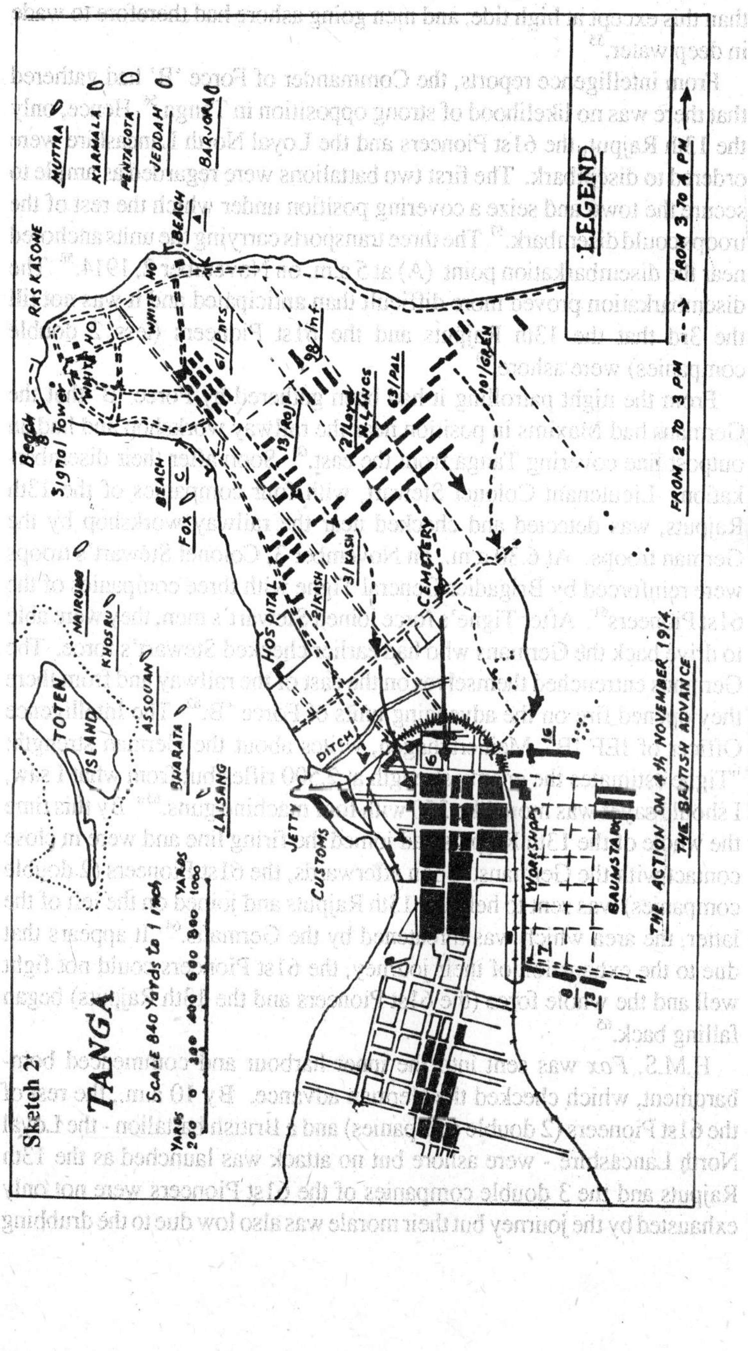
Sketch 2
TANGA
SCALE 840 Yards to 1 inch
THE ACTION ON 4th NOVEMBER 1914
THE BRITISH ADVANCE
LEGEND
FROM 2 TO 3 PM
FROM 3 TO 4 PM
RAS KASONE
Signal Tower
Beach
BEACH A
BEACH C
WHITE HO
TOTEN ISLAND
MUTTRA
KARMALA
PENTACOTA
JEDDAH
BARJORA
NAIRUBI
KHOSRU
ASSOUAN
BHARATA
LAISANG
FOX
61/Pnrs
98 Inf.
13/RAJP
2/Loyal N. LANCS
63/PAL
101/GREN
2/KASH
3/KASH
HOSPITAL
CEMETERY
DITCH
JETTY
CUSTOMS
WORKSHOPS
BAUMSTARK

from the shore, and tugs and lighters could not come closer to the shore than this except at high tide; and men going ashore had therefore to wade in deep water.[55]

From intelligence reports, the Commander of Force 'B' had gathered that there was no likelihood of strong opposition in Tanga.[56] Hence, only the 13th Rajput, the 61st Pioneers and the Loyal North Lancashire were ordered to disembark. The first two battalions were regarded as ample to secure the town and seize a covering position under which the rest of the troops could disembark.[57] The three transports carrying the units anchored near the disembarkation point (A) at 5 a.m. on November 2, 1914.[58] The disembarkation proved more difficult than anticipated and it was not till the 3rd that the 13th Rajputs and the 61st Pioneers (less 2 double companies) were ashore.[59]

From the night patrolling it had been gathered by Force 'B' that the Germans had Maxims in position near the railway workshop and had an outpost line covering Tanga from the east.[60] Soon after their disembarkation, Lieutenant Colonel Stewart, with four companies of the 13th Rajputs, was detected and checked near the railway workshop by the German troops. At 6.30 a.m., on November 3, Colonel Stewart's troops were reinforced by Brigadier General Tighe with three companies of the 61st Pioneers[61]. After Tighe's force joined Stewart's men, they were able to drive back the Germans who had earlier checked Stewart's force. The Germans entrenched themselves on the east of the railway and from there they opened fire on the advancing units of Force 'B.[62] The Intelligence Officer of IEF 'B', Meinertzhagen, writes about the German strength: "Tighe estimates the enemy strength at 2,500 rifles but from what I saw, I should say it was more like 250 with four machine guns.[63]" By this time the whole of the 13th Rajputs had joined the firing line and were in close contact with the Germans. Soon afterwards, the 61st Pioneers (2 double companies) was sent to help the 13th Rajputs and joined on the left of the latter, the area which was threatened by the Germans.[64] It appears that due to the exhaustion of their journey, the 61st Pioneers could not fight well and the whole force (the 61st Pioneers and the 13th Rajputs) began falling back.[65]

H.M.S. *Fox* was sent into the inner harbour and commenced bombardment, which checked the German advance. By 10 a.m., the rest of the 61st Pioneers (2 double companies) and a British battalion - the Loyal North Lancashire - were ashore but no attack was launched as the 13th Rajputs and the 3 double companies of the 61st Pioneers were not only exhausted by the journey but their morale was also low due to the drubbing they had received from the Germans in the engagement. According to reports, the 13th Rajputs had fought well upto a point, but the 61st Pioneers were of little value throughout the operations.[66] The Germans, also, did not attack Force 'B' during the rest of the day. Had they attacked, they might probably have been able to drive out the units of Force 'B', as most of the units were not prepared for their defence either due to exhaustion or because of their low morale, and there was little likelihood of getting these units of Force 'B' reinforced as the other ships carrying units could not be brought to the inner harbour due to the piloting difficulties.[67]

By nightfall of November 3, 1914, only the 2nd Kashmir Rifles, half of the 3rd Battalion of Kashmir Rifles and two companies of the 3rd Gwalior had also been got ashore.[68] At 5 p.m. Brigadier General Aitken took command of Force 'B' at Tanga, but no effort was made to capture the town, which had been vacated by the Germans. The whole force remained in the vicinity of the harbour to the east and north-east of the town.

By the morning of November 4, 1914, the other units, namely the 63rd Light Infantry, the 101st Grenadiers, and the 98th Infantry had disembarked.[69] At 1.30 a.m. orders were issued to the units of Force 'B' at Tanga to attack the town.[70] The disposition of the force was as follows:

In front, on the right one and a half Battalions of the Kashmir Rifles (their flanks resting on the harbour, and on the left the North Lancashire and the 63rd Light Infantry were placed, the whole line at two paces interval. To the left rear of the 63rd were positioned the 101st Grenadiers. The 98th Infantry was behind the North Lancashire, about 200 paces distance. As the 61st and the 13th were demoralised, the latter was placed in the rear of and about 300 yards behind the centre of the Kashmir Rifles, and the 61st in the rear of and about 300 yards behind the 13th Raputs[71].

The Commander of the force left the Mountain Artillery aboard as the dense jungle which spread over the whole theatre of operations was regarded as unsuitable for the employment of artillery. However, in the town the artillery units could have been successfully employed. The artillery units were placed on board the ship *Bharata* which moved as far up the inner harbour as possible to help the advancing troops.[72] The *Fox* was also brought to the inner harbour for the same purpose. The plan was to take the town and then to swing the left flank of the force, round the south of the railway workshop, to cut off the German line of retreat.

Meanwhile, Vorbeck placed his units in the following order: the 6th Field Company was placed to hold the eastern edge of Tanga on the broad front; to its night rear, outside Tanga was the 16th and 17th companies; to the rear were placed two European companies, the 7th and 8th Rifle Companies; and the 13th Field Company, was stationed on the Tanga-Pangani road.[73] The total number of German companies on November 4, 1914, was about six, with a total strength of 932 men. Two more companies (the 4th and 9th Field Companies) were on their way to Tanga[74] (See Sketch 2).

The advance of IEF 'B' was unopposed until it reached 800 yards from Tanga town.[75] The battle took place at about 3 p.m. on November 4, between the Germans and Force 'B'

As soon as the rival forces came into contact, some of the units of Force 'B' got demoralised by the heavy fire from the German force. The German force concentrated their attack, on the right flank of Force 'B' i.e. they adopted 'the Principle of Concentration', which implies concentrating superior force than the enemy at the decisive point. Some of the 13th Rajputs and 61st Pioneers fell back from the battlefield.[76] No effort was made by Brigadier General Tighe, who was with the 13th Rajputs or by Major General Aitken who was with the 61st Pioneers to raise the morale of these men. At this juncture, Major General Aitken ordered the Loyal North Lancashire to support the right flank. However, in the meantime, the 63rd Light Infantry also got demoralised and withdrew from the battlefield, leaving a considerable gap which the 101st Grenadier did its best to fill.[77] The 98th Infantry was ordered to move up which it did but the men of this unit were so half-hearted as to be quite useless.[78]

At about 3.30 p.m. the Loyal North Lancashire succeeded in entering the town in spite of the heavy gunfire of the German troops. At the same time, the Kashmir Rifles and three companies of the 13th Rajputs entered the town from the northern end. There ensued regular street fighting. For some time all went well. The Kashmir Rifles captured a Machine gun and killed a few Germans in hand to hand combat, while the half battalion of the Loyal North Lancashire was engaged with the enemy to the south of the town and other parties of the regiment joined hands with the Kashmir Rifles.[79] The Kashmir Rifles and the two companies of the 13th Rajputs did well in the town.[80] These units along with the Loyal North Lancashire fought well but due to the lack of additional troops for effective support[81] and the strong German pressure these units had to retire across the railway.

In this attack, the artillery units on board the ships did not help the attacking units on land due to lack of coordination. The Commander of Force 'B' should have ordered a simultaneous attack on the town by land and sea. Though, later, some shots were fired from the *Fox* to help the Kashmir Rifles, the ship was not close enough to give any effective aid to the Kashmir Rifles.[82] There was no cooperation between the Artillery and Infantry.[83] In short, 'the Principle of Cooperation' was ignored.

Later, the Indian troops made a powerful attempt to push back the Germans and by 5.30 p.m., all the units of Force 'B' were across the railway line. According to Major General Aitken, there was no water whithin the area held by Force 'B' near the railway cutting line, so he ordered retirement by about 500 yards to the precincts of the German hospital, the only place between the town and Ras-Kasone where water was available.[84]

However, later Aitken found that some of the units of Force 'B', some companies of the 13th Rajputs, the 61st Pioneers, the 98th Infantry, the 63rd Light Infantry and the 101st Grenadiers which had suffered heavy losses were unable to mount a second attack.[85] Aitken decided to re-embark. During the evening, he consulted his officers and chalked out a plan for re-embarkation. Since Beaches B and C were in full view of the German force, it was decided to re-embark Force 'B' at Beach A situated to the east of the town.[86] The time for re-embarkation was fixed at 1 p.m. on November 5.

The German force did not attack during the night of 4th-5th November. On November 5, a defensive position was taken up by a covering party to cover the re-embarkation. The covering party consisted of the Loyal North Lancashire and the 2nd Kashmir Rifles, and half a battalion of the 3rd Kashmir Rifles with Brigadier General Tighe in command.[87] The ship *Bharata* was shifted about a mile to the east, off Red House, to assist with fire from the Mountain guns in case of an attack from the Germans.[88] The ship *Barjora* was also brought close to the *Bharata* for the same purpose.

While the preparations were being made for re-embarkation, Force 'B' pretended to prepare for an attack on the town.[89] For this purpose, the ship H.M.S. *Fox* took on the *Bharata's* billet of the 4th, in the inner harbour, as if to support the attack on the town.[90]

Though the time agreed upon for re-embarkation was 1 p.m., as low tide was at 12 noon, wfth the distance between the lighters and the shore at the minimum, the re-embarkation commenced at 12 noon.[91] To begin with everything went well but soon after 1 p.m. a party of the Germans appeared in front of the covering party. This force of Germans was driven back by the covering party but the sound of the firing created panic among some of the troops re-embarking.[92] German patrol parties approached the covering party of Force 'B' a number of times but they were driven back. At the same time, to deceive the 'German force, efforts were made to convince them that the attack was going to be made on the town. To this end many bogus messages were sent to the *Fox* from the signal tower.[93] These messages were intended to fall into the hands of the Germans and they were deliberately sent 'in clear' so that the Germans may not find any difficulty in understanding them. These messages read: "Take up a position whence the houses, which checked us Yesterday, can be shelled. Advance commences 1 p.m. . . .[94] This was one of the effective steps taken by Major General Aitken during this battle. No major attack was delivered afterwards on Force 'B' during the re-embarkation and it was completed by about 4 p.m.[95]. In the evening, arrangements for the removal of the wounded were made. An officer was sent with a white flag of truce to the German Commandant. The Germans behaved very courteously and did their best for the comfort of the patients. After this, Force 'B' left Tanga for Mombasa in British East Africa.

In spite of the fact that Force 'B' was six and a half times the German strength in this battle, it met with disaster at Tanga. Force 'B' had seven battalions while the German force had about six companies. The Force 'B' met with disaster mainly because of defective strategy and tactics. A thorough study of this battle shows that Major General Aitken, Commander of IEF 'B', did not prove a good commanding officer. The disaster at Tanga was due to many reasons. First, the German force was not given a surprise attack. Not only was the date of arrival well-known to the Germans.[96], but even after their arrival the Germans were given ample time to reinforce themselves. Secondly, before launching the attack, the troops should have been given enough rest to remove their fatigue. Meinertzhagen describes the condition of the force in the following words: "We disembarked at Tanga after a fortnight's hell on crowded ships in tropical heat. All the Indian troops were dispirited and disgruntled before landing.[97] Thirdly, as noted earlier, the "Principle of Cooperation" was not properly applied. The *Fox* on which the Mountain artillery was left was not brought close enough to be able to render effective help to the force on land. The Mountain Artillery should have been ordered to bombard the city from the sea before attacking it on the ground. This would have broken the morale of the German units and created panic among both the soldiers and civilians within the town. The artillery should also have been employed at the left flank of Force 'B', in order to enfilade the German force entrenched along the railway line. Fourthly, the deployment of the units was defective. The left flank of Force 'B' had not covered the right flank of the German force fully, i.e., the 'Principle of Security' was disregarded. Fifthly, the whole operation was taken lightly because Aitken was convinced that there would be no resistance at Tanga from the Germans. And, lastly, it appears that the force had no knowledge of the topography of the theatre of the battle. The force should have collected this information and selected landing place before hand, instead of wasting time searching for the disembarkation point after its arrival.

During two days of fighting, Force 'B' lost 1,152 men in killed, wounded and missing.[98] Meinertzhagen estimated the losses of Force 'B' at 800[99] while Vorbeck estimated them at 2,000.[100] Besides, 16 Machine guns, 455 rifles and 600,000 rounds of ammunition were left behind at Tanga.[101] The German losses were 84 killed and 80 wounded with 1 missing.[102]

In his defence Major General Aitken wrote that the total number of the German force who opposed them at Tanga was about 2,000 Europeans[103] and 2,000 Askaris.[104] He also stated that the Germans had been reinforced by reservists from China and Australia.[105] From the available sources, it seems that the above figures were not correct. Regarding the reinforcements from China and Australia, the Intelligence Officer of Force 'B' wrote that there was no evidence to support this claim and he regarded it as incorrect.[106]

Action at Longido

Longido is an isolated hill situated to the north-west of Kilimanjaro mountain. Just after the outbreak of the war, reports were received by the British Intelligence that it was occupied by German troops.[107] A plan to attack the hill was made immediately, but, as the Germans were reinforced, it was postponed.[108]

In October 1914, when the remainder of Force 'C' arrived, it was decided to attack Longido simultaneously with the landing of Force 'B' at Tanga.[109] On October 31, 1914 this plan was discussed between Major General Aitken, Commanding Officer IEF 'B' and Brigdier General Stewart, Commanding Officer IEF 'C'. Before the attack, it was gathered that the German strength at Longido was betwen 400 and 500 soldiers though after the attack it was found that there were between 800 and 1200 German soldiers.[110]

As mentioned earlier, Longido was an isolated hill. There was no water, for about 30 to 40 miles around it except on the hill itself.[111] To the north of Longido Mountain is the Nyiri desert. It was decided to launch an attack on Longido hill from a place on Manga River in British East Africa. The operation was a difficult one as there was no water between the Manga and Longido, and therefore, it was decided that till the water source on Longido was secured, the attacking column must return every day to its base on the Manga River.[112]

The units detailed for the attack on Longido were the East African Mounted Rifles (5 squadrons), two sections of the 27th Mountain Battery, the 29th Punjabis (less 2 companies), the Kapurthala Imperial Service Troops (half a battalion), a section of the Volunteer Maxim Battery and a detachment of Masai Scouts. The movements of the attacking force took place in three columns.[113] The decisive attack column was composed of the 29th Punjabis (less 2 companies), a section of the 27th Mountain Battery, a section of the Volunteer Maxim Battery and a detachment of Masai Scouts, commanded by Lieutenant-Colonel Drew. It was to attack the German position on the eastern face of the mountain. The second column, known as the left column, was to secure the water supply and cut off the enemy's retreat; it was composed of two squadrons of the East African Mounted Rifles commanded by Captain Bingley. This column was to attack the German position from south-east. The third column was the Frontal Attack Column. It was composed of the East African Mounted Rifles (three squadrons) and the Kapurthala Imperial Service Troops (one company) and a section of the 27th Mountain Battery and was commanded by Major Leverton[114]. This force was to hold the enemy on the northern face of the mountain. By the morning of November 3, all these columns reached Longido from the different sides near the German position, after marching in the night.[115] The combined strength of all the units which took part in this expedition was 1487 men.[116]

On the morning of November 3, a small column of Germans suddenly opened fire in the mist on Decisive Column at 7.45 a.m.[117] The 29th Punjabis replied with rifle and Machine gun fire. The exchange of fire continued for five minutes. The number of causalties was 2 on each side.[118]

At 9.15 a.m. the mist cleared and the general action began. A section of the 27th Mountain Battery opened fire on the position from where the German troops were firing on the advancing troops of the Decisive Column. In turn, the Germans attacked this section of the 27th Mountain Battery. As a first step Lieutenant Colonel Drew decided to send a force to occupy the main spur which had been shelled. At 9.25 a.m. one (double) company, the 29th Punjabis, began to securing the main spur with the help of fire from the 27th Mountain Battery and by 10 a.m. had occupied the main spur.[119] The (double) company of 28th Punjabis continued its advance along the ridge towards the German position in that direction. At 11.45 a.m. half a company of the 29th Punjabis captured a position to the west of the main German position.[120] From then till 2 p.m., desultory firing continued on both sides.

At 2.10 p.m. it was observed that the main camp of the Germans was receiving reinforcements from the German base in the middle of the south side of the hill.[121] By 4 p.m. the German troops occupied a place to the south of the water course running towards the east of Longido, opposite the Frontal Column.[122]

At this juncture, already short of water, it was realised that there was no possibility of getting water there.[123] Therefore, it was decided to retire during the night. At 5.20 p.m. 20 to 30 Germans gained a position unobserved on the left flank of the Decisive Column and started firing on the main position of this Column. One company of 29th Punjabis and some troops of the East African Mounted Rifles were entrusted with the work of driving them back, but the Germans were reinforced and the engagement became general and all round.[124] The Germans were resisted in front but they advanced as darkness came on, the guns opening fire with fuzes at zero.[125]

Next, the Decisive Column was ordered to withdraw. At 6.15 p.m. the retirement of the Reserve Ammunition commenced, followed by the Ambulance Section under great difficulties as most of the stretcher bearers had deserted.[126] Meanwhile, the 29th Punjabis resisted the German attack.[127] As the Kapurthala Infantry was tired, it was withdrawn[128]. The retirement of the 29th Punjabis commenced at 6.35 p.m. and was carried out in orderly manner.[129] The Germans were seen occupying the vacated positions and also firing upon the retiring column. The 29th Punjabis returned to Manga camp during the course of the night.[130]

The Frontal Column left the Manga river at 6.15 p.m. on November 2 and arrived at a *donga* (the African name for a channel formed by the flow of water) a few miles north of Longido during the night[131]. The advance of this column began in the morning of November 3. A section of the 27th Mountain Battery was left to the south of the *donga*. Eighty men of the East African Mounted Rifles moved up the water course.[132] A (single) company of the Kapurthala Imperial Service Troops followed as reserves.[133]

This Frontal Column was shortly checked by a German force at the foot of the Longido.[134] The main object of this column was to hold the German force in the north.[135] The section of the 27th Mountain Battery opened fire on the German guns to support the advancing troops, but their fire was not accurate because of the bushes and trees.[136] Fighting continued the whole day. The German fire was so accurate that the attacking party had to withdraw by 3 p.m.[137] At about 4.45 p.m. a fresh attack was launched by the Frontal Column but in the evening it too had to retire.[138] By 9 a.m. of the November 4, it reached the Manga river camp.[139]

The Left column set out to find the water supply line of the Germans and to cut off their lines of retreat. The search party of this column became engaged with a German force on the morning of November 3, but as the number of German soldiers was twice (about 200) that of the column they commenced to outflank it. Finally, it retired without achieving the object.[140] This column also reached the Manga river camp at about 2 a.m. on November 4.

The total losses of the British force were 19 killed, 33 wounded and 1 missing[141] while the German losses were 118 men killed and wounded.[142] This expedition was also a failure. It required a through knowledge of the topography of that area, which the British force did not possess, to gain victory. Due to this, the guns could not fire accurately on the Germans. The other difficulty was the lack of water in this area that forced the troops to rush back to the base camp in the evening. Thus, the geographical factors played the dominant role in determining the fate of this expedition.

Defensive Battles

After the disaster at Tanga, Force 'B' was ordered to go to British East Africa. The Commander of Force 'B' felt that with the small number of troops under him, it was not feasible to capture German East Africa and for that purpose two more brigades of troops with greater fighting capacity were required.[143] Hence, it was decided that unless the required number of troops join up to make an offensive action possible, only a defensive strategy should be adopted.[144] From that time onwards, for more than a year till the arrival of the South African troops, defensive and defensive-offensive operations alone were undertaken.

Meanwhile, the War Office took over control of the operations in East Africa on November 22, 1914.[145] Immediately after, on December 4, 1914, Major General Aitken was ordered to hand over command of the IEF 'B' to Brigadier General Wapshare,[146] who re-organised the troops for the purpose of the defence of British East Africa.

After the retreat from Tanga, for some time no major battle took place. Only slight skirmishes occurred along the border between German East Africa and British East Africa.

On December 25, Jasin, a point just to the south-east of the Anglo-German frontier, under German control, was attacked by two companies of the King's African Rifles and one company of the 101st Grenadiers. After a short engagement, these forces captured the place.[147] On January 9, 1915, Sherati, a place on the eastern coast of lake Victoria, just to the south of the Anglo-German frontier, was also captured.[148]

Occupation of Mafia Island

The Mafia Island lies some 10 miles off the mouth of the Rufiji. In January 1915, the strategic importance of this island was realised as it was well-placed and could be of use as a base from which to operate against the German ships hiding in the Rufiji delta. It was reportedly held by about 45 men.[149] On January 8, 1915 about 500 men under Lieutenant Colonel Ward left for Mafia Island.[150] The force was composed of 1 (double) company of the 101st Grenadiers, 4 companies of the King's African Rifles and 1 section of Machine guns, the King's African Rifles.[151] The force was followed the next day by one company of the 63rd Carnatics detailed as the permanent garrison of the island.[152] On January 10, this force landed unopposed,[153] at Kisimani about four miles from Ngombeni, where the Germans had entrenched themselves.[154] The next day the force under Lieutenant Colonel Ward attacked the Germans at Ngombeni.[155] After some opposition, the German force surrendered. The Expeditionary Force re-embarked and the double company of the 63rd Carnatics was left in occupation.[156] The success here over the Germans was mainly because the German force was less than one tenth the attacking force.

Operations Around Jasin (Jassini)

The post of Jasin was held by the two companies of the 2nd Kashmir Rifles.[157] On January 12, 1915, this post was attacked[158] by a German force consisting of 4 Sch. K. And half of 15 F.K.[159] The two companies of the 2nd Kashmir Rifles, with the help of a company of the 3rd Kings's

African Rifles, two companies of the Jind Infantry and a section of the 28th Mountain Battery were able to drive back the German attacking party.[160]

In the meantime, the expeditionary force from the Mafia returned. At this moment, the garrison at Jasin, which consisted of two companies of the 2nd Kashmir Rifles and one company of the 101st Grenadiers, was placed under the command of Colonel Raghubir Singh, commander the 2nd Kashmir Rifles.[161]

The Germans had decided to recapture the Jasin post and for this purpose Vorbeck gathered nine companies (about 1,458 men) with two Machine Guns at Totohown plantation by January 17, seven miles south of Jasin.[162] Early in the morning of January 18, Jasin was attacked by the German force.[163] The total number of British force at Jasin was 296 (the 101st Grenadiers, 138; the 2nd Kashmir Rifles, 144; the Machine Gunners of the King's African Rifles, 9; and the Signallers, 5).[164] A few miles ahead of Jasin 40 men of the 2nd Kashmir Rifles were posted at the Sisal factory.[165] The Germans were definitely superior in number. Soon after the fighting broke out, three companies of the King's African Rifles were sent to help the forces at Jasin and Sisal factory but they proved of no avail.[166] The force of 40 men of the 2nd Kashmir Rifles at the Sisal factory was subjected to heavy fire by the Germans to which it replied bravely and having fired their last round by 11 a.m., its men charged out with bayonets and Khukris, scattering into the bush. Eventually 29 of the 40 men of the 2nd Kashmir Rifles reached Umba Camp.[167] This was one of the finest examples of bravery, courage and initiative taken by the Indian soldiers in the campaign. This force was led by an Indian officer, Subedar Mardan Ali.[168]

On receipt of the information that the three companies of King's African Rifles were unable to relieve the force of Jasin, another three companies of the Ist King's African Rifles, two companies (single) of the Jind Infantry and a section of the 28th Mountain Battery were despatched.[169] The section of the 28th Mountain Battery was soon engaged by the German gun fire.[170] The reinforcement, however, did not bring any change to the situation as these units were repulsed by the Germans. By this time Brigadier General Tighe, who had taken over command of this operation, decided to renew the attack the next day in the morning.[171] Unfortunately, the ammunition of the forces at Jasin had been expended by the night of the 18th and the Commanding Officer, Colonel Reghubir Singh had been killed.[172] These things had badly shaken the morale of the troops. Besides, the climatic conditions were so bad that many men had fallen sick.[173] On the morning of January 19, the force at Jasin surrendered to the Germans.[174] According to Vorbeck the total number of casualties of the Indian Expeditionary Force was bout 700[175]. The German casualties, according to military reports, were 300 Germans and 1,500 Blacks including porters.[176] In the encounter, great gallantry was displayed by the Jind Infantry.[177] After this, Brigadier General Tighe wished to attack Jasin with the help of the Navy.[178] H.M.S. *Weymouth* actually shelled Jasin on January 20, 1915.[179] But meanwhile a telegram was received from England forbidding further offensive action and so the idea of attacking Jasin was dropped.[180]

Germans were successful in this battle for various reasons. The scene of the operation was difficult and was covered with dense bush making it difficult for Force 'B' to reinforce the besieging force quickly. Moreover, technically speaking, 'the Principle of Security' was not fully applied by Force 'B'. First, the quantity of ammunition at the front post was not enough. Secondly, the number of soldiers was not sufficient to defend the post. And lastly, there was no naval ship to assist the force in case of an emergency.

Construction of the Voi-Maktau and the Railway Line

Major General Wapshare realised that to make an offensive in the north of German East Africa, it was necessary to have a line of communication upto Maktau. He decided to link Maktau by a road and a railway line with Voi which was situated at the Ushambara Railway line[181]. A track had already existed between Voi and Maktau. The conversion of the Voi-Maktau track into a road for wheeled traffic was begun in January 1915 by the Faridkot Sappers and the 61st Pioneers along with a large number of the Africans.[182] It was completed in March 1915. The road, 37 miles in length was taken across the Voi River on a fine suspension bridge over which 5 tons load could be carried. This road proved of great value during the advance in 1916. In March, 1915, the construction of the railway line from Voi to Maktau was undertaken. For this purpose, the 25th and the 26th Railway Companies, the Faridkot Sappers and the 61st Pioneers along with 300 railway coolies and a unit of 1,500 African labourers were employed.[183] By July 1915, this railway line was completed. It proved invaluable during the advance of Force 'B' in 1916.

In the meantime, a blockade was imposed on German East Africa from midnight 28th February-1st March 1915[184] in order to check German efforts to send arms, ammunition and men, to German East Africa. Deprived of help from Germany, Vorbeck utilised other resources to continue the struggle. He enrolled many natives and trained them. The strength of the German force at the end of 1915 was 2,998 Europeans and 11,300 Askaris.[185]

Surrender of Bukooba by the Germans

Until June 1915, no major battle was fought in East Africa and only minor skirmishes took place all along the border. Major General Tighe, then Commanding Officer of Force 'B', adhering to the principle that the best defence is offence decided to undertake some offensive enterprise. He thought this would not only relieve the pressure on the long border but also prove that Force 'B'could repulse the attacks of the Germans.[186] The object he selected was Bukoba town, situated on the western shore of lake Victoria.[187] This town had a powerful wireless station and it was thought that its capture would dislocate the German line of communication.

Before making an attempt on Bukoba, all precautions were taken to keep the plan of attack on Bukoba secret, to take it by surprise.[188] To capture Bukoba, a force was dispatched under Brigadier General J.M. Stewart. This force consisted of one section of the 28th Mountain Battery, two companies of the 2nd Loyal North Lancashire Regiment, four companies of the 25th Royal Fusiliers, one company (double) of the 29th Punjabis, three companies of the 3rd Cing's African Rifles, a Machine gun section of the East Africa Regiment, 'C' Section of the 26th British Field Ambulance and C-22 Indian Clearing Hospital.[189] Their total fighting strength was about 1,600 men.[190] The whole force assembled at Kisumu and started for Bukoba by ship at 2 p.m. on June 20.[191] On the following night, it reached off the western shore north of Bukoba. As there was bright moonlight, it was difficult to remain unnoticed by the Germans. The German observation post at the Busira island noticed the arrival of the force and fired a rocket signal at about 1 a.m. on June 22, 1915.[192] For the rest of the night, the ships remained there without any disturbance from the German side. At 5.30 a.m. H.M.S. *Nyanza* was sent to threaten Bukoba while the rest of the fleet moved to the point of disembarkation, about 3 miles north-east of Bukoba.[193] The disembarkation was completed by about 1 p.m.[194] Originally, it had been planned to land three companies of the 3rd King's African Rifles at the Customs House situated south of Bukoba, but before the disembarkation could take place it was found that the German force had a gun in that area, and therefore the three companies of the King's African Rifles were disembarked north of Bukoba (a few yards south of the main landing place).[195]

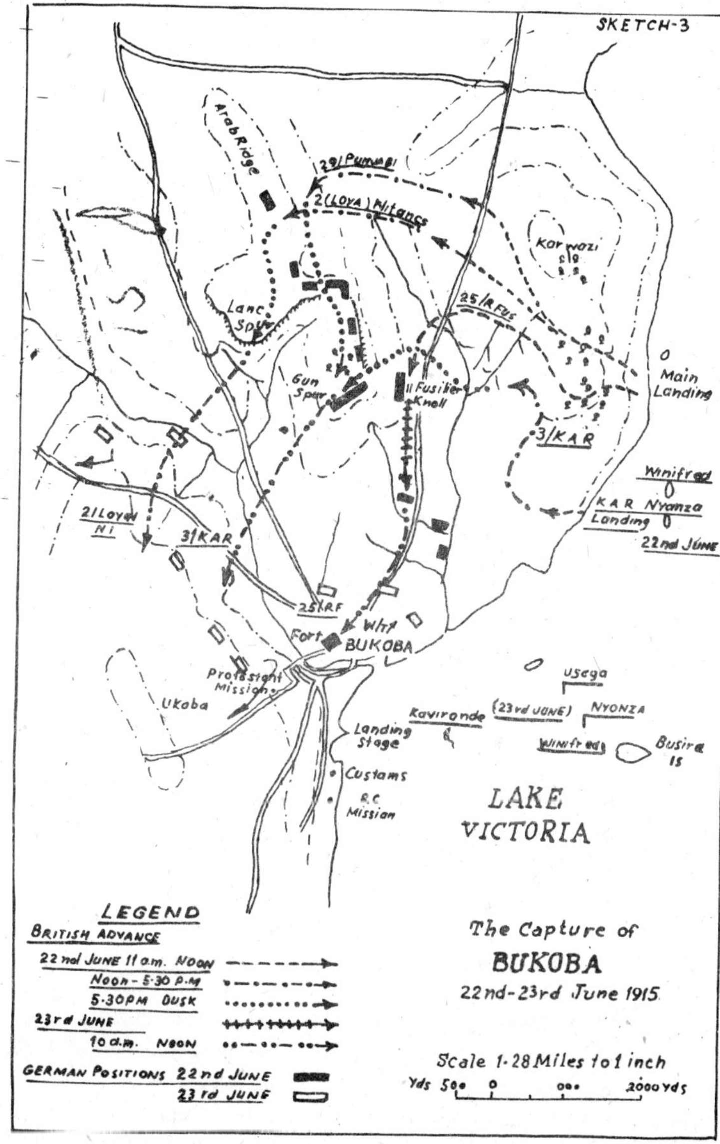
SKETCH-3
Arab Ridge
29/Pumnbi
2(Loya) N/Lancs
Karwazi
Lanc Spur
25/R Fus
Main Landing
Gun Spur
Fusilier Knoll
3/KAR
Winifred
KAR Nyanza Landing
22nd JUNE
2/Loyal N I
3/KAR
25/RF
W/T
Fort
BUKOBA
Protestant Mission
Usega
Ukoba
Kavironde
(23rd JUNE)
NYONZA
Landing Stage
Winifred
Busira Is
Customs
R.C Mission
LAKE VICTORIA
LEGEND
BRITISH ADVANCE
22nd JUNE 11 a.m. NOON
Noon - 5.30 p.m
5.30PM DUSK
23rd JUNE
10 a.m. NOON
GERMAN POSITIONS 22nd JUNE
23rd JUNE
The Capture of BUKOBA
22nd-23rd June 1915
Scale 1.28 Miles to 1 inch
Yds 500 0 2000 Yds

The troops were disposed from the left, in the following order; 'The 3rd King's African Rifles, the 25th Royal Fusiliers with the Machine guns of the East Africa Regiment, the 2nd Loyal North Lancashire Regiment and the 28th Mountain Battery in position on the Summit of Karawazi (east-north-east of Gun Spur) escorted by the 29th Punjabis. The Faridkot Sappers and Miners and the British section were behind the 25th Royal Fusiliers.[196]

The German force, consisting of 200 rifles and Maxim guns, was holding a strong opposition from Arab Ridge to Gun Spur.[197] The 2nd Loyal North Lancashire advanced towards Arab Ridge with the help of the section of 28th Mountain Battery and occupied it by 6 p.m.[198] The 29th Punjabis advanced towards Gun Spur turning right in order to reach the left flank of the German force which was also occupied by 6 p.m. with support of the 3rd King's African Rifles.[199] In the meantime, Fusilier Ridge was also occupied by the 25th Royal Fusiliers.[200] There was little opposition. No further event took place that night. (See Sketch 3).

The next morning it was decided to attack Bukoba town. The 2nd Loyal North Lancashire regiment was sent to the hills at the south-west of Bukoba, to cut off the German, line of retreat.[201] The 25th Royal Fusiliers were ordered to advance directly on Bukoba and the 2 guns of the 28th Mountain Battery and the guns of all the ships were employed to cover the advance.[202] The 3rd King's African Rifles and the 29th Punjabis were to serve as reserve on Gun Spur while the two engineering units (Faridkot Sappers and Miners and Bridging section) were to follow the 25th Royal Fusiliers into Bukoba to remove useful instruments from the wireless station and demolish the rest of the constructions[203].

Desultory firing started at 6.15 a.m. At 7 a.m. the 2nd Loyal North Lancashireo began moving towards Bukoba and the guns of the 28th Mountain Battery started firing from Gun Spur on men seen digging entrenchments around the Rest House.[204] The German force, replied to this fire from a position at Bukoba where they had a gun. This gun was soon knocked out of action by the 28th Mountain Battery.[205] The German force had to retire under pressure of the fire of the 28th Mountain Battery and the guns of the ships.[206] At 1.15 p.m. the 25th Royal Fusiliers entered the wireless station and the German flag was hauled down.[207]

The victory in this engagement was due to the superior number of Force 'B'. Moreover, the Germans were unable to reinforce their troops at Bukoba quickly because of the difficult geographical conditions. The fire of the Mountain Battery was accurate and of great value.[208] Yet, the planning of this battle too was faulty. On June 22, all the troops disembarked and moved in different directions to occupy various places. There was no reserve force.[209] Besides, Brigadier General Stewart was himself in the firing line.[210] And lastly, no attempt was made to capture Bukoba as quickly as possible, specially when the Germans had come to know of the British plans, and they gained ample time to remove ammunition etc. During the two days' fight, the total casualties of Force 'B' were 32 killed and wounded and the casualties of the Germans were 45 killed and wounded.[211]

On July 11, 1915, an important event occurred in this theatre. On this day, the career of the German cruiser *Königsberg* came to an end. With the help of some aircraft, the Royal Navy located the *Königsberg* in the Rufiji delta and destroyed it. The crew consisting of 322 men joined the German force and most of the arms and ammunition were salvaged.[212] Arms and ammunition had also been salvaged from the ship *Rübens*, which was sunk by the Royal Navy in April 1915.[213]

Action Near Mbuyuni

By the beginning of July 1915, a railhead had been established at Maktau.[214] The German force around Mbuyuni then started making frequent raids on Maktau. It was reported that the Germans were in *large number there*. Meinertzhagen, the Intelligence Officer of Force 'B' had reported to Malleson, leader of the force to Mbuyuni, that about 800 Germans with 6 Machine Guns were at Mbuyuni and they could be easily reinforced upto the strength of 3,000 men and 20 Machine Guns.[215]

Malleson, who was in-charge of the force around Maktau, decided to push back the Germans from Mbuyuni. For this purpose, he marched with a force from Maktau, on the afternoon of July 13, 1915, and bivouacked for the night 8 miles west of Maktau.[216] From there, he proceeded to attack Mbuyuni the next morning[217]. The force was divided into two columns, the Main and the Right. The Main Column, composed of troops of the Mounted Infantry of the 3rd King's African Rifles, one section of the 27th Mounted Battery, two companies of the 2nd Loyal North Lancashire, four (single) companies of the 29th Punjabis, and two companies of the 1st King's African Rifles (total 762 men[218]), was ordered to make a frontal attack on the German force at Mbuyuni.[219] The Right Column, composed of Cole's Scouts, two companies of the 2nd Rhodesians, two (single) companies of the 130th Baluchis, and two companies of the 4th King's African Rifles (total 461 men[220]) was ordered to attack the German forces on the left flank.[221]

The Main Column advanced to attack with the 29th Punjabis on the right and the 1st King's African Rifles on the left, while the 2nd Loyal North Lancashire regiment was kept in reserve.[222] The Right Column advanced to attack in the following order, from the right Cole's Scouts and the 4th King's African Rifles in centre, the 130th Baluchis on the left, and the 2nd Rhodesians behind the 4th King's African Rifles.[223]

A patrol party of Germans approached the Main Column on the morning of July 14. It was soon spotted by the 29th Punjabis, who fired on the German party with their Machine Guns.[224] This served as a warning to the main German force, which immediately took up the challenge. By 7.30 a.m. the Main Column came under heavy fire that brought it to a halt.[225] In the meantime, the Right Column encountered a German party which checked its advance by 8 a.m.[226]

Thinking that the Germans were in too great a strength (estimated approximately at 2,000 rifles and 10 to 20 Machine Guns).[227] Malleson ordered his force to withdraw.[228] By 1 p.m. all the advancing troops had retired.[229] The total casusalties of Force 'B' were 33 killed and 127 wounded.[230] and on the German side it was 5 killed and 30 wounded.[231]

Certain mistakes were committed by Force 'B' the engagement. First the white force moved during daylight, disclosing themselves to the German force.[232] Secondly, Malleson, who had been informed that the enemy's strength around Mbuyuni was over 3,000 men before he set out for Mbuyuni[233], made no effort together a sufficient number of troops to meet the German force there. Thirdly, the firing by the 29th Punjabis on the German patrol before the fixed time of attack warned the German force that Force 'B' was advancing to attack and thus removed the element of surprise. And lastly, Malleson delivered a frontal attack on a carefully prepared position held by the German force. It is true that he made a flank movement as well, but that was never intended to be the decisive attack which it should have been.[234] It was reported afterwards that the German force at Mbuyuni on July 14, 1915 was composed of 45 Germans, 600 Askaris and 69 irregulars with 6 Machine Guns.[235] As such, the German force was not superior in strength. Had a well-planned attack been made on the German force, Malleson's force would have been successful in its mission.

Raids From August 1915 to January 1916

As it was decided that offensive action should be adopted after the arrival of reinforcements, only minor engagements took place during this period. On August 14, 1915, a German patrol launched a surprise attack on 87 men of the 130th Baluchis at Kasigau.[236] On September 14, 1915, a part of 100 men of the 130th Baluchis and 60 men of the European Mounted Infantry ambushed a German patrol of 60 to 70 Askaris around Maktau. In this encounter, the German patrol lost heavily.[237]

On September 20, 1915, reports were received that a German force of about 80 men with 2 Machine Guns was at Longido west, covering the water.[238] It was decided to attack the German force there. For the same purpose, a reconnaissance force of about 450 men, consisting of one squadron of the 17th Cavalry, one company of the King's African Rifles (Mounted Infantry), two companies of the 3rd King's African Rifles and the East African Mounted Rifles was ordered to go to Longido west.[239] The force attacked the enemy on September 21 [240] and found that the Germans were well entrenched there. It was very difficult to continue the fight without artillery support. Moreover, the men were exhausted as they had to march for 16 to 17 miles in the night.[241] The attack came to a standstill. Yet as this force was superior in strength the German party vacated the camp by the evening.[242] The total causalties of Force 'B' were 13 killed, 33 wounded, 4 missing and 2 deserted to the enemy.[243] The exact number of German causalties could not be ascertained but 12 dead bodies were found later.[244]

Minor engagements continued till the beginning of 1916, In the meantime, the British protectorates of Uganda, Rhodesia and Nyasaland also joined in the attack on the borders of German East Africa and the Government of Belgian Congo, too, agreed to cooperate in the attacks from the west on the enemy.[245] Towards the end of 1915, the British Government decided to send the South African troops to German East Africa.[246] These units started moving to British East Africa from December 1915[247] onwards and by the end of March 1916, all the units, comprising about 18,700 men, which had been detailed for East Africa, had reached there.[248]

During the period from the outbreak of hostilities upto the beginning of 1916, Force 'B' in East Africa was not successful on the whole because no proper planning was done beforehand. There was no topographical information with Force 'B' when it arrived at Tanga, which is why it took so long to disembark the troops and the British were not able to properly deploy their units. The artillery units were not used effectively against the Germans. The troops were not given sufficient time to recoup from the fatigue of the journey. In addition, there was no alternative plan with Force 'B'. One of the prerequisites of success in battle is to have alternative plans, so that in case of failure of one plan, the alternative plan immediately be executed. As soon as the original plan of Force 'B' failed, it had to sail to British East Africa.

After the Tanga affair, Force 'B' had to go on the defensive as it was realised that without a greater number of troops it could not launch an offensive on the Germans. As Great Britain was busy in the other theatres of the war, it could not spare more troops for East Africa until the beginning of 1916. During this period it undertook defensive-offensive operations in which only meagre success was achieved.

NOTES

1. *History of the Great War - Military Operations, East Africa,* Vol. 1, London, 1941, pp. 15-16.
2. *Ibid.*, p. 53.
3. *Ibid.*, p. 54.
4. Von L. Vorbeck, *My Reminiscences of German East Africa,* London, 1920, p. 3.
5. *Ibid.*, p. 4.
6. *Ibid.*, p. 4.
7. *History of the Great War. op.cit.*, pp. 16-18.
8. M.D., H.S., Plans, Operations Against German East Africa, p. 10.
9. *History of the Great War, op.cit.*, p. 31.
10. See Chapter II.
11. *History of the Great War, op.cit.*, p. 20.
12. Von L. Vorbeck, *op.cit.*, p. 27.
13. *History of the Great War, op.cit.*, p. 21 fn.
14. Von L. Vorbeck, *op.cit.*, p. 28.
15. *History of the Great War, op.cit.*, p. 21.
16. Von L. Vorbeck, *op.cit.*, p. 15.
17. *History of the Great War, op.cit.*, pp. 20-21.
18. *Ibid.*, pp. 20-21. See also Von L. Vorbeck, *op.cit.*, p. 21.
19. Von L. Vorbeck, *op.cit.*, pp. 28-29. See also *History of the Great War, op.cit.*, p. 28.
20. *Ibid.*, p. 37.
21. M.D., H.S., G.S.B., The European Crisis, Vol. 5, pp. 876-877.
22. *History of the Great War, op.cit.*, p. 37.

23. The War Diary, IEF 'C', Vol. 3, pp. 17-19, states that $3\frac{1}{2}$ companies were moved to Tsavo. Therefore, it appears a half company was left at Voi.
24. *History of the Great War, op.cit.*, pp. 37-38.
25. *Ibid.*, p. 38.
26. *Ibid.*, p. 38.
27. M.D., H.S., G.S.B., The European Crisis, Vol. 6, p. 918.
28. *History of the Great War, op.cit.*, p. 38.
29. M.D., H.S., G.S.B., The European Crisis, Vol. 6, p. 918.
30. *Ibid.*, p. 918.
31. M.D., H.S., War Diary, IEF 'C', Vol. 4, p. 51.
32. *History of the Great War, op.cit.*, pp. 41-42.
33. It consisted of the half battalion of Imperial Service Troops from Bharatpur, Jind, Kapurthala and Rampur, 27th Mountain Battery, Calcutta Volunteer Battery and Volunteer Maxim Battery.
34. *History of the Great War, op.cit.*, p. 47 fn.
35. *Ibid.*, p. 47.
36. It was composed of half a company of Volunteer Machine Gun Company, two companies of 29th Punjabis, Jind Imperial Service Troops, one Arab company, half a company of King's African Rifles (reservists). M.D., H.S., War Diary, IEF 'C', Vol. 4, pp. 19-20.
37. *Ibid.*, pp. 19-20.
38. *History of the Great War, op.cit.*, p. 65.
39. *Ibid.*, p. 65.
40. M.D., H.S., War Diary, IEF 'B', Vol. 3, p. 74. This plan was chalked out in England.
41. According to Meinertzhagen, Intelligence Officer of IEF 'B', the convoy was left about 15 miles away. R Meinertshagen, *Army Diary*, London, 1936, p. 87.
42. M.D., H.S., War Diary, IEF 'B', Vol. 4, p. 15.
43. *Ibid.*
44. R. Meinertzhagen, *op.cit.*, p. 87.
45. Von L. Vorbeck, *op.cit.*, p. 35.
46. *Ibid.*
47. *History of the Great War, op.cit.*, p. 103.
48. Von L. Vorbeck, *op.cit.*, p. 36. The two companies were the 15th and 16th (F.K. Companies) according to the offical history of the campaign.

49. Along the Ushambara Railway were small protective detachments of 4 Sch. and 5 Sch. K. German Headquarters were at New Moshi, the terminus of the railway, 150 miles from Tanga, together with 1 and 6 F.K. And 6 Sch. K. Along the border were distributed three advanced detachments: at taveta under Captian von Prince, 7 Sch. and 8 Sch. K and 19 K, with three small guns, on Kilimanjaro under Major Kapler, 4, 8, 9, and 13 F.K. With Hering's "batter" of two obsolete field guns at Longido under Major Kraut, 10, 11 and 21 F.K., 9 Sch. K. *History of the Great War, op.cit.*, p. 103.
50. Von L. Vorbeck, *op.cit.*, p. 35. See also History of the Great War, *op.cit.*, p. 104.
51. *Ibid.*, p. 36.
52. *Ibid.*
53. J.J. Collyer, *op.cit.*, p. 38.
54. M.D., H.S., War Diary, IEF 'B', Vol. 6, p. 30.
55. *Ibid.*
56. *Ibid.*, Vol 4, p. 15.
57. *Ibid.*, Vol. 6, p. 30.
58. *Ibid.*
59. *Ibid.*
60. *Ibid.*
61. *Ibid.*
62. *Ibid.*
63. R. Meinertzhagen, *op.cit.*, p. 89.
64. M.D., H.S., War Diary, IEF 'B', Vol. 6, p. 31.
65. *Ibid.*
66. *Ibid.*
67. *Ibid.*, Vol. 4, p. 15.
68. *Ibid.*, Vol. 6, p. 31.
69. *Ibid.*, Vol. 4, p. 15.
70. *Ibid.*
71. *Ibid.*, p. 16.
72. *Ibid.*
73. Von L. Vorbeck *op.cit.*, pp. 39-41.
74. *Ibid.*, p. 40.
75. M.D., H.S., War Diary, IEF 'B', Vol. 4, p. 16.
76. R. Meinertzhagen, *op.cit.*, p. 90. See also M.D., H.S., War Diary, IEF 'B', Vol. 4, p. 16.
77. M.D., H.S., War Diary, IEF 'B' Vol. 6, p. 32.
78. *Ibid.*, Vol. 4, p. 16.

79. *Ibid.*, Vol. 6, p. 32.
80. R. Meinertzhagen, *op.cit.*, p. 91.
81. M.D., H.S., War Diary, IEF 'B', Vol. 6, p. 32.
82. R. Meinertzhagen, *op.cit.*, p. 95.
83. *Ibid.*
84. M.D., H.S., War Diary, IEF 'B', Vol. 6, p. 33.
85. *Ibid.*
86. *Ibid.*, p. 34.
87. *Ibid.*
88. *Ibid.*
89. *Ibid.*
90. *Ibid.*, p. 35.
91. *Ibid.*
92. *Ibid.*
93. *Ibid.*
94. *Ibid.*
95. *Ibid.*
96. *Ibid.*, p. 27.
97. R. Meinertzhagen, *op.cit.*, p. 103.
98. M.D., H.S., War Diary IEF 'B', Vol. 4, p. 9.
99. R. Meinertzhagen, *op.cit.*, p. 96.
100. on L. Vorbeck, *op.cit.*, p. 44.
101. R. Meinertzhagen, *op.cit.*, p. 104.
102. J.J. Collyer, *op.cit.*, p. 47
103. M.D., H.S., War Diary, IEF 'B', Vol. 4, p. 17.
104. R. Meinertzhagen, *op.cit.*, p. 104.
105. M.D., H.S., War Diary, IEF 'B', Vol. 4, p. 17.
106. R. Meinertzhagen, *op.cit.*, p. 104.
107. M.D., H.S., War Diary, IEF 'B', Vol. 6, p. 13.
108. Ibid.
109. *Ibid.*
110. *Ibid.*
111. *Ibid.*
112. *Ibid.*
113. *Ibid.*
114. *Ibid.*, p. 15
115. *Ibid.*, p. 13.
116. *Ibid.*
117. *Ibid.*, p. 14.
118. *Ibid.*

119. *Ibid.*
120. *Ibid.*
121. *Ibid.*
122. *Ibid.*
123. *Ibid.*
124. *Ibid.*
125. *Ibid.*
126. *Ibid.*
127. *Ibid.*
128. *Ibid.*
130. *Ibid.*
131. *Ibid.*
132. *Ibid.*
133. *Ibid.*
134. *History of the Great War, op.cit.*, p. 98
135. M.D., H.S., War Diary, IEF 'B', Vol. 6, p. 15.
136. *Ibid.*
137. *Ibid.*
138. *Ibid.*
139. *Ibid.*
140. *Ibid.*, p. 16
141. *History of the Great War, op.cit.*, p. 98.
142. M.D., H.S., War Diary, IEF 'B', Vol. 6, p. 16.
143. M.D., H.S., G.S.B., The European Crisis, Vol. 4, p. 30.
144. *Ibid.*, p. 28.
145. *History of the Great War, op.cit.*, p. 117.
146. *Ibid.*, p. 100.
147. *Ibid.*, p. 121.
148. M.D., H.S., War Diary, IEF 'B', Vol. 6, p. 45.
149. *Ibid.*, p. 60.
150. *Ibid.*, p. 9.
151. *Ibid.*, p. 60.
152. *History of the Great War, op.cit.*, p. 122 fn.
153. M.D., H.S., War Diary, IEF 'B', Vol. 6, p. 60.
154. *History of the Great War, op.cit.*, p. 123.
155. *Ibid.*
156. M.D., H.S., War Diary, IEF 'B', Vol. 6, p. 60
157. *History of the Great War, op.cit.*, p. 124.
158. M.D., H.S., G.S.B., The European Crisis, Vol. 23. p. 3335.
159. *History of the Great War, op.cit.*, p. 123.

160. *Ibid.*, p. 124.
161. *Ibid.*
162. Von L. Vorbeck, *op.cit.*, p. 57.
163. M.D., H.S., G.S.B., The European Crisis, Vol. 23, p. 3412C.
164. *History of the Great War, op.cit.*, p. 124 fn.
165. *Ibid.*
166. *Ibid.*, p. 125.
167. *Ibid.*
168. *Ibid.*
169. *Ibid.*
170. *Ibid.*
171. *Ibid.*
172. *Ibid.*, pp. 126-127.
173. *Ibid.*, p. 127
174. M.D., H.S., G.S.B., The European Crisis., Vol. 23, p. 3417.
175. Von L., Vorbeck, *op.cit.*, p. 127.
176. M.D., H.S., G.S.B., The European Crisis., Vol. 23, p. 3426.
177. M.D., H.S., War Diary, *IEF 'B'*, Vol. 6, P. 86.
178. M.D., H.S., G.S.B., The European Crisis, Vol. 23, p. 3426.
179. *History of the Great War, op.cit.*, p. 127.
180. *Ibid.*
181. *Ibid.*, p. 130.
182. *Ibid.*, p. 130 fn.
183. *Ibid.*, p. 130.
184. M.D., H.S., G.S.B., The European Crisis, Vol. 27, p. 3837.
185. Von L. Vorbeck, *op.cit.*, p. 72.
186. M.D., H.S., War Diary., *IEF 'B'*, Vol. 12, p. 1.
187. *Ibid.*
188. *Ibid.*
189. *Ibid.*, p. 3.
190. *History of the Great War, op.cit.*, p. 151.
191. M.D., H.S., War Diary, *IEF 'B'*, Vol. 12, p. 1.
192. *Ibid.*
193. *Ibid.*
194. *Ibid.*, pp. 3-4.
195. *Ibid.*
196. *Ibid.*, p. 4.
197. *Ibid.*
198. *Ibid.*
199. *Ibid.*

200. *Ibid.*
201. *Ibid.*, p. 5.
202. *Ibid.*
203. *Ibid.*
204. *Ibid.*, p. 6.
205. A. Buchanan, *Three Years of War in East Africa*, London, 1919, p. 23.
206. M.D., H.S., War Diary, *IEF 'B'* Vol. 12, p. 6.
207. *Ibid.*
208. R. Meinertzhagen, *op.cit.*, p. 134.
209. *Ibid.*
210. *Ibid.*
211. M.D., H.S., War Diary, *IEF 'B'*, Vol. 12, P. 7.
212. *History of the Great War, op.cit.*, p. 153.
213. *Ibid.*, p. 154.
214. M.D., H.S., G.S.B., The European Crisis, Vol. 58, p. 8169.
215. R. Meinertzhagen, *op.cit.*, p. 137.
216. M.D., H.S., G.S.B., The European Crisis, Vol. 58, p. 8169.
217. *Ibid.*
218. *Ibid.*, p. 8169.
219. R. Meinertzhagen, *op.cit.*, p. 138.
220. M.D., H.S., G.S.B., The European Crisis, Vol. 58, p. 8169.
221. R. Meinertzhagen, *op.cit.*, p. 138.
222. From the sketch of the battle, *History of the Great War, op.cit.*, Sketch 17.
223. *Ibid.*
224. *Ibid.*, p. 157
225. *Ibid.*
226. *Ibid.*, p. 157.
227. M.D., H.S., G.S.B., The European Crisis, Vol. 58, p. 8169.
228. *Ibid.*
229. *Ibid.*
230. M.D., H.S., War Diary, *IEF 'B'*, Vol. 13, p. 50.
231. *History of the Great War, op.cit.*, p. 158 fn.
232. R. Meinertzhagen, *op.cit.*, p. 138.
233. *Ibid.*, p. 137.
234. *Ibid.*
235. *History of the Great War, op.cit.*, p. 158 fn.
236. M.D., H.S., War Diary, *IEF 'B'*, Vol. 14, p. 23.
237. M.D., H.S., G.S.B., The European Crisis. Vol. 57, p. 10647.

238. *Ibid.*
239. *Ibid.*
240. *Ibid.*
241. *Ibid.*
242. *Ibid.*
243. *Ibid.*
244. *Ibid.*
245. *History of the Great War, op.cit.*, pp. 106-209.
246. J.J. Collyer, *op.cit.*, p. 50.
247. *History of the Great War, op.cit.*, p. 216 fn.
248. J.J. Collyer, *op.cit.*, p.50.

5

Duel For Kilimanjaro

The British Government could not spare more Indian troops for the German East African Campaign during 1914-1915, after the Tanga disaster, as it had to send the bulk of the Indian units to the other theatres, especially to Mesopotamia and Gallipoli. Only the 17th Cavalry (one squadron), the 130th Baluchis, the 17th Infantry, the 40th Pathans, the 129th Baluchis and the 5th Light Infantry reached East Africa by March 1916. Before the arrival of the 5th Light Infantry, the effective strength of Force 'B' was 13,355 men[1] and after the arrival of the 5th Light Infantry, it rose to 13,880 men.

As mentioned earlier, the British Government decided to send the South African troops to East Africa at the end of 1915. During that year, the situation had not improved much in favour of England in the other theatres of war while in Africa some gains had been registered for the British armies. On July 9, 1915, German South-West Africa was captured by the troops of the Union of South Africa who had been assigned this task. After the capture of German South-West Africa, the British Government decided to send the South African troops to East Africa, expecting that they would be very useful there as they had fought in German South-West Africa under similar conditions. By the end of March 1916, the original draft of 18,700 South Africa troops reached British East Africa to launch an offensive against German East Africa.[2] The command of all the forces in British East Africa was given to General Sir Horace Smith-Dorrien.[3] General Smith-Dorrien started for British East Africa on December 24, 1915 from Plymouth to take up the new assignment. On the way, he stopped at the Cape to confer with the authorities of the Union of South Africa about their military units and their equipment.[4] Unfortunately, he fell ill there and it became impossible for him to take up his new assignment.[5] On February 6, 1916,

Lieutenant-General Jan C. Smuts was appointed as Commander-in-Chief of the forces in British East Africa.[6] He left Pretoria on February 11, and arrived at Mombasa on February 19, 1916.[7]

By the first week of February, 1916, the Ist Mounted Brigade commanded by Brigadier General Van Deventer, the 2nd Infantry Brigade commanded by Brigadier General P.S. Beves and five field batteries of the South African Field Artillery had reached British East Africa and, even while Lieutenant General J.C. Smuts was on his way to British East Africa, an action had already taken place at Salatia hill.[8]

Attempt at Salatia Hill.

Salatia hill, situated midway along the Taveta-Maktau road formed a part of British East Africa. It was occupied by the Germans after the outbreak of hostilities in East Africa. Salatia hill was known to the Germans as Oldorobo hill.[9] The 2nd Division under Brigadier General Malleson was commissioned to recapture the hill. The whole force of about 6,000 men, comprised the Ist East African Brigade (the 2nd Loyal North Lancashire, the 2nd Rhodesians and the 130th Baluchis), the 2nd South African Infantry Brigade (the 5th, 6th and 7th South African Infantry battalions), and the Divisional troops (the Mounted Infantry Company and Belfield's Mounted Scouts) and the 4th Indian Mountain Artillery Brigade (less one battery) which included the 28th Mounted Battery, the No. 1 Light Battery, the Calcutta Volunteer Battery, the No. 3 and No. 4 Heavy Batteries, four Armoured Cars, the Volunteer Machine Gun Battery and the 61st Pioneers.[10]

At Salatia hill there was a German force under Major Kraut[11] consisting of about 120 Germans, 1,200 Askaris with 12 Machine Guns and 2 small guns.[12] In the west of Salatia hill, at Taveta, a German detachment under Captain Schulz was encamped.[13] This detachment was composed of about 600 men, i.e. three companies[14] (by that time a company's strength had risen to about 200 men). Vorbeck's plan was to let the British force come to Salatia hill and then to defeat it by launching a counter-attack.[15]

The British plan was to deliver the main attack from the north of the hill and simultaneously attacking from the east to contain the German force there.[16] On February 12, 1916, in the morning, the British force started from Serengeti, the 2nd South African Infantry Brigade towards the north-west and the Ist East African Brigade towards the west.[17] Both the forces reached the Nyoro *nullah,* about one and a half miles apart at about 6.45 a.m.[18] The 2nd South African Infntry Brigade continued its advance until it reached about 1,000 yards from the German position while the Ist East African Infantry Brigade with most of the artillery units (except two 4" guns, which were left at the *nullah*), moved up to within 3,000 yards of Salatia hill.[19]

The 7th South African Infantry Battalion of the 2nd South African Infantry Brigade advanced up to 500 yards short of the foot of the hill with the help of the covering fire of a section of the 28th Mountain Battery.[20] The Germans replied to it with the fire. At 10.45 a.m. the Ist East African Infantry Brigade was sent to assist the 2nd South African Infantry Brigade by attacking the eastern face of the hill. By noon its advance brought it, with the 2nd Loyal North Lancashire in the centre, flanked by the 2nd Rhodesian on the left and the 130th Baluchis on the right rear, to the edge of the hush about 1,000 yards from the German trenches.[21] A heavy German attack on this brigade checked its advance. By that time the German detachment under Captain Schulz was ordered to march from Taveta along the rear of Kraut's detachment, to make a decisive attack on the right flank of the 2nd South African Infantry Brigade.[22] Soon after, being pressed by the German counter-attack, the British force began withdrawing. The retirement was well covered by the fire of the 28th Mountain Battery assisted by the No. 1 Light Battery, the Volunteer Machine Gun Battery and the Machine Guns of the 2nd Loyal North Lancashire.[23]

Later, when the British force was retiring, a bayonet charge was made by the Germans upon the 2nd Loyal North Lancashire and the 130th Baluchis. Its was successfully checked by the 130th Baluchis,[24] saving not only the lives of many soldiers of the British force but also retaining much of the arms and ammunition, which would otherwise have fallen into German hands. In the battle at Salatia hill, the British losses were 138 in the 2nd South African Brigade. The losses were slight in the remainder of the force.[25] The German losses although not on record could safely be deemed negligible. (See Sketch 4).

The strategy of this battle was not sound. No attempt was made to prevent the Germans from reinforcing their units at Salatia hill. For this purpose, the British force should have sent a detachment to the Taveta-Salatia road by a wide turning movement, either from the north or the south of Salatia hill, before delivering the attack. Tactically speaking, there was no reserve. Both the brigades were on the firing line and that is why, when the Germans counter-attacked, the British force could not get reinforcements. Moreover, there was little coordination of the efforts between the two brigades.[26]

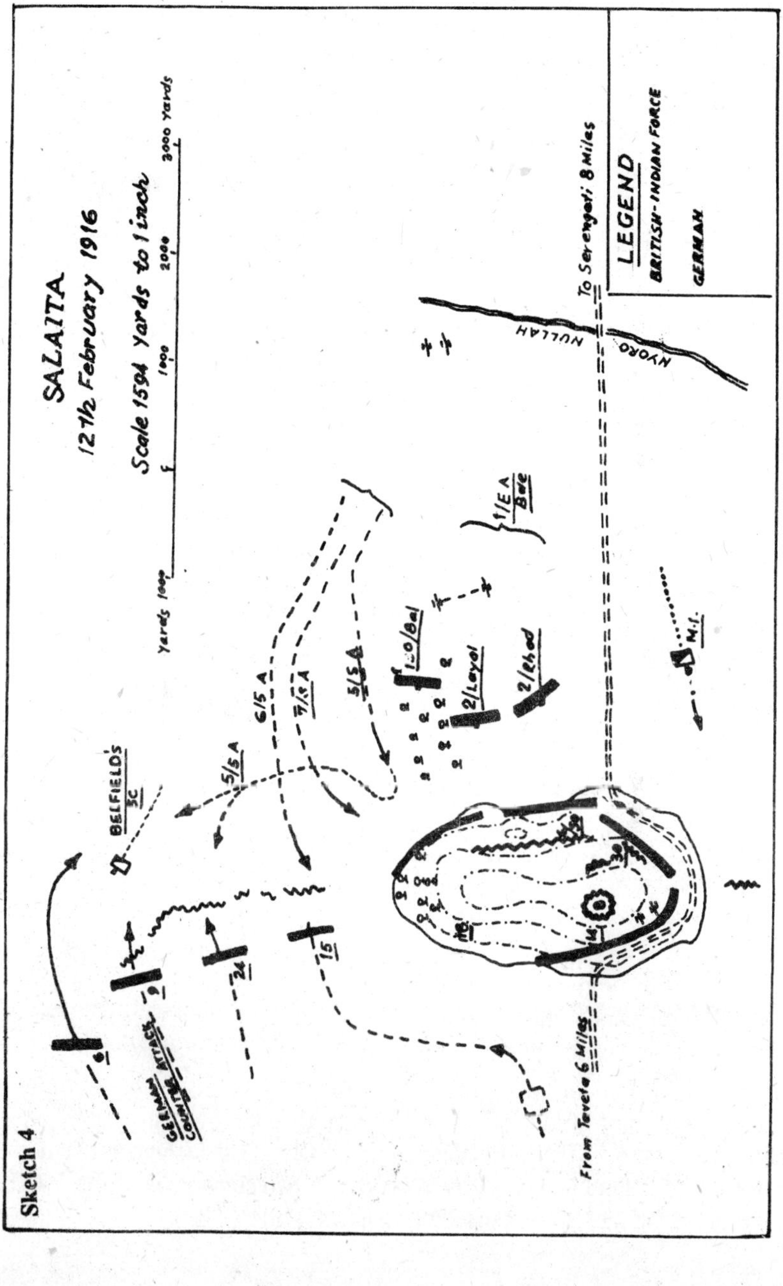
Sketch 4
SALAITA
12 1/2 February 1916
Scale 1594 Yards to 1 inch
Yards 1000
1000
2000
3000 Yards
LEGEND
BRITISH-INDIAN FORCE
GERMAN
To Serengeti 8 Miles
NYORO NULLAH
From Taveta 6 Miles
BELFIELD'S 3C
GERMAN COUNTER ATTACK
5/S A
6/S A
7/S A
1/E A Bde
2/Loyal
2/Rhod
M.I.
9
24
15
6

Capture of the Kilimanjaro

With the coming of Lieutenant General Smuts to East Africa, the offensive was resumed. By the beginning of March 1916, as most of the troops of the original draft had come from South Africa, Lieutenant-General Smuts decided to capture German East Africa and, as the first step in that direction, he planned to capture the Kilimanjaro area, which was free from the Tsetse fly. The southern foot of the Kilimanjaro could be reached by only two ways - from the east by the Taveta-Moshi road, which was flanked by the Kilimanjaro hills to the north and the Pare, the Latema and the Reata hills to the south, and from the west by the Longide-Moshi route which was flanked on the left by the Kilimanjaro hills and on the right by the Meru hills. Smuts decided to attack from both sides. According to a despatch, outlining the plan, Smuts wrote:[27]

The task of the Ist Division was to cross the 35 miles of waterless bush which lay between Longido and the Engare Namjuki River, occupy the latter and then advance between Meru and Kilimanjaro to Vieh Bomaja Ngombe (Somali Hauser). My intention was thereafter to direct this division on Kahe and cut the enemy's line of communications by Ushambara Railway. The task of the Ist S.A.M. Brigade and of the 2nd Division was to advance through the gap between Kilimanjaro and the Pare hills against the enemy's main force, which was reported to be concentrated in the neighbourhood of Taveta with strong detachments at the head of the Lake Jipe in the bush, east of the River Lumi, and at Salatia. The total force with which the enemy could oppose our advance into the Kilimanjaro area was estimated at 6,000 rifles with 37 m.gs. and 16 guns. (See Sketch 5)

The German force in the Kilimanjaro area, according to their official document, was composed of twentysix companies on March 5, 1916.[28] According to Vorbeck, the German force around the Kilimanjaro area consisted of 4,000 rifles.[29] To defeat this force, Smuts sent a force of 18,400 men, 57 guns and 99 Machine Guns, which included the Ist and the 2nd Divisions, the Reserve Force and the Flanking Force.[30] The detailed composition of the British force is given in Appendix B.[31]

According to the plan, the Ist Division started from Longido hill towards its first destination Vieh Bomaja Ngombe (Somali Hauser) on March 5, 1916.[32] The following morning, a German detachment met this force at Ngaserai and was driven off by the two companies of the 29th Punjabis and a section of the 27th Mountain Battery.[33]

Sketch 5

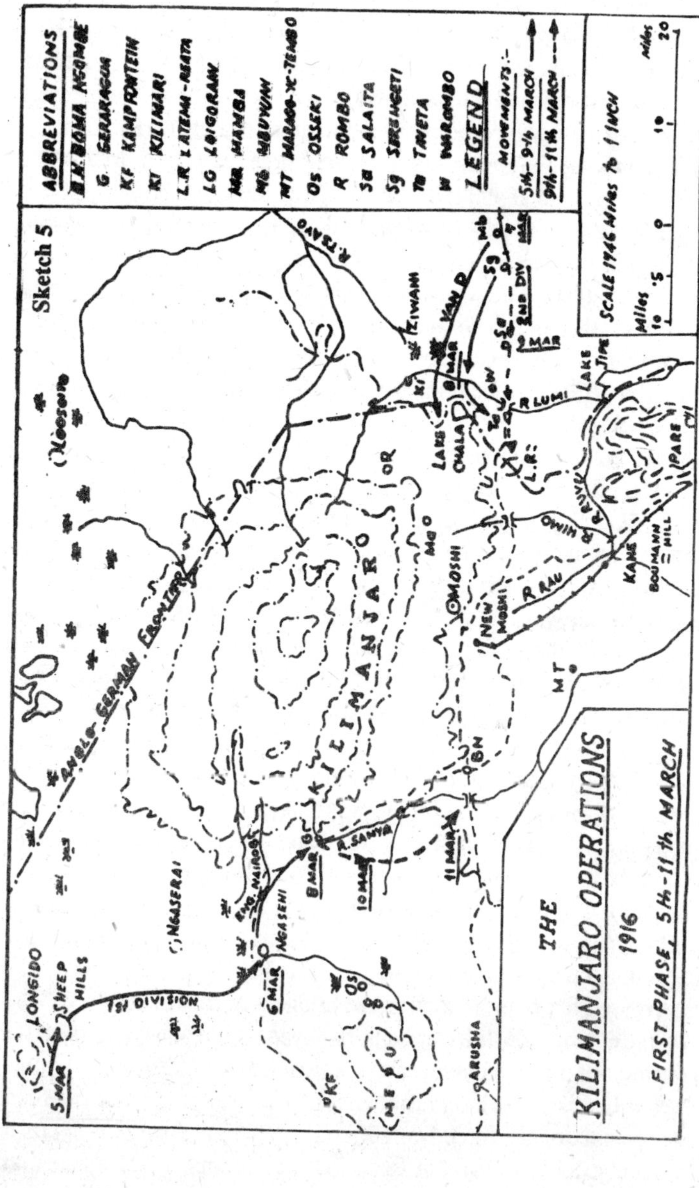

THE KILIMANJARO OPERATIONS 1916

FIRST PHASE, 5th-11th MARCH

On March 8, the Ist Division reached Geraragua from where it became difficult for the Division to move fast as the roads became practically impassable following heavy rains.[34] The Faridkot Sappers and Miners repaired the roads and made them passable.[35] The force started from Geraragua and reached Sanja (Sanya) river bridge about 3 miles west of Vieh Bomaja (Boma) Ngombe by the night of March 12/13.[36]

The Flanking Force and the Reserve Force started on March 7 and reached Lumi river at about 6 a.m. on March 8.[37] Lumi river was bridged by the 61st Poineers[38] which facilitated the further movement of the forces. The Flanking Force occupied Chala hill on the same day without any resistance and on the next day a fort was occupied near the Kilimari hill.[39] On March 10, the 2nd South African Horse had an encounter with a German force near Taveta and after a sharp skirmish the German force was driven off.[40] The 2nd South African Horse, after this skirmish, retired to the Chala hill.

While the Ist Division, the Flanking Force and the Reserve Force were thus engaged, the 2nd Division advanced towards Salatia hill. A frontal attack was delivered with the help of aeroplanes on March 8 at Salatia, which drove away the Germans and the next day the Salatia hill was occupied by the 2nd Division.[41] During the advance towards Salatia, the road and the railway line from Voi to Maktau, which had been constructed by the units of the Indian Army, namely the Faridkot Sappers, the 61st Pioneer, and the 25th and 26th Railway Companies proved very useful. On March 10, in the morning, the 2nd Division moved towards Taveta by road. At intervals, the Germans had dug trenches in the road (3 feet deep and 2 feet wide) to obstruct the movement of wheeled traffic.[42] On the way to Lumi river, the bridge was found unsuitable for most of the artillery units. The bridge was repaired and the bulk of the artillery units crossed it by the evening of March 11.[43] Meanwhile, the infantry units and the 8th (Calcutta) and the 13th Howitzer Batteries (these two artillery units had crossed the Lumi river with the help of oxen) moved up to Taveta and occupied it by the noon of March 10, 1916.[44] The remaining artillery units crossed the river as soon as the bridge was repaired.

On the enemy side, the Germans deployed their troops for a fresh stand on the mountains - the Latema and the Reata.[45] A detachment was posted in the north-west of the Latema mountain and another on the road to Moshi, while the bulk of the force was kept near the Himo river.[46] Reports had been received by the British force that the Germans had concentrated around the Reata and the Latema hills.[47] Smuts decided to drive out this force before advancing. He ordered a frontal attack at the neck between the Latema and the Reata hills.[48] In the morning of the March 11, reconnaissance was made, and it was found that the Germans were entrenched along the hills. As Malleson was sick, the command was taken over by Tighe.[49] During the day, the 130th Baluchis and the 3rd King's African Rifles advanced but under the pressure of the heavy fire of the Germans, they had to retire.[50] By the evening, the 2nd Rhodesians had also moved in but a strong counter-attack by the Germans had compelled all the units to retire to lower ground.[51]

Later, Tighe decided to push forward and endeavour to clear the ridge with a bayonet charge.[52] He ordered the 2nd Rhodesians and the 3rd King's African Rifles to advance on the left side and the 5th South African Infantry and the 130th Baluchis on the right side towards the crest.[53] The 2nd Rhodesians and the 3rd King's African Rifles were able to make their way to the crest.[54] The 130th Baluchis and the 5th South African Infantry were joined by the 7th South African Infantry.[55] The 7th South African Infantry succeeded in taking both sides of the neck while the 5th South African Infantry reached the neck itself.[56] The Germans attacked the British forces in the night of March 11/12.[57] The 130th Baluchis were ordered to help the 5th South African Infantry.[58] In the fight which ensued, the British forces were driven back. The following morning, the Germans evacuated their position at the hills.[59] Consequently, the British forces occupied these positions on March 13. The number of casualties on the British side was about 300,[60] while the number of casualties on the German side, according to Dr. H. Schnee, Governor of German East Africa, was 123.[61]

This expedition was a failure due to ill-planning. First, there should also have been an attack on the northern flank of the German position at the hills, i.e., from the north of the Latema mountain. This would have contained some of the German troops there. Only then, should the frontal attack have been delivered. Second, there was not enough force in reserve to check the German counter-attack. Most of the British units were far off, near Taveta, and were unable to reinforce the fighting units, quickly. Besides, because of the dense bush, it was not possible to have communication between the different units and the different fighting units could not support each other.

Occupation of Kahe

After vacating the Latema and Reata hills, the German forces moved along the Reata-Kahe road and encamped in the South-West area of Reata hill.[62] The German force employed between Kilimanjaro and Meru, which had been pushed to New Moshi by the British forces, was also ordered to move up to Kahe while one of the detachments of this force, which was energetically pursued by a British unit, made its way to Kondoa-Irangi via Arusha.[63]

On the British side, the Flanking Column under Van Deventer, was ordered to move up to New Moshi by the Taveta Moshi road.[64] The Ist South African Mounted Brigade reached the Himo river and found that the bridge on it had been blown up by the Germans.[65] The Ist South African Mounted Brigade crossed the river by an old drift at a short distance from the bridge and reached Old Moshi by March 15.[66] The Ist Division had by this time reached New Moshi.[67]

Smuts then decided to push back the Germans southwards and issued orders accordingly for a general advance. On March 18, at 8.30 a.m., the 2nd South African Brigade advanced from the Himo bridge towards Unterer Himo hill.[68] This Brigade was assisted by the Ist East African Brigade (less two battalions) and the 9th South African Battery.[69] By the evening, Unterer Himo hill was occupied.[70] At the same time, the 3rd South African Brigade with the 28th Mountain Battery advanced towards the Kifumu and Euphorbien hills and occupied the latter by the evening.[71] On the same day, the 2nd East African Brigade along with the 17th Cavalry advanced towards Massai Kraal where it faced German fire. On March 19, with the help of the 129th Baluchis, the Germans were pushed back.[72]

On the same day, the 2nd South African Brigade and the 5th South African Battery advanced southwards from Unterer Himo hill to Rasthaus but soon came to a standstill because the bush was practically impenetrable.[73] At the same time, the 3rd South African Brigade also advanced towards Rasthaus, while the Ist East African Infantry Brigade formed the reserve.[74] This force was attacked by the Germans as soon as it neared Rasthaus.[75] In spite of the invaluable support of the 28th Mountain Battery, which silenced many German guns, the British force could not advance much further because of the dense bush.[76] By the evening, a German detachment succeeded in bypassing the bush to a position on the western flank of the advancing British troops, from where it opened the enfilade fire upon the British troops and forced them to retire to Euphorbien hill.[77] The British casualties were 40.[78]

Smuts then ordered the 2nd South African Brigade to reinforce Sheppards' Brigade (the 2nd East African Brigade) which was at Store on the Kile-Kahe road, facing the main body of Germans numbering 2,000 men.[79] The Ist South African Mounted Brigade of Van Deventer was ordered to make a wide turning movement southwards from New Moshi to Kahe to reach the rear of the Germans.[80] At this juncture, Major General Stewart relinquished command of the Ist Division prior to his returning to India and the Division was placed under the command of Brigadier General Sheppared.[81]

On the 20th, Sheppard sent patrols out on reconnaissance. A patrol of the 129th Baluchis located a German detachment at the junction of the Soke Nassai and Defu rivers.[82] About these partrols, Vorbeck writes: "With considerable skill patrols worked close up to the detachment and so concealed the movements of the enemy."[83] Vorbeck then decided to push back the British.[84] The Germans launched an attack on the outposts manned by one company of the 29th Punjabis, which was soon reinforced by one and a half companies of the 129th Baluchis.[85] By 1 a.m. (in the night of March 20/21) the Germans drew away.[86] The German casualties were over 150 while the British casualties were about 30. The 129th Baluchis played a very important role in this engagement.[87]

On receipt of the information that Van Deventer's Brigade was nearing Kahe, Smuts decided to attack Kahe from the north, on March 21. The plan was that Van Deventer's Brigade would reach Kahe station and cut off the German line of retreat while the main attack was to be delivered from the north.[88]

On March 21, in the morning, Van Deventer Ist South African Mounted Brigade alongwith the 2nd and the 4th South African Batteries moved towards Kahe.[89] On the way, it found a German detachment holding Kahe hill. Two squadrons of the South African Horse (one each from the 2nd and the 3rd) occupied the hill after a minor engagement by 11 a.m.[90] The Germans tried to recapture it, realising its strategic importance, but in vain.[91] In the meantime, the main column of Van Deventer advanced towards Kahe station.[92] The German Commander, Vorbeck, deployed eight companies to resist the advance,[93] but this column under Van Deventer was able to occupy Kahe station and the German companies retired upto the railway bridge at Kahe which, after crossing, they blew up.[94]

From the north, the Ist Division under Sheppard advanced to capture Kahe, on March 21. The disposition of the troops was as follows: Between the Defu and the main road, the 61 Pioneers and 8 South African Infantry were deployed, each on a two-platoon frontage, with the 7th South African Infantry in support. From the road to the Soke Nassai, the 29th Punjabis were in front, supported by the 129th Baluchis. In reserve were the 25th Royal Fusiliers and the Ist King's African Rifles of the Ist Division, with the 5th South African infantry. Artillery support was given by the No. 1 and the No. 3 Batteries of the South African Field Artillery and the No. 12 (How) Battery, with the 27th Mountain Battery, [95] moving in close support of the infantry. Two armoured cars took the main road.[96]

The Germans had posted a detachment, under Stemmermann, at Kahe where they had a four-inch *Königsberg* gun.[97] Vorbeck stationed himself at Kahe village.[98] Besides, there were some detachments around Rasthaus.[99]

The advance of the Ist Division was narrowed down by the two rivers (the Defu and the Soke Nassai), which were not only wider and deeper than was expected by the British force but were also full of crocodiles.[100] The Germans attacked from their position in the north-west of Kahe on this British advancing column and also used the *Königsberg* gun, which wreaked havoc on the British.[101] In spite of the efforts of the 29th Punjabis, the 8th South African Infantry and a section of the 27th Mountain Battery, it became impossible for the column to advance further.[102] At this juncture, the British force endeavoured to envelop the Germans' right by crossing the Soke Nassai.[103] A (double) company of the 29th Punjabis was ordered to cross the river.[104] Half Battalion of 129th Baluchis was also sent to assist it.[105] With great difficulty, this force crossed the river and advanced towards the German force but their advance was checked by firing of the German force.[106] In the night, the troops, which had crossed the Soke Nassai river were recalled and Brigadier General Sheppard was ordered to dig in and hold the ground.[107] The work of the 27th Mountain Battery in this engagement, was remarkably effective. From the commencement of the attack, it was in action in the infantry firing line and kept up a heavy fire till darkness put an end to the fighting.[108]

Vorbeck had received information in the afternoon that the British force was concentrating at Kisangire.[109] Therefore, he ordered all his companies to move to Kisangire and decided to attack the British force there, with all his units.[110] The German units withdrew from Kahe in the night and the four-inch Königsberg gun, which they could not carry with them due to its lack of mobility, was blown up by them.[111] The following morning, Brigadier General Sheppard's force occupied the area around Kahe.[112] Thus, by March 22, the whole area around the Kilimanjaro mountain, came into the hands of the British.

During the action at Kahe on March 21, the British casualties were about 240 men while the German casualties were 121 men.[113]

The plan of attack at Kahe, was sound. This time, efforts were made to cut off the line of retreat of the Germans. There were also sufficient troops in reserve. Yet, the plan could not be executed well because of the geographical factors. The bush was so dense that it was not possible to ensure coordination between the different units, and the artillery units could not fire accurately. This also retarded the movement of the troops. The rivers were not only deep and wide but were full of crocodiles, and it was not an easy task to cross them quickly.

Reorganisation of the British Force

After capturing the Kilimanjaro area, Smuts re-organised the whole force and divided the field army into three divisions, in early April 1916.[114] The composition of these divisions was as follows:[115]

1. Division	Major-General A.R. Hoskins. Ist East African Brigade (Brigadier General S.H. Sheppard): 2nd East African Brigade (Brigadier General J.A. Hannyngton). Artillery units : 5th, 6th and 7th South African Field Batteries : 27th Mountain Battery : One section 38th Howitzer Brigade.
II Division	Major General J.L. Van Deventer. Ist South African Mounted Brigade (Brigadier General Maine Batha); 3rd South African Infantry Brigade (Brigadier General A.L. Berrange). Artillery units: Group 2 - 2nd and 4th Batteries, South African Field Artillery; 28th Mountain Battery; 12th Howitzer Brigade.
III Division	Major General Brits. 2nd South African Mounted Brigade (Brigadier General B.G.L. Enslin); 2nd South African Infantry Brigade (Brigadier General P.S. Beves). Artillery Units : Group - 3 - Ist and 3rd Batteries, South African Field Artillery; 8th (Calcutta) Battery; One section 38th Howitzer Brigade.

The IInd Division under Van Deventer was ordered to advance from Arusha to Kondoa-Irangi[116] while the remainder of the force was ordered to stay in the area occupied by the end of the March, and to advance towards the Central Railway only after the rains.[117] In March 1916, the position of the German force improved as it received arms and ammunition in considerable quantities from the German blockade runner, the *Marie*. On March 17, the *Marie* reached Lindi port in German East Africa, evading the British Navy and brought the German force much needed arms and ammunition.

Plan for Further Advance Towards South

Smuts planned to reach to the Central Railway by the end of August 1916.[118] There were two ways to advance from the Kilimanjaro area to the Central Railway - one was along the Pangani river up to Morogoro and the other was through the interior upto Dodoma, via Kondoa-Irangi. Smuts thought of capturing Kondoa-Irangi to cut the German line of retreat to Tabora and he further assumed that, if the Germans were unable to retire to Tabera, they would cling on to Ushambara hill.[119] But as the rainy season was approaching, Smuts decided to postpone the advance till the end of the season. Later, however when he was informed that the rains would not interfere with the advance towards Kondoa-Irangi,[120] he decided to send a force immediately to occupy Kondoa-Irangi, determining to advance along the Pangani river after the rains.

The area from Arusha to Kondoa-Irangi forms the eastern part of the plateau. There are no rivers in this area. The rainfall in this area is not normally heavy. At Kondoa, during the three years prior to 1916, the annual rainfall was less than $3\frac{1}{2}$ inches.[121] The temperature in this area like the rest of the plateau varies greatly, from 110°C during the day to below freezing point at night. Some of the area is covered with bush.

Kondoa-Irangi was of immense strategic importance as it was then the most valuable road junction east of the Central Railway line.[122] So the occupation of Kondoa-Irangi was regarded essential as first step. (See Sketch 6).

The 2nd Division was ordered to push upto Kondoa Irangi. At this juncture, information was received that a small German force was holding Lolkisale, situated about 35 miles south-west of Arusha.[123] On April 2, the Ist South African Mounted Brigade with the 2nd and the 4th South African Batteries marched to Lolkisale.[124] After a hard fight, the Germans were compelled to surrender on April 6. The German force, which was

Sketch 6

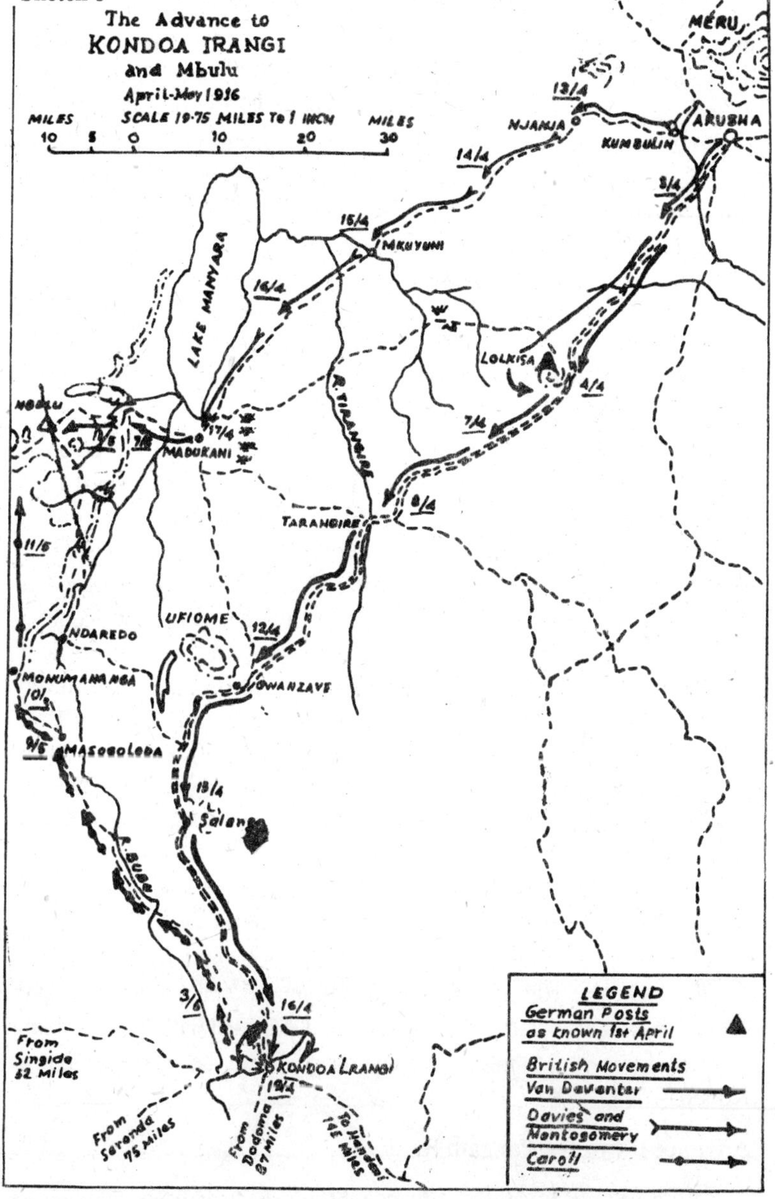
The Advance to
KONDOA IRANGI
and Mbulu
April-May 1916
MILES
SCALE 19·75 MILES To 1 INCH
MILES
10 5 0 10 20 30
MERU
ARUSHA
KUMBULIN
NJANJA
13/4
14/4
3/4
15/4
MKUYUNI
16/4
LAKE MANYARA
LOLKISA
4/4
7/4
17/4
MADUKANI
R. TIRANGIRE
8/4
TARANGIRE
11/5
UFIOME
12/4
NDAREDO
MONUMANANGA
GWANZAVE
10/5
9/5
MASOGOLEDA
19/4
Salera
R. BUBU
3/6
16/4
KONDOA IRANGI
19/4
From Singida 62 Miles
From Seronda 75 Miles
From Dodoma 87 Miles
To Handeni 145 Miles
LEGEND
German Posts as known 1st April
British Movements
Van Deventer
Davies and Montgomery
Caroll

captured, was composed of 17 whites and 414 natives (2 officers, 15 other Germans, 114 Askaris, 300 Company porters[125]). It was learnt from the prisoners of war and captured documents that the Germans were concentrating at Kondoa-Irangi and Ufiome,[126] with the intention of barring the advance of the British forces by that route to the Central Railway.

Simultaneously, a small detachment (one squadron of the 2nd South African Horse) was sent on April 2, to capture Madukani (Mbugwe) and this force was later followed by the three squadrons of 4th South African Horse.[127] Madukani was captured on April 10.[128] On the same day the 10th South African Infantry Battalion, accompanied by the 28th Mountain Battery, was ordered to go to Madukani, from where it was to march towards Mbulu,[129] where a German force was camping. This force left Kumbulin on April 13 but before it could reach Mbulu, the bulk of the German force at Mbulu had left for Ufiome.[130]

In the meantime, the Ist South African Mounted Brigade had resumed its advance and reached six miles north of Kondoa-Irangi by April 17.[131] Due to unexpected heavy rain the advance of the troops was delayed. On the 18th, the Ist South African Mounted Brigade (about 650 rifles) advanced with the cooperation of the artillery units towards Kondoa-Irangi.[132] The German force (about 400 rifles) withdrew and Kondoa-Irangi was occupied by the British force on the 19th.[133] It was difficult to move from Kondoa-Irangi for the British force because of the heavy rain.[134] This force stayed there and by May 1, the 3rd South African Brigade (less the 10th South African Infantry Battalion) and the 4th South African Horse, which were following the Ist South African Mounted Brigade, joined the latter at Kondoa-Irangi.[135] On the 9th, the Germans, numbering about 4000 men, attacked the British force of about 1000 men which was holding the hill south of Kondoa-Irangi but were successfully driven back by the latter.[136] The British casualties were 24 while the German casualties were much more than the 147 which they claimed.[137] On the 18th, the 10th South African Infantry Battalion with the 28th Mountain Battery occupied Mubulu, after a skirmish with the remaining German force at Mubulu.[138] They later joined the British force at Kondoa-Irangi.

Advance Down the Pangani River

Before commencing the advance Smuts had realised that unless supplies were available, the troops would find it impossible to proceed towards the Central Railway. Considering this, he ordered the construction of a railway line from Voi to Kahe, which was built by March 23.[139] This greatly facilitated the movement of supplies.

Before advancing towards south, Smuts re-distributed the Ist and the IInd Divisions.[140] These divisions were divided into three columns to suit his plan. The plan was that the greater part of his force should follow the Pangani river, a second portion would at the same time work down the railway, while a small third force, moving from Mbuyuni up the valley of the Ngulu, would cooperate from the east.[141]

The country, over which the advance was to take place, is such as almost to preclude all rapid movement. There are two huge blocks of mountains - the Pare and the Ushambara - with fertile valley in the north of the area and the Nguru hills in the south. The whole area is covered with dense bush. Besides, there are many rivers.[142]

The force was re-grouped by Smuts. He placed the whole force under the command of Major General A.R. Hoskins while retaining the Reserve Force in his own hands.[143]

River Column (Brigadier General S.H. Sheppard)	Centre Column (Brigadier General J.A. Hannyngton)	Eastern Column (Lieutenant Colonel T.O. Fitzgerald)
One squadron 17th Cavalry; 2nd Rhodesia Regiment; 130th Baluchis; One composite battalion, Kashmir Rifles; No. 5 Battery of the South African Field Artillery; 27 Mountain Battery (less one section); One (double company), 61st Pioneers; Ambulance and Supply columns.	East African Mounted Rifles; 40th Pathans; 129th Baluchis; 2nd Kashmir Rifles (half battalion); No. 6 Field Battery; No. 7 Field Battery; One section, East African Pioneers; Ambulance and Supply columns.	One Company, King's African Mounted Infantry; 3rd King's African Rifles; One section, 27th Mountain Battery; Ambulance and Supply columns.

Divisional Reserve
(Major General A.R. Hoskins)
Headquarters Ist Division Mounted Infantry Company (composed of the soldiers of the 2nd Loyal North Lancashire and the 25th Royal Fusiliers);
East African Mounted Rifles;
25th Royal Fusiliers;
29th Punjabis;
Machine Gun Company, 2nd Loyal North Lancashire;
No. 1 Armoured Car Battery;
One section East African Pioneers;
Ambulance and Supply columns.

Reserve Force 2nd South African Brigade (less two battalions):
Belfield's Scouts;
No. 8 (Calcutta) Battery;
134th (Howitzer) Battery;
5th South African Infantry;
6th South African Infantry

(See Sketch 7)

These columns started moving towards the south by their designated three routes in the third week of May, after the rains were over. The River Column successfully captured Buiko on May 31, though meeting some resistance on the way. The Central Column advanced on its route and reached Mandi hill on May 25. There, the Eastern column joined it on the 26th and both Columns reached Mkemazi on June 1, 1916.[144] The Germans withdrew as these columsn advanced.[145]

At this juncture, Smuts decided to halt as the troops were exhausted and required rest. The line of communication was damaged by the destruction of bridges by the German troops.[146] The time was utilised in repairing the bridges, crossings etc. This work was completed by the 25th, 26th and 28th Railway Companies of the Sappers and Miners who rendered inestimable service.[147]

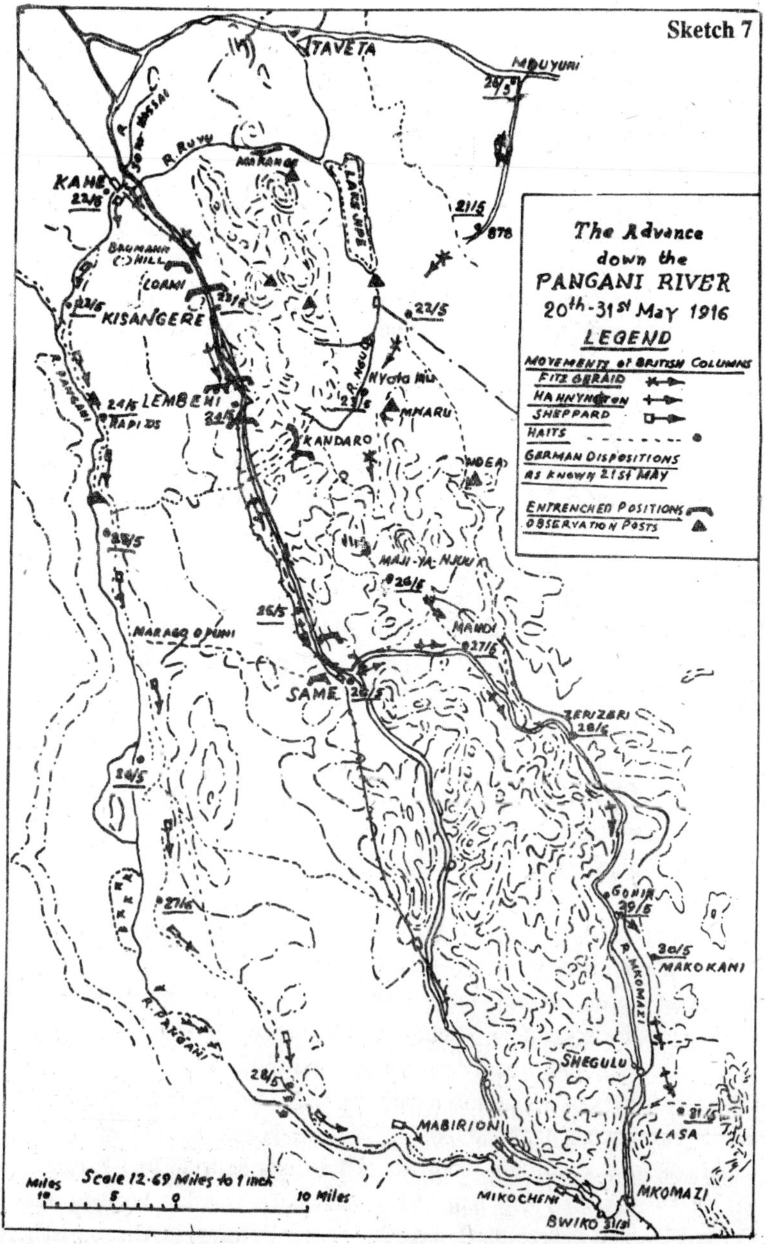
Sketch 7
The Advance down the PANGANI RIVER 20th-31st May 1916
LEGEND
MOVEMENTS of BRITISH COLUMNS
FITZGERALD
HANNYNGTON
SHEPPARD
HALTS
GERMAN DISPOSITIONS AS KNOWN 21st MAY
ENTRENCHED POSITIONS
OBSERVATION POSTS
TAVETA
MBUYUNI
KAHE
R. RUVU
LAKE JIPE
BAUMANN HILL
LOANI
KISANGERE
LEMBENI
KANDARO
MNARU
NDEA
MAJI-YA-NJUU
MANDI
SAME
MARAGO OPUNI
ZERIZERI
GONJA
R. MKOMAZI
MAKOKANI
R. PANGANI
SHEGULU
LASA
MABIRIONI
MIKOCHENI
MKOMAZI
BWIKO
Scale 12·69 Miles to 1 inch
Miles
10 Miles

Action at Mkalamo

Air reconnaissance had revealed that the German troops were entrenched at Mkalamo and Mkumbala.[148] Having decided to capture these places, Smuts despatched two columns. The column under Hannyngton[149] was sent towards Mkumbala and the column under Sheppard was sent towards Makalamo.[150]

Hannyngton's force marched on June 4 from Mkomazi and advanced along the railway. On the 8th, it occupied Mazinde station, meeting little opposition. On approaching Mombo hill, the following day, the Advance Guards[151] was fired on from the hill, which together with the bush south of the railway was held by the Germans.[152] The German guns were soon silenced by the guns of the 27th Mountain Battery (one section).[153] The Germans left their position and the British infantry advanced and occupied the hill.[154] On the 10th, Wilhelmstal was also occupied by this force.[155]

Meanwhile, the column under Sheppard advanced from Buiko towards Mkalamo on June 3. On the 5th, it met a strong German patrol at Makaya, which was pushed back by the 29th Punjabis.[156] The advance was resumed the following day, and on the 8th this force reached near Mkalamo. On the 9th, at 5 a.m., the Advance Guards started towards Mkalamo.[157] The Advance Guards was composed of the 29th Punjabis, 130th Baluchis, a company of the 61st Pioneers and a section of the 27th Mountain Battery.[158] At about 1 p.m., the two leading companies of the 130th Baluchis came up against the German force, which was well entranched and a bush fight ensued.[159] In the fighting, the companies of the 130th Baluchis lost heavily. Later, detachments were sent to move around the Germans' left flank and cut off their line of retreat.[160] Two companies of the 29th Punjabis were sent to the right of the 130th Baluchis, and the remainder of the 29th Punjabis were ordered to the left to ascertain the strength of the Germans.[161] At about 2.30 p.m., Brigadier General Sheppard assumed command of the operations and later the main force also came near the fighting line.[162] The visibility was so poor that it was difficult to fire accurately. According to Sheppard, "The bush was so thick that one could literally not see beyond thirty yards in any direction."[163] As it was difficult to locate the main German force, Sheppard decided to shove in hard and look out for counter-attacks.[164] He had two battalions in reserve - the 25th Royal Fusiliers and the 2nd Kashmir Rifles.[165] At about 3.15 p.m., a counter-attack was launched by the Germans, which was repulsed by the 2nd Kashmir Rifles.[166] After pushing the Germans back a considerable distance, the British force dug in on the ground gained as darkness was coming.[167] By the 10th, the Germans had left Mkalamo and the trolley line from Mombo to Handeni was found intact.[168]

At Mkalamo the British force had five battalions [169] while the Germans had three field companies and one platoon on June 9, 1916.[170] The British casualties were 15 killed and 33 wounded[171] while the German casualties, according to Dr. Shnee, were 3 killed and 11 wounded.[172]

The plan of the attack was sound. The geographical factors made the execution of the plan difficult. The bush was so dense that it was difficult to fire accurately. Moreover, the units of the British force were not accustomed to bush warfare while the soldiers of the German force were mostly natives, well acquainted with bush warfare. In this respect, the German force had an edge over the British force. In spite of these odds, the 2nd Kashmir Rifles was able to push back the Germans.

March Upto Handeni

According to British intelligence reports, the Germans were holding a strong position near Handeni.[173] Smuts decided to attack the Germans. Again, a turning movement was planned - the main body was to march to Sangeni on the Masangozi river, 17 miles west of Handeni while the force under Sheppard was to move south-west to Nguguini.[174] (See Sketch 8).

The force under Sheppard had advanced upto Mbagui, reaching there on June 15. On the way, it met a German patrol at Luchomo, which was driven off by the 17th Cavalry.[175] It further advanced upto Kilimanjaro village by the 16th, from where it had to move to the south-west of Nguguini. The main column (the 2nd south African Brigade) set out on the 16th and reached Sangeni on the 17th. The following day, the 2nd South African Brigade advanced to the south of Sangeni to cut the German line of retreat, while Sheppard advanced towards Handeni.[176] Seeing this, the German force withdrew and on the 19th Sheppard occupied Handeni and Nderma.[177]

The force under Hannyngton moved from Mombo and reached Korogwe on the 16th, which it captured on the same day after an engagement.[178] Hannyngton was then ordered to join the main force at Handeni where he reached on the 20th.[179]

The British troops were tired and supplies were not available because of the difficulties of transportation.[180] Above all, many troops had fallen sick.[181] Yet, considering that the Germans had to be pursued so that they

Sketch 8

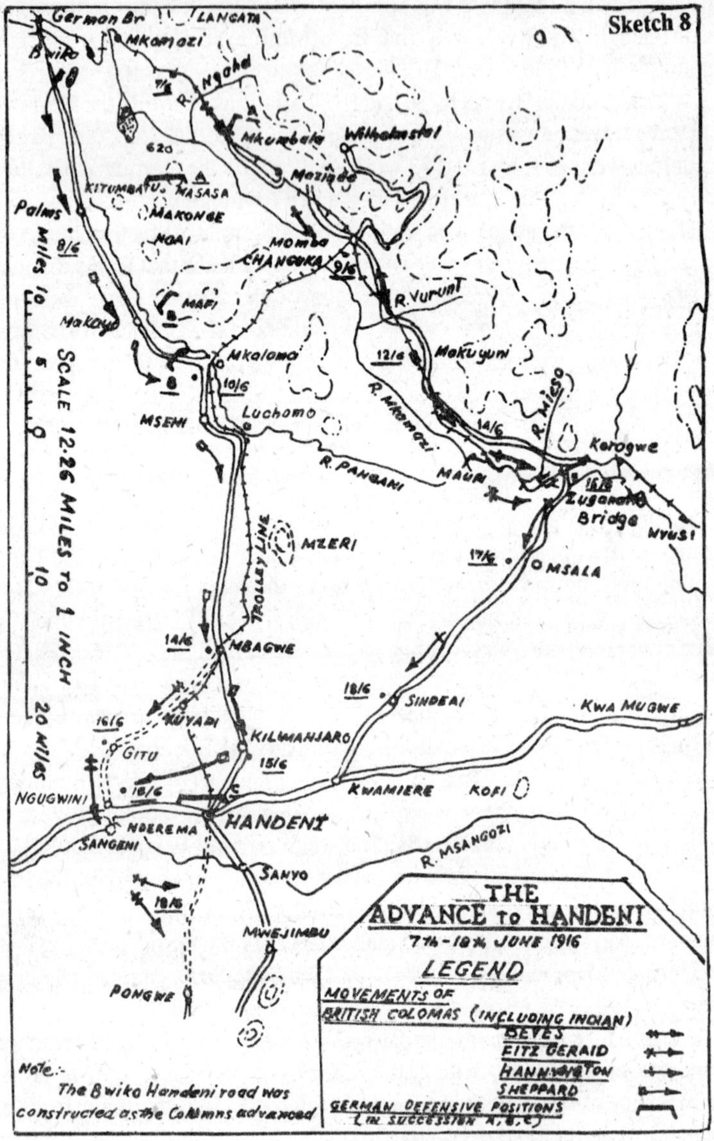
THE ADVANCE to HANDENI
7th–19th JUNE 1916
LEGEND
MOVEMENTS OF BRITISH COLOMAS (INCLUDING INDIAN)
BEVES
FITZ GERAID
HANNYNGTON
SHEPPARD
GERMAN DEFENSIVE POSITIONS (IN SUCCESSION A, B, C)
SCALE 12·26 MILES TO 1 INCH
Miles 10 5 0 10 20 MILES
Note:- The Bwiko Handeni road was constructed as the Columns advanced
German Br
LANGATA
Bwiko
Mkomozi
R. Ngoha
Mkumbala
Wilhelmstal
Mazinde
KITUMBATU
MASASA
Palms
MAKONGE
NGAI
MOMBO
CHANGUKA
R. Vuruni
MAFI
Makayu
Mkalamo
Mokuyuni
R. Mkomozi
MSENI
Luchomo
R. PANGANI
R. Mligo
Korogwe
MAURI
Zuganato Bridge
NYUSI
MZERI
TROLLEY LINE
OMSALA
MBAGWE
SINDEAI
KWA MUGWE
KUYADI
KILIMANJARO
GITU
NGUGWINI
KWAMIERE
KOFI
HANDENI
NDEREMA
SANGENI
R. MSANGOZI
SANYO
MWEJIMBU
PONGWE

were not given sufficient time to entrench somewhere or launch an attack after reorganising their force, Smuts decided to push forward. In other words, Smuts decided to apply' the Principle of Offensive Action'.

On June 20, the main body moved to Pongwe. On the same day, in the afternoon, the 5th South African Infantry left to occupy Kangata, which they occupied after an encounter with the Germans.[182] By June 22, 1916, the whole force, except Hannyngton's column, was at Kangata.[183]

Success Near the Lukigura River

All ground and air reports showed that the Germans had withdrawn to a defensive position on the river Lukigura, 13 miles beyond Kangata.[184] Smuts decided to push on. Hoskins was put in command of a column consisting of the East African Mounted Rifles, the 27th Mountain Battery (less one section), the 25th Royal Fusiliers, the 2nd Kashmir Rifles, the Machine Gun Company of the 2nd Loyal North Lancashire, and the 5th and 6th South African Infantry, with instructions to march via Kwa Negeru and to get behind the German position, which was reported to be in the vicinity of the bridge on the Lukigura.[185] This force was to turn to the German's left, while at the same time Sheppard's column, comprising the 29th Punjabis, the 130th Baluchis and the 2nd Rhodesians, the No. 5 and No. 8 Field Batteries and the two cars of the No. 1 Light Battery was to attack the German front.[186] (See Sketch 9).

Sheppard's force reached Msinga hill at 5.35 p.m. on June 23, 1916, and resumed its march the next day at 3.30 a.m.[187] Hoskin's column had reached the low hills near Lukigura bridge.[188] At 7 a.m., Sheppard's column came into contact with the Germans but this force did not push forward quickly as its aim was to attract the attention of the German force at the Lukigura.[189] In the afternoon Hoskin's Advance Guard consisting of the 2nd Kashmir Rifles, noticed the Germans holding a bridge ahead.[190] After being reinforced by the remainder of the 2nd Kashmir Rifles, the Advance Guard occupied the ridge near the bridge.[191] Hoskins then sent the 2nd Kashmir Rifles along with two Machine Gun companies of the 2nd Loyal North Lancashire forward to attack the Germans, who were then holding the next ridge. He also placed the 25th Royal Fusiliers to the left of the 2nd Kashmir Rifles.[192] This force advanced towards the German position and a heavy fight took place. At 1.30 p.m., Hoskins ordered the 6th South African Infantry to advance round the German's left flank. At 2 p.m., Hoskins received information from the frontal column, that its Advance Guard had reached the bridge and was pushing along the road in the rear of the German position.[193] He ordered his force to push

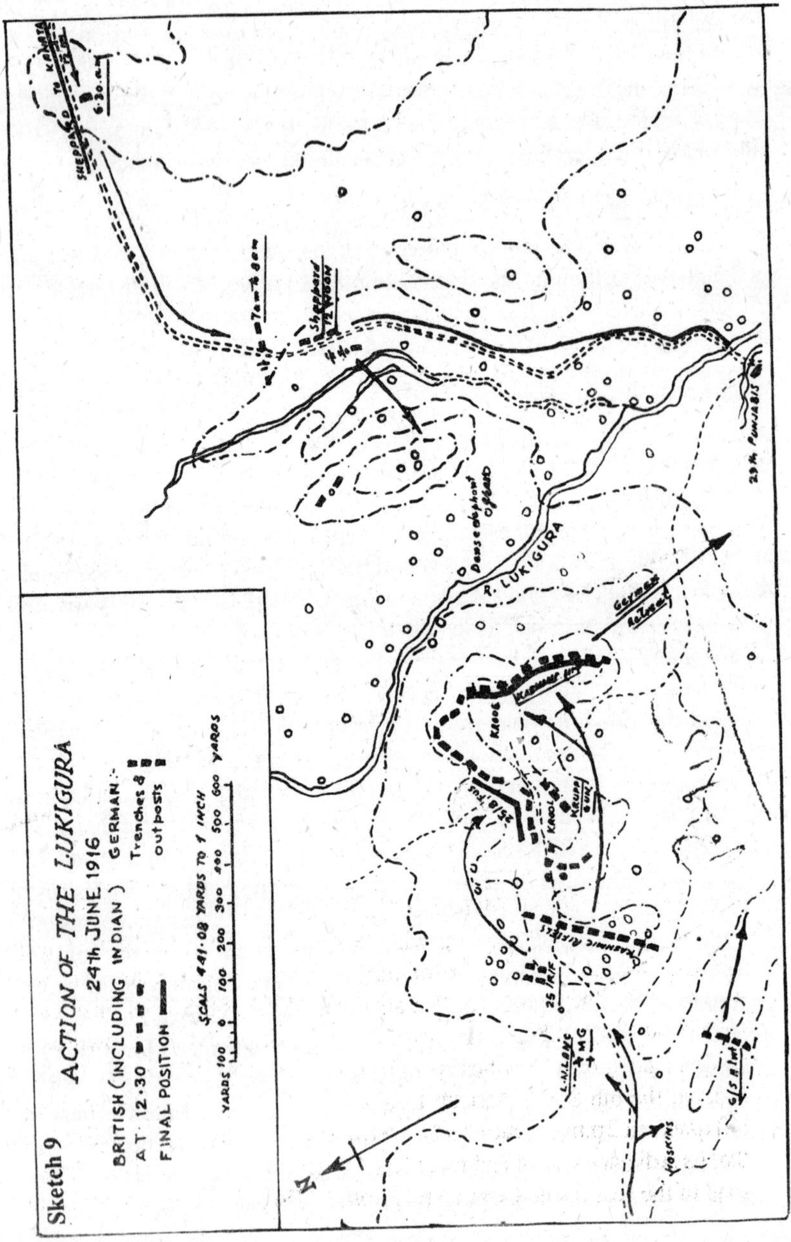
Sketch 9
ACTION OF THE LUKIGURA
24th JUNE 1916
BRITISH (INCLUDING INDIAN)
AT 12·30
FINAL POSITION
GERMAN:-
Trenches & out posts
SCALE 441·08 YARDS TO 1 INCH
YARDS 100 0 100 200 300 400 500 600 YARDS
N
R. LUKIGURA
German Retreat
29th PUNJABIS
HOSKINS
25/R.F.
KASHMIR RIFLES
KROOL
Dense elephant grass
SHEPPARD

forward. The 2nd Kashmir Rifles and the 25th Royal Fusiliers rushed in and took the position at the point of bayonet.[194] The German force retired through the grass and only small parties came under the fire of the 29th Punjabis while the bulk of the German force escaped.[195] The line of the Lukigura river was occupied. After a few days, the force moved on to Msiha.[196]

The total number of troops in the German force was about 500.[197] The total strength of the two battalions (the 2nd Kashmir Rifles and the 25th Royal Fusiliers) of the British force, which actively participated, was about 650 men.[198] The German losses were 34 killed and 53 captured while the British force lost 10 killed and 36 wounded.[199]

The strategy of this attack was realistic. The Germans were attacked from two sides. The 2nd Kashmir and the 25th Royal Fusiliers had very high morale and that is why they could easily advance to the German position. However, at one place, a mistake was committed. The efforts made to cut off the German line of retreat failed because the forces employed for this purpose were insufficient. Had the whole German force been captured, the morale of German forces at other places would have broken and it would have become easier to force a surrender.

Simultaneous Troop Movements

While the main attack launched in to capture Central Railway was on, a few important events occurred in other parts of German East Africa. On July 7, 1916, Tanga, where the British troops had met disaster in November 1914, was occupied.[200] On the 16th, Segera hill was occupied by a British force after driving out the Germans.[201] The British force which occupied Segera hill consisted of the 25th and the 26th Railway Companies, a detachment of the Jind Infantry and others.[202] In the meantime, an Indian battalion (the 57th Rifles) joined the British force in German East Africa.[203] On the western front, the Belgian forces advanced up to Kigoma and Ujiji and occupied a considerable area in the west of German East Africa.[204]

The II Division's Advance Up to the Central Railway

By mid July, the supply and transport difficulties, which had held up the 2nd Division at Kondoa-Irangi, had been overcome sufficiently to make further advance possible.[205] Smuts ordered the main body of the IInd Division to move towards Dodoma, a small column towards

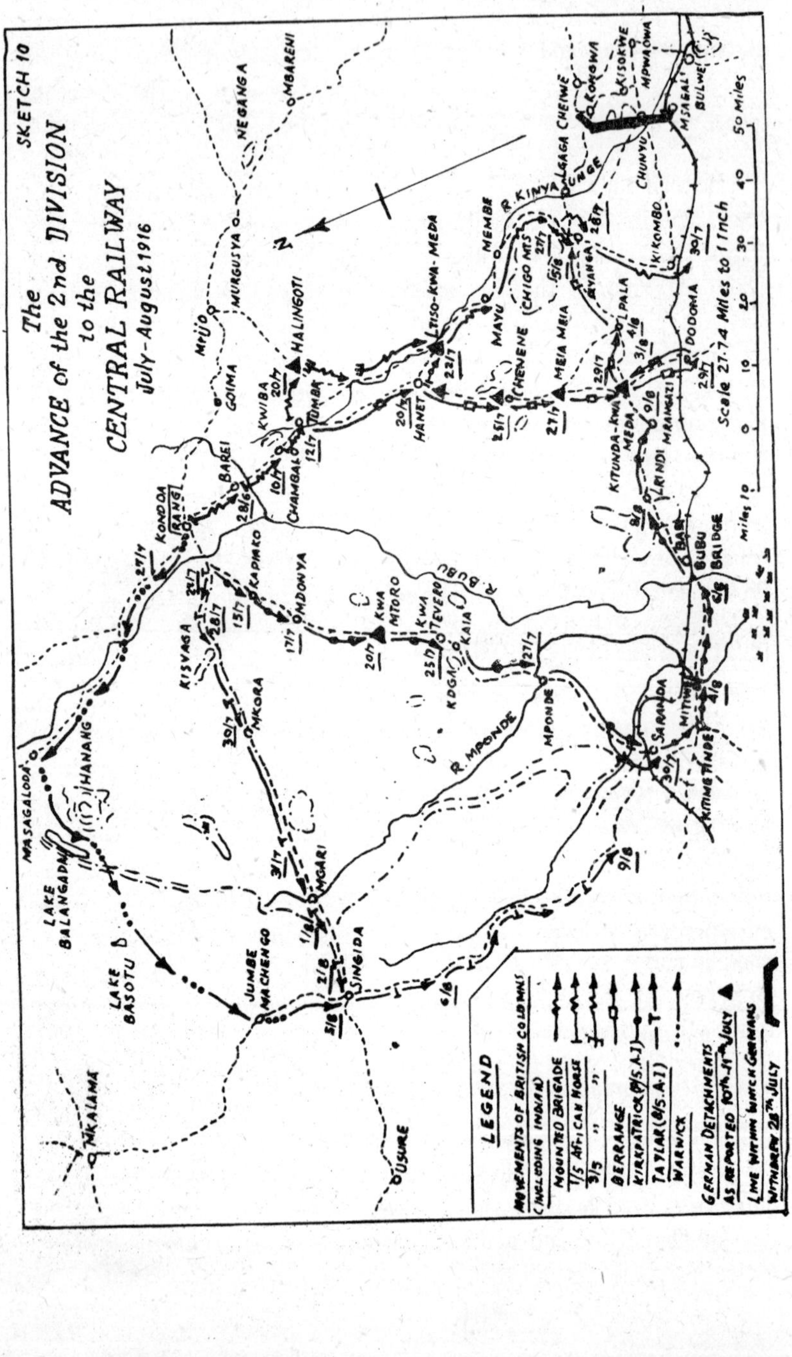
SKETCH 10
The
ADVANCE of the 2nd. DIVISION
to the
CENTRAL RAILWAY
July-August 1916
LEGEND
MOVEMENTS OF BRITISH COLUMNS (INCLUDING INDIAN)
MOUNTED BRIGADE
1/5 AFRICAN HORSE
3/5 " "
BERRANGE
KIRKPATRICK (9/S.A.I)
TAYLAR (8/S.A.I)
WARWICK
GERMAN DETACHMENTS AS REPORTED 10TH-11TH JULY
LINE WITHIN WHICH GERMANS WITHDREW 28TH JULY
Scale 27.74 Miles to 1 Inch
Miles 10
50 Miles
KONDOA IRANGI
SINGIDA
DODOMA
MPWAPWA
R. BUBU
R. MPONDE
R. KINYA
LAKE BALANGADA
LAKE BASOTU

Kilimantinde, and a detachment to clear the right flank to Singida (Ssingida).[206] On July 7, the 9th South African Horse had also joined the 2nd Division.[207] (See Sketch 10).

The Kilimantinde column, consisting of a squadron of the 9th South African Horse, a section of the 28th Mountain Battery and the 9th South African Infantry moved off under Colonel Kirkpatrick on July 14, 1916.[208] This force, reached in the vicinity of Mpondi, where it came under heavy fire of Machine Guns and rifles from the German force located there.[209] With the help of firing of the guns of the 28th Mountain Battery, the section of the 9th South African Horse was able to push on and drove off the Germans.[210] From Mpondi, this column advanced to Kilimatinde and reached there on July 30 without being opposed.[211] The Singida Column, consisting of the 8th South African Infantry, one squardon of the 4th South African Infantry, one squardon of the 4th South African Horse, one section of the No. 1 Battery of the South African Field Artillery and a Wirless Section, under Lieutenant Colonel A.J. Taylor, left Kondoa-Irangi on July 26.[212] This column reached Singida on August 2, defeating a German detachment near Magari.[213] After leaving a detachment there, Lieutenant-Colonel Taylar moved towards Kilimatinde, which he reached on August 11.[214]

The main column consisting of the Ist South African Mounted Brigade (less two squadrons of the 4th South African Horse), the 3rd South African Infantry Brigade (less the 9th South African Infantry), Attached troops of the IIIrd Division (the 7th South African Infantry and the Volunteer Machine Gun Company), the Division Artillery (less one section of the Ist South African Field Artillery and one section of the 28th Mountain Battery) and the Divisional Troops[215] advanced from Kondoa-Irangi and reached Chambalo on July 18.[216] There, the main column was divided into two columns - the Ist South African Mounted Brigade with the South African Field Artillery Brigade which was to move via Tissa Kwa Meda and Njangalo and strike the railway at Kikombo, under the command of Brigadier General Botha, and the remainder of the force which was to move via Tschenene and Meia Meia to Dodoma, by the direct road.[217] Brigadier General Botha reached Kikombo on the Central Railway on July 30, after defeating two German detachments at Tissa Kwa Meda and Njangalo on the 22nd and the 29th respectively.[218] The other column consisting of the remainder of the units of the main column reached

Dodoma on July 29, after defeating two German detachments at Tschenene on the 25th and at Meia Meia on the 27th.[219] Thus, by July 30 the Central Railway from Kilimatinde to Kikombo was captured by the British forces.

Occupation of Morogoro

In the early part of the August, Smuts found that further advance could be made from the Lukigura river towards the Central Railway as the supply difficulties had been sufficiently removed. His plan was to advance Sheppard's Brigade from the Msiha camp and make a holding attack on the main Kanga position of the Germans at Ruhungu, to link up with the column advancing down the Mdjonga valley. The 2nd East Africa Brigade under Hannyngton and the Divisional Reserve along with the Ist Division's Headquarters were to enter the mountains at Mabasi and advance down the Mdjonga valley to Matomondo and Turiani. The IIIrd Division, under Brits, was to move along the north of the mountains by the valley of the Lukigura and advance by the western valley up to Mhonda to arrive in the rear of the German forces at Ruhungu and farther up the Mdjonga valley.[220]

On August 5, the 2nd South African Mounted Brigade (Enslin) and the 2nd South African Infantry Brigade (less two battalions) of the IIIrd Division, left the Lukigura camp and the 2nd South African Infantry Brigade (less two battalions) reached Wiadigwa on August 8, while the 2nd South African Mounted Brigade reached Mhonda on the same day, where it defeated a German force in an engagement.[221] The 2nd South African Infantry Brigade from Wiadigwa was ordered to join Hannyngton's force at Kwa Chenga, where the latter had reached by August 8.[222] Hannyngton's force (the 2nd East African Brigade) along with the 2nd South African Infantry Brigade marched up to Matmondo, where it fought the German force on August 10, and which the Germans evacuated the next day.[223] By August 13, the 2nd South African Mounted Brigade and the 2nd East African Brigade reached Turiani. The 2nd East African Brigade was ordered to move forward along Kilosa road while the 2nd South African Mounted Brigade with two battalions of the 2nd South African Infantry Brigade were to go towards Morogoro.[224] The former force reached Mwomero on August 15, while the latter reached near Dakawa on August 16, and after a fight captured Dakawa on August 18.[225] On August 21, the 2nd South African Mounted Brigade with the No. 3 Battery under Enslin was ordered to move to Mkata on the Central Railway, where it reached on August 22.[226] This force, with the help of

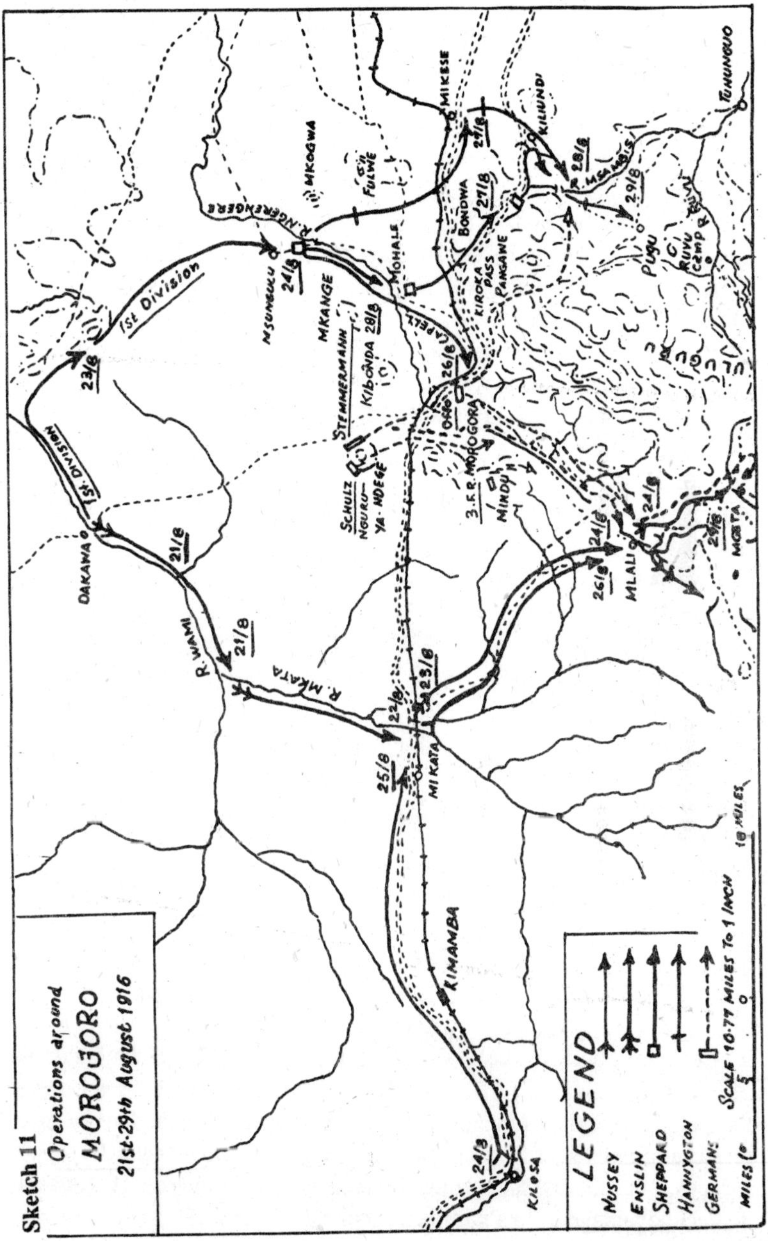
Operations around
MOROGORO
21st-29th August 1916
1st Division
1st DIVISION
DAKAWA
R. WAMI
R. MKATA
MIKATA
KIMAMBA
KILOSA
NSUNGULU
R. NGERENGERE
MKOGWA
FULWE
MKANGE
STEMMERMANN
KIBONDA
SCHULZ
NGURU-YA-NDEGE
MOROGORO
3.S.R.
MINDU
MIKESE
KILIUNDI
BONDWA
KIROKA PASS
PANGAWE
MOHALE
R. MSAMBISI
PUGU
RUVU CAMP
R. RUVU
ULUGURU
TUHUNGUO
MLALI
MGETA
21/8
22/8
23/8
24/8
25/8
26/8
27/8
28/8
29/8
LEGEND
NUSSEY
ENSLIN
SHEPPARD
HANNYNGTON
GERMANS
SCALE 10.77 MILES TO 1 INCH
MILES 10 5 0 10 MILES

Sketch 11

the Ist South African Mounted Brigade (less the Ist South African Horse) of Van Deventer drove the Germans from Mlali, a few miles south of the Central Railway, after a hard fight for 3 days from the 24th to the 26th.[227] (See Sketch 11).

The 1st East Africa Brigade under Sheppard left Misha camp on Angust 7 moving towards the south reached a place at the Wami river, a few miles north-east of Dakawa, on August 17.[228] There, it met a German force, which was driven off with the help of the 2nd South African Mounted Brigade.[229] On August 19, the 2nd East Africa Brigade joined the Ist East African Brigade at Dakawa. Smuts then decided to move towards Morogoro.[230] His force left Dakawa on August 23 for Morogoro, where the Advance Guard consisting of the Rhodesians and two companies of the 130th Baluchis reached on August 26.[231] On August 27, Smuts entered Morogoro with his Advance General Headquarters.[232] On the same day, the 2nd East African Brigade occupied Mikese on the Central Railway.[233] The IInd Division had advanced along the Central Railway capturing Kilosa by August 22.[234] Thus by the end of August 1916 the British force had pushed the Germans south of the Central Railway.

The British force, as had been planned by Smuts, was able to reach the Central Railway by the end of August 1916. The strategy of Smuts during this period was sound. Before making an advance towards the south along the Pangani up to Morogoro, he sent a sufficient force under Van deventer to Kondoa-Irangi, which not only cut off the German line of retreat to the west but also ensured that the German detachments in the north-west of German East Africa which were facing the Belgian forces would not be able to join hands with Vorbeck. The time chosen for Van Deventer's advance was based upon information available to Smuts. He was informed that the rains would not be heavy and so would not interfere with the advance. Unfortunately, the rains were exceptionally heavy around Kondoa-Irangi that year and so Van Deventer's force faced many difficulties. Smut's force which advanced along the Pangani also faced difficulties. The country precluded rapid movement. Many roads, railway lines and bridges were to be either repaired or constructed. This work was done brilliantly by the engineering units of Force 'B'. The other units of Force 'B' which proved very useful in the military operation during this period were the Mountain Batteries. The aeroplanes rendered useful service to Smuts's force, not only by locating the German forces by aerial surveys, but also by supporting the land forces in attacks. This was a distinct advantage Smuts's force had over the Germans.

From February 1916 to August 1916, the German forces adopted 'the Strategy of Attrition' or 'the Fabian Strategy', i.e., avoiding direct confrontation and attacking the enemy whenever a suitable opportunity was found. At one place, Vorbeck writes that he decided to withdraw further to the south and to continue the war for a long time.[235] In this way, he was able not only to prolong the struggle but also kept the British forces engaged for a considerable time. In the beginning of this period the German forces experienced a shortage of arms and ammunition but this problem was solved to some extent by the arrival of the German ship, the *Marie* which brought with her a considerable amount of arms and ammunition in March 1916.

NOTES

1. M.D., H.S., War Diary IEF 'B', Vol. 21. pp. 30-38.
2. J.J. Collyer, *The South Africans with General Smuts in German East Africa,* Pretoria, 1939, p. 50.
3. *Ibid.*
4. *History of the Great War, Military Operations, East Africa,* Vol. I, London, 1941, p. 213.
5. *Ibid.*, p. 214
6. *Ibid.*,
7. J.J. Collyer, *op.cit.*, p. 52
8. *Ibid.*
9. Von L. Vorbeck, *My Reminiscences of East Africa,* London, 1920, p.103.
10. J.J. Collyer, *op.cit.*, p. 103.
11. Von L. Vórbeck, *op.cit.*, p.103.
12. *History of the Great War.*, *op.cit.*, p. 231 fn.
13. Von L. Vorbeck, *op.cit.*, p. 103. According to the official History this detachment was somewhere between Taveta and Salatia hill.
14. *History of the Great War, op.cit.*, p. 231 fn.
15. Von L. Vorbeck, *op.cit.*, p. 103
16. *History of the Great War, op.cit.*, p. 231
17. *Ibid.*, pp.231-232.
18. *Ibid.*, p. 232.
19. *Ibid.*
20. *Ibid.*
21. *Ibid.*
22. Von L. Vorbeck, *op.cit.*, p. 103.

23. *History of the Great War, op.cit.*, p.233.
24. *Ibid.*, p. 232.
25. J.J. Collyer, *op.cit.*, p.56.
26. *Ibid.*, p. 58.
27. J.H.V. Crowe, *General Smuts, Campaign in East Africa.* London, 1918, p. 60.
28. *History of the Great War, op.cit.*, pp. 260-261.
29. Von L. Vorbeck, *op.cit.*, p. 109.
30. *History of the Great War, op.cit.*, p. 248.
31. See Appendix 'B'.
32. J.H.V. Crowe, *op.cit.*, p. 62
33. *History of the Great War, op.cit.*, p. 238.
34. J.J. Collyer, *op.cit.*, p. 84.
35. *History of the Great War, op.cit.*, p.239 fn.
36. J.H.V. Crowe, *op.cit.*, pp. 74-75.
37. *Ibid.*, pp. 71-72.
38. *History of the Great War, op.cit.* p. 241 fn.
39. J.H.V. Crowe, *op.cit.*, p. 72.
40. *Ibid.*, p. 74.
41. *Ibid.*, pp. 65-66.
42. *Ibid.*, pp. 67.68.
43. *History of the Great War, op.cit.* p. 242.
44. J.H.V. Crowe, *op.cit.*, pp. 69-70.
45. Von L. Vorbeck, *op.cit.*, p. 110.
46. *Ibid.*, p. 111.
47. R. Meinertzhagen, *op.cit.*, p. 70.
48. J.H.V. Crowe, *op.cit.*, p. 70.
49. *History of the Great War, op.cit.*, p. 244.
50. *Ibid.*
51. *Ibid.*
52. J.H.V. Crowe, *op.cit.*, p. 81.
53. *Ibid.*, pp. 82-83.
54. *Ibid.*, p. 82.
55. *Ibid.*
56. *Ibid.*, pp. 82-83.
57. *Ibid.*, p. 83.
58. *Ibid.*
59. Von L. Vorbeck, *op.cit.*, p.116.
60. J.H.V. Crowe, *op.cit.*, p. 85. According to the Official History the casualties were is about 270.

61. H. Schnee, *Deutsch - Ostafrika in Weltkriege*, Leipzing, 1919, p. 115. (in German), Dr. H. Schnee was the Governor of German East Africa during World War I.
62. Von L. Vorbeck, *op.cit.*, p. 116.
63. *Ibid.*, p. 119.
64. J.H.V. Crowe, *op.cit.*, p. 87.
65. *Ibid.*
66. *Ibid.*
67. *Ibid.*, p. 90.
68. *Ibid.*, p. 93.
69. *Ibid.*, pp. 93-94.
70. *Ibid.*, p. 94.
71. *Ibid.*
72. *History of the Great War, op.cit.*, p. 252.
73. J.H.V. Crowe, *op.cit.*, p. 95.
74. *Ibid.*
75. *Ibid.*
76. *Ibid.*, pp. 95-98.
77. *Ibid.*
78. *Ibid.*
79. *Ibid.*, p. 97.
80. *Ibid.*
81. *History of the Great War, op.cit.*, p. 253.
82. *Ibid.*
83. Von L. Vorbeck, *op.cit.*, pp. 120-121.
84. *Ibid.*, p. 121.
85. *History of the Great War, op.cit.*, p. 254.
86. *Ibid.*
87. J.H.V. Crowe, op.cit., p. 98.
88. *History of the Great War, op.cit.*, pp. 251-152.
89. J.H.V. Crowe, op.cit., p. 98.
90. *Ibid.*, p. 99.
91. *Ibid.*
92. *Ibid.*, p. 100.
93. Von L. Vorbeck, *op.cit.*, p. 122.
94. J.H.V. Crowe, *op.cit.*, p. 100.
95. In the *History of the Great War, East Africa (op.cit.)* it has been wrongly mentioned that the 27th and the 28th Mountain Batteries belonged to the Royal Artillery. They belonged to the Indian Mountain Artillery.

96. *Ibid.*, pp. 255-256.
97. Von. L. Vorbeck, *op.cit.*, p. 121.
98. *Ibid.*, p. 122.
99. *History of the Great War, op.cit.*, Sketch 27.
100. *Ibid.*, p. 256.
101. Von L. Vorbeck, *op.cit.*, p. 121.
102. *History of the Great War, op.cit.*, p. 256.
103. J.H.V. Crowe, *op.cit.*, p. 101
104. *History of the Great War, op.cit.*, p. 257.
105. J.H.V. Crowe, *op.cit.*, p. 103.
106. *Ibid.*
107. *History of the Great War, op.cit.*, p.257.
108. J.H.V. Crowe, *op.cit.*, p. 103.
109. Von L. Vorbeck, *op.cit.*, pp. 122-123. This report was later found untrue.
110. *Ibid.*, p. 123.
111. *Ibid.*
112. J.H.V. Crowe, *op.cit.*, p. 103.
113. *History of the Great War, op.cit.*, p. 257. The German casualties, according to it, are underestimated.
114. J.H.V. Crowe, *op.cit.*, p. 108.
115. *History of the Great War, op.cit.*, p. 264. (Artillery units at fn.)
116. J.J. Collyer, *op.cit.*, p. 103.
117. *History of the Great War, op.cit.*, p.296.
118. J.J. Collyer, *op.cit.*, p. 102.
119. *Ibid.*
120. *Ibid.*
121. J.H.V. Crowe, *op.cit.*, p. 114.
122. *Ibid.*, p. 113.
123. *Ibid.*, p. 111.
124. *Ibid.*, pp. 111-112.
125. *History of the Great War, op.cit.*, p.271.fn.
126. J.J. Collyer, *op.cit.*, p. 106.
127. *History of the Great War, op.cit.*, p. 272.
128. *Ibid.*
129. J.H.V. Crowe, *op.cit.*, p. 114.
130. *History of the Great War, op.cit.*, p. 273.
131. J.H.V. Crewe, *op.cit.*, p. 144.
132. J.J. Collyer, *op.cit.*, p. 106.
133. *Ibid.*

134. J.H.V. Crowe, *op.cit.*, p. 118.
135. *Ibid.*
136. J.J. Collyer, *op.cit.*, p. 116.
137. *Ibid.*
138. J.H.V. Crowe, *op.cit.*, p. 120.
139. History of the Great War, *op.cit.*, p. 278.
140. *Ibid.*, pp. 288-289.
141. *Ibid.*, p. 288.
142. M.D., H.S., War Diary, IEF 'B', Vol. I. Map. 1 (in Pocket)
143. *History of the Great War, op.cit.*, p. 289.
144. J.H.V., Crowe, *op.cit.*, pp. 135-137.
145. Von L. Vorbeck, *op.cit.*, p. 141.
146. J.H.V. Crowe, *op.cit.*, p. 137.
147. *History of the Great War, op.cit.*, p. 292 fn.
148. *Ibid.* p. 294.
149. The force consisted of the Central and the Eastern columns.
150. *History of the Great War, cp.cit.*, p. 294.
151. *Ibid.*, p. 295. Composed of the 40th Pathans and a vanguard of the Mounted Infantry of the King's African Rifles.
152. J.H.V. Crowe, *op.cit.*, p. 143.
153. *Ibid.*
154. *Ibid.*
155. *Ibid.*, pp. 143-144.
156. *Ibid.*, pp. 140.141
157. *History of the Great War, op.cit.*, p. 296.
158. *Ibid.*
159. *Ibid.*
160. J.H.V. Crowe, *op.cit.*, p. 141.
161. *History of the Great War, op.cit.*, p. 296.
162. *Ibid.*, pp. 296-297.
163. S.H. Sheppard, 'East African Campaign' U.S.I. *Journal,* April 1919, p. 143.
164. *Ibid.*
165. *History of the Great War, op.cit.*, p. 297.
166. *Ibid.*
167. S.H. Sheppard, *op.cit.*, p. 143.
168. *Ibid.* In *History of the Great War (op.cit.),* it is mentioned that the trolley line had been damaged by the Germans. pp. 297-298.
169. S.H. Sheppard, *op.cit.*, p. 143.
170. *History of the Great War, op.cit.*, p. 296 fn.

171. *Ibid.*, p. 297 fn.
172. *Ibid.*
173. J.H.V. Crowe, *op.cit.*, p. 144.
174. *Ibid.*
175. *Ibid.*, p. 143
176. *Ibid.*, p. 163.
177. *Ibid.*
178. *Ibid.*, pp. 146-147.
179. *Ibid.*, p. 148.
180. *Ibid.*
181. *History of the Great War, op.cit.*, p. 301.
182. J.H.V. Crowe, *op.cit.*, p. 150.
183. *Ibid.*, p.151.
184. *History of the Great War, op.cit.*, p. 303.
185. J.H.V. Crowe, *op.cit.*, p. 151.
186. *History of the Great War, op.cit.*, p. 304.
187. *Ibid.*
188. J.H.V. Crowe, *op.cit.*, p. 152.
189. *History of the Great War, op.cit.*, p. 304.
190. J.H.V. Crowe, *op.cit.*, p. 152.
191. *Ibid.*
192. *Ibid.*, p. 153.
193. *Ibid.*
194. *Ibid.*
195. *Ibid.*
196. *Ibid.*, pp. 154-155.
197. *History of the Great War, op.cit.*, p. 306 fn.
198. *Ibid.*, p. 304.
199. *Ibid.*, pp. 305-306 fn.
200. M.D., H.S., The European Crisis, Vol. 152, p. 24176.
201. *Ibid.*, p. 318 fn.
202. *Ibid.*, p. 318 fn.
203. *Ibid.*, p. 231, In return the 101st Grenadiers was sent to Egypt on August 28, 1916.
204. M.D., H.S., The European Crisis, Vol. 155, p. 24632 b.
205. *Ibid.*
206. J.H.V. Crowe, *op.cit.*, p. 165.
207. *History of the Great War, op.cit.*, p. 237 fn.
208. J.H.V. Crowe, *op.cit.*, p. 165.
209. *Ibid.*

210. *Ibid.*, pp. 165-166.
211. *History of the Great War, op.cit.*, p. 331.
212. *Ibid.*, pp. 331-332.
213. *Ibid.*, p. 232.
214. J.H.V. Crowe, *op.cit.*, p. 166.
215. The list of units of the IInd Division is given in the *History of the Great War, East Africa,* Vol. I, on page 327. From the total units, the units of other two columns have been reduced to arrive at the composition of the main column.
216. J.H.V. Crowe, *op.cit.*, p. 166.
217. *Ibid.*
218. *Ibid.*
219. *Ibid.*, p. 167.
220. *Ibid.*, p. 174.
221. *History of the Great War, op.cit.*, p. 337.
222. *Ibid.*
223. *Ibid.*, pp. 338-339.
224. *Ibid.*, p. 343.
225. J.H.V. Crowe, *op.cit.*, pp. 181-183.
226. *History of the Great War, op.cit.*, p. 355.
227. *Ibid.*, pp. 356-357.
228. J.H.V. Crowe, *op.cit.*, p. 180.
229. *Ibid.*, p. 181.
230. *History of the Great War, op.cit.*, p. 358.
231. *Ibid.*, p. 354.
232. *Ibid.*, p. 359.
233. J.H.V. Crowe, *op.cit.*, p. 190.
234. *History of the Great War, op.cit.*, pp. 349-354.
235. Von L. Vorbeck, op.cit., p. 141.7

6

The Last Push

By the end of August 1916, the situation for the Germans had deteriorated in the other theaters of the war. The Germans were engaged in heavy fighting with the Allies on many other fronts and their resources were being steadily exhausted. In May 1916, the German navy suffered badly in the battle of Jutland. In August 1916, Rumania joined the Allies. Under these circumstances, it was not possible for Vorbeck to receive any assistance from his homeland.

By this time, the strength of Vorbeck's force had been considerably depleted. Before the operations around Morogoro, the strength of the German force facing Smuts' force was about 4,500 men. After those operations, it went down to 3,500 men.[1] In the west of the colony, the strength of the German force was about 3,000 men which faced a Belgian force of about 10,000 men.[2] Thus, the total strength of the German force was about 6,500 men in August 1916.

By the end of August 1916, the 57th Wilde's Rifles, and the 27 and 28th Railway Companies from India had joined Smuts' force in German East Africa. In September 1916, the effective strength of the units from India in German East Africa was 12,353 men.[3] By the end of the year, the 30th Punjabis also joiined force 'B'.[4] Besides the 30th Pubjabis, a few more units arrived from India in 1917. They were the Ist Kashmir, and the 22nd and 24th Mountain Batteries. In addition to these, the British force also received reinforcements from other parts of the British Empire. By December 1916, the Gold Coast Regiment[5] and a Nigerian brigade[6] had also joined the British forces. Moreover, the British enrolled new recruits in East Africa. The total strength of the British forces in December 1916 had risen to 98,580 men.[7]

The area to the south-east of the Central Railway, in which the military operations took place after September 1916 is better watered compared to the area to the north of the Central railway. It is watered by many rivers, some filled with deadly fish and crocodiles. But the area to the south-west of the Central Railway does not have many rivers. There are three separate blocks of hills, the Uluguru hills, the Mtumbi hills and the Mahenge hills. Most of the area is covered with dense bush.[8]

Occupation of Kisaki

When the British troops reached Morogoro on the Central Railway by the end of August 1916, the German troops were just south of Morogoro in the Uluguru hills.[9] Vorbeck received information that the British troops were trying to reach Kisaki, situated south of the Uluguru hills and decided to reach beyond Kisaki in order to avoid encirclement by the British troops.[10] The German troops managed to get around Kisaki before the arrival of the British troops, because of their superior mobility and topographical knowledge of the area.[11]

Smuts decided to advance towards the south from Morogoro. Before starting, he regrouped his troops as follows[12]

First Division

Major General A.R. Hoskins

1st East African Brigade

Brigadier General
S.H. Sheppard
2nd Rhodesian Regiment;
29th Punjabis;
130 Baluchis;
2nd Kashmir;
5th King's African Field Artillery;
One Section, 27th Mountain Artillery;
One Squadron, 17th Cavalry;

2nd East African Brigade

Brigadier General J.A. Hannyngton
57th Rifles;
3rd Kashmir (half battalion);
3rd King's African Rifles;

Third Division

Major General C. Brits

2nd South African Mounted Brigade

Brigadier General
B. Enslin
5th South African Horse;
6th South African Horse;
7th South African Horse;
8th South African Horse;

2nd South Africa Infantry Brigade

Brigadier General P.S. Beves
5th South African Infantry;
6th South African Infantry;
3rd Battery, South African Field Artillery;

7th South African Field Battery;	8th Battery, South African Field Artillery
27th Mountain Battery (less one section);	
East African Mounted Rifles;	
Mounted Infantry Company;	
King's African Rifles;	
Divisional Troops	*Divisional Troops*
25th Royal Fusiliers;	13th Howitzer Battery;
Gold Coast Regiment;	
Cape Corps Battalion;	
	Army Troops
	9th Field Artillery;
	14th Howitzer Battery;
	134th Howitzer Battery;

Having re-grouped the units, Smuts ordered the Ist Division to advance to the east of the Ulguru hills.[13] The Ist East African Brigade (Sheppard) reached Kiroka Pass on August 28, and on the same day the 2nd East African Brigade (Hannyngton) reached the Msambisi (Mssambissi or Msumbisi) river.[14] On August 29, the Advance Guards (the 3rd Kashmir Rifles) of the 2nd East African Brigade was fired at by a German detachment.[15] The 3rd King's African Rifles along with the 27th Mountain Battery were brought up in support.[16] With the help of firing by the 27th Mountain Battery, the 3rd King's African Rifles were able to move forward and drive off the German detachment.[17] Then the 2nd East African Brigade resumed its advance and on September 7, its advance unit - the 3rd King's African Rifles - reached the hills above Kissanga.[18] Meanwhile, the 29th Punjabis of the Ist East African Brigade (Sheppard) reached Tule via Tunungua, where the leading units of the Ist Division assembled on September 9.[19] While these units were advancing, Sheppard, with the bulk of his force, was busy repairing the road above Sheppard's Pass, near Bukubuku.[20]

On August 28, the Ist South African Mounted Brigade (Nussey) was holding Mgeta Mission and the 2nd South African Mounted Brigade (Enslin) was holding Mombossa, a little south-west of Mlali.[21] Realising that the Germans had withdrawn to Kisaki, Smuts ordered Nussey to move on to Kisaki from the north through the mountains along the Mgeta river while Enslin was ordered to move to Kisaki by way of the Mahalaka road.[22] The whole movement was placed under the command of Major General Brits, who remained at Mlali awaiting the arrival of Beves's infantry - the 5th and the 6th South African Infantry Battalions - which reached him on August 21.[23] The Ist South African Mounted Brigade under Nussey started from Mlali on September 1, and reached Kikeo, a few miles north of Kisaki, on September 7.[24] This force had to face many difficulties as the route assigned to it was covered with dense bush. The 2nd South African Mounted Brigade under Enslin and the 2nd South African Infantry Brigade under Beves reached near Tyaduma on September 5.[25] Brits then decided to capture Kisaki at the earliest[26]. Accordingly, he directed the 5th and the 6th South African Infantry Battalions under Beves to move to Kisaki from the north-west by way of the Mgeta river while the 2nd South African Mounted Brigade was ordered to reach the Iringa-Kisaki road and thence to advance towards Kisaki.[27] These two forces set out from Tyaduma for Kisaki on September 7 by the above mentioned routes.[28]

The 5th and the 6th south African Infantry Battalions (approxmately 600 rifles[29]) under Beves, crossed the Mgeta river and reached near a German position around Kisaki by 4.30 p.m. on September 7.[30] Then, Beves decided to dig in on the left bank of the river till the next morning. At 10 p.m., a German force attacked Beves' left wing but the attack was successfully repulsed.[31] In the night, Brits ordered Beves to retire to Whigu hill. By 4.30 a.m. on September 8, Beves and his force reached Whigu hill.[32] (See Sketch 12).

The 2nd South African Mounted Brigade (about 600 rifles[33]) advanced towards Kisaki along the Iringa-Kisaki road and at noon on September 7 came before a German force of 1,200 rifles.[34] The German force attacked the 2nd South African Mounted Brigade and the latter had to retire after a loss of 16 killed, 24 wounded and some missing.[35] By the next day, this force reached Whigu hill.

Nussey's force (about 500 rifles[36]) advanced towards Kisaki. On September 8, it came before a German force of about 700 rifles.[37] Nussey had not received any information about what had happened to Beves's force or Enslin's force. Nussey's force soon became engaged with this German force. The fight continued the whole day. In the afternoon, during the course of fight, the Germans were reinforced by 400 rifles.[38] The German force inflicted 44 casualties (23 killed and 11 wounded) on Nussey's force.[39] Later, the German force retired from Kisaki to take up defensive positions around the Dutumi. Vorbeck knew that this British force would soon be reinforced there and it would be difficult for the Germans to face the British force.

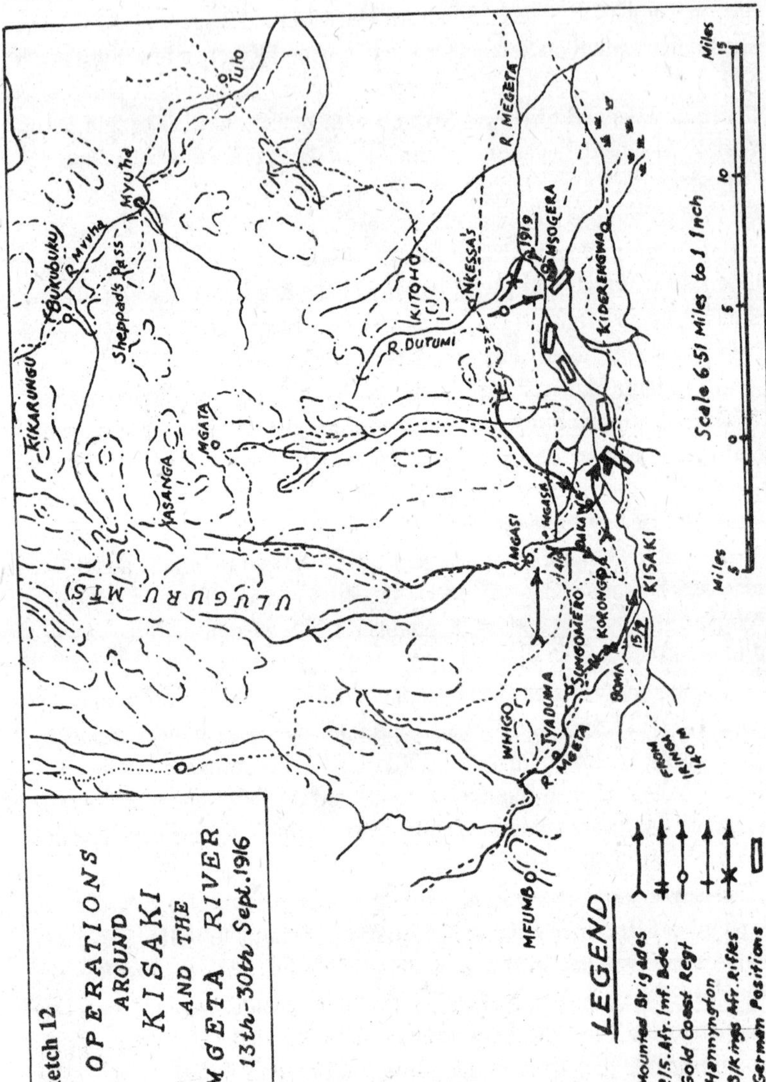

Sketch 12
OPERATIONS AROUND KISAKI AND THE MGETA RIVER
13th-30th Sept. 1916

The total strength of the Germans at Kisaki was not less than 2,500 rifles [40] while the British had about 1,700 rifles. But as withdrawal from Kisaki was vital for Vorbeck he did not allow his force to fight longer to destroy the British force there. The defeat of the British force was due to two reasons. First, the different British columns were unaware of each other's movements as there was no communication between them. Hence, they had to face the German forces individually. The Germans could easily defeat the three British columns as the latter could not apply 'the Principle of Cooperation'. Secondly, the German applied 'the Principle of Surprise' and delivered surprise attacks on the British who were easily defeated by the Germans.

Action Near the Dutumi River.

At this juncture, Smuts ordered the 1st Division to advance towards Kisaki from the east to cooperate with Brits's force.[41] The 2nd East African Brigade (Hannyngton) with the 3rd Kashmir Rifles as Advance Guard moved from Kiroka along the Kisaki road and at 10 a.m. on September 10, found a German force consisting of six companies. This force was later reinforced by eleven more companies.[42] They were entrenched some 1,200 yards east of the Dutumi river.[43] Hannyngton decided to capture the Kitoho (Kitovo) hill which commanded the road.[44] At 10.30 a.m. the 57th Rifles with the Machine Guns of the 129th Baluchis and a section of the 27th Mountain Battery were sent forward to occupy this hill, which was occupied after some resistance.[45] The Mountain Guns were brought up and put into action and they very soon silenced the German guns which had opened fire from a position on the far bank of the river[46]. The 57th Rifles were reinforced by the 3rd King's African Rifles, which were instructed to pass the former and turn the German left flank.[47] By the evening, both the battalions had reached near a small stream, without facing any opposition fresh water being of great importance to the forces.

The 3rd Kashmir Rifles along with the guns of the 2nd loyal North Lancashire, and supported by the remainder of the 27th Mountain Battery, moved forward on the road but little progres could be made before night fall of September 10 because of the elephant grass.[49]

On September 11, in the morning, the 57th Rifles and the 3rd King's African Rifles, leaving behind a double company to hold the area, started off in a south-westerly direction to envelop the German left flank.[50] The 3rd Kashmir Rifles also continued to march towards the Dutumi river under covering fire of the Mountain guns[51] The 57th Rifles wheeled to their left and occupied the next lower ridge to the south of Kitoho hill, the 3rd King's African Rifles continuing the turning movement could not make much progress because of the thick bush, which rendered it difficult for the artillery to provide them any direct support.[52] The 3rd King's African Rifles were checked by the German fire in the afternoon and by 5 p.m. they were forced back by a German counter-attack.[53] (Crowe states that the German counter-attack was repulsed by the 3rd King's African Rifles.[54])

Meanwhile, on the same morning, the 5th Battery of the South African Field Artillery, which had arrived the previous day, moved into action on the Kisaki road. The Gold Coast Regiment came up from reserve, and sent two of its companies round Kitoho hill to reinforce the 3rd King's African Rifles on the extreme right while the remainder of the battalion extended the left of the attacking line in the plain.[55]

The night of September 11/12 passed quietly.[56] The 29th Punjabis, which had been sent up by Hoskins to reinforce the 2nd East African Brigade, joined Hannyngton and were sent to support the Gold Coast Regiment.[57]

On September 12 in the morning, the 57th Rifles started towards Nkessa[58] while the 3rd King's African Rifles advanced along the river (the 3rd King's African Rifles had been reinforced by two companies of the Gold Coast Regiment and a section of the Mountain Guns[59]). On the left of the road, the Gold Coast Regiment (less two companies) was advancing towards the Dutumi river.[60] In the late afternoon, a German counter-attack was launched against the Gold Coast regiment on the left but due to the thick vegetation the German effort failed.[61] By this time, the 3rd Kashmir Rifles had moved along the road. In the afternoon confused fighting began all along the line which came to an end at 7.30 p.m.[62] By the morning of September 13, the Germans had withdrawn their forces from the Dutumi area.[63] The British force suffered 100 casualties in the operation.[64]

By this time, the two Mounted Brigades (the 1st and the 2nd south African Brigades) under Enslin were ordered to Korongo, east of Kisaki, on September 12.[65] This force reached Korongo on September 14 to learn that the Germans had evacuated Kisaki. Realising this, Brits sent the 5th and the 6th South African Battalions to Kisaki, which was occupied by them on September 15[66].

The strategy of Smuts around the Dutumi river was sound. By advanceing from both sides of Uluguru hill, it was expected that the Germans would be forced to a show-down. That Vorbeck was yet able to elude the British forces was creditable. It cannot be denied that Vorbeck had certain advantages. The main advantage was that he knew the country very well. He had the Askaris with him, who were used to those climatic conditions which were proving disastrous to the British troops. And last, due to the thick vegetation, it had become extremely difficult for the British troops to fire on the Germans accurately. On the other hand, the British force had certain disadvantages. First, they did not know the country well. Second, they were not used to the unfamiliar climatic conditions. And last, because of the thick bush, cooperation between the various units was impossible. Yet, in a way, the thick bush proved helpful to them also. When the Germans counter-attacked on the Gold Coast Regiment on September 12, the thick bush proved a good shelter for the latter, preventing the Germans from driving them back.

Second Division's Advance to Kidodi

Smuts decided to send the 2nd Division, which was at Kilossa, to Kidodi to dislodge the Germans entrenched to the south of Kilossa[67]. This division reached Kidodi on September 10, successfully removing the opposition by the German troops on the way.[68] The opposition was overcome with the help of the artillery units. In this engagement, the 28th Mountain Battery proved of great value.[69]

Occupation of Dar-es-Salaam

On August 15, 1916, the port of Bagamoyo was occupied by the Royal Navy.[70] At Bagamoyo, a force totalling about 1,900 men with 20 Machine Guns was assembled to capture Dar-es-Salaam.[71] The force advanced in four columns.[72] The first column composed of the 40th Pathans, was to secure the important railway bridge over the Kingani river at Ruwu station on the Central Railway line.[73] The second column, comprising the Jind Infantry, was to march on Ngrengere station about 40 miles west of Ruwu, on the Central Railway.[74] The third, consisting of the 2nd Loyal North Lancashire, the 129th Baluchis and the 5th Light Infantry (composed as one battalion), and the fourth the 2nd West Indian Regiment, a detachment of the South African Infantry and the Zanzibar Column were to advance directly to Dar-es-Salaam from Bagamoyo by two parallel routes.[75] The fourth column was to advance along the coast and the third column was to advance by a route a little west of the former's route.

The 129th Baluchis, acting as the Advance Guard of the third column, reached Dar-es-Salaam on September 4, without meeting any opposition on the way.[76] The rest of the units of the third column followed the 129th Baluchis. The fourth column also reached Dar-es-Salaam by the route running along the coast without any opposition. The first column marched around Ruwu on September 1, successfully routing a German party 3 miles east of Ruwu station.[77] From there, it moved on towards Dar-es-Salaam, where it reached on September 6, successfully encountering the German detachments on the way.[78] The second column reached Ngerengere on the 3rd, meeting little opposition, and from Ngerengere it returned to Bagamoyo on September 5.[79]

After the capture of Dar-es-Salaam, Smuts decided to capture the other sea ports.[80] Within a short time, Kilwa Kivinge,[81] Kilwa Kisiwani,[82] and Mikindani[83] were occupied.

By this stage, the Belgian troops had occupied Tabora while Brigadier-General Northey's force (Nyasaland-Rhodesia Field Force) occupied Lupembe near the upper Rujiji river.[84]

At the end of September 1916, Smuts reviewed the whole situation and found it necessary to reorganise the whole force. The effective number had gone down considerably because of the diseases prevalent in German East Africa.[85] The 3rd Division and the 2nd Mounted Brigade were disbanded.[86] About 12,000 white troops were sent back to South Africa.[87] Howevr, Smuts formed additional King's African Rifle battalions[88] and received as reinforcement a Nigerian Brigade under Brigadier Gemeral Cunlife; the 30th Punjabis[89] and two batteries of the Kashmir Imperial Service Mountain Artillery[90] - the 22nd and the 24. The Ist Kashmir Mountain Artillery had already joined a few days earlier.

Capture of Kibata

Smuts expected Vorbeck would withdraw his troops to the south of the Rufiji river and so he decided to land a force at Kilwa to operate from the coast, to confine the German troops in the north of the Matandu river[91]. Hannyngton was selected to command the Field Force which was to operate from Kilwa[92].

While preparations were on to send a force to Kilwa, it was reported that a German detachment was at Kissangire, 40 miles due south of Ruwu Railway Station.[93] A force, consisting of half a battalion of Jind Imperial Service Troops was sent, which attacked this German detachment, but was repulsed.[94] Later, it was reinforced by the South African Infantry and the 57th Rifles but before any action could be taken, the German party had left Kissangire.[95]

The force placed under Hannyngton consisted of the 2nd Loyal North Lancshire, the 40th Pathans, two battalions of the 2nd King's African Rifles, a composite battalion of India troops from the lines of communication and the 8th and the 14th Howitzer Batteries.[96] This force had reached Kilwa by the first week of October. On receiving information that a German detachment was holding a post at Kibata, Hannyngton decided to capture it.[97] A force of 800 rifles was sent, which occupied Kibata on October 10 without any opposition, as the Germans had withdrawn from there.[98]

Keeping in view the changing situation, Smuts made certain changes in the distribution of the force. The headquarters and the remainder of the 1st Division was transferred from Tule to Kilwa.[99] Reconstitution of the 1st Division was ordered - the 3rd East African Brigade took the place of the 1st East African Brigade. Sheppard was ordered to remain on the Mgeta front under the direct orders of Smuts.[100] Hoskins was placed in command of the force at Kilwa.[101]

Hoskins took charge on November 15, 1916[102]. The German force had about ten companies in the Kilwa area according to British intelligence reports.[103] Hoskins, therefore, prepared his force to meet the opposition from this German force. On December 5, 1916, the Germans attacked at Kibata with a 4.1" *Königsberg* gun, a 4.1" Howitzer and a field gun, and until the 7th the fighting continued in heavy rain.[104] At that time, there were about 800 soldiers of the King's African Rifles.[105] Hoskins sent the 2/2nd King's African Rifles with one section of the 28th Mountain Battery, which reached Kibata on the 9th at 2.a.m.[106] On the night of the 9th/10th the Germans made a night attack which was repulsed by Hoskins' force.[107] The British force at Kibata was reinforced with one more section of the 28th Mountain Battery.[108] The 40th Pathans and the Gold Coast Regiment were also sent to help the force at Kibata and were ordered to attack the German right flank to the north of Kibata.[109] On December 15, heavy fighting took place, after which the German force withdrew.[110]

Advance Up the Rufiji River

Smuts decided to attack the German troops after crossing the Rufiji, and then closing in on the main German force along the river.[111] (See Sketch 13). Simultaneously, two forces (one under Northey and other under Van Deventer) were to advance to the Ulanga and the Ruhudje.[112]

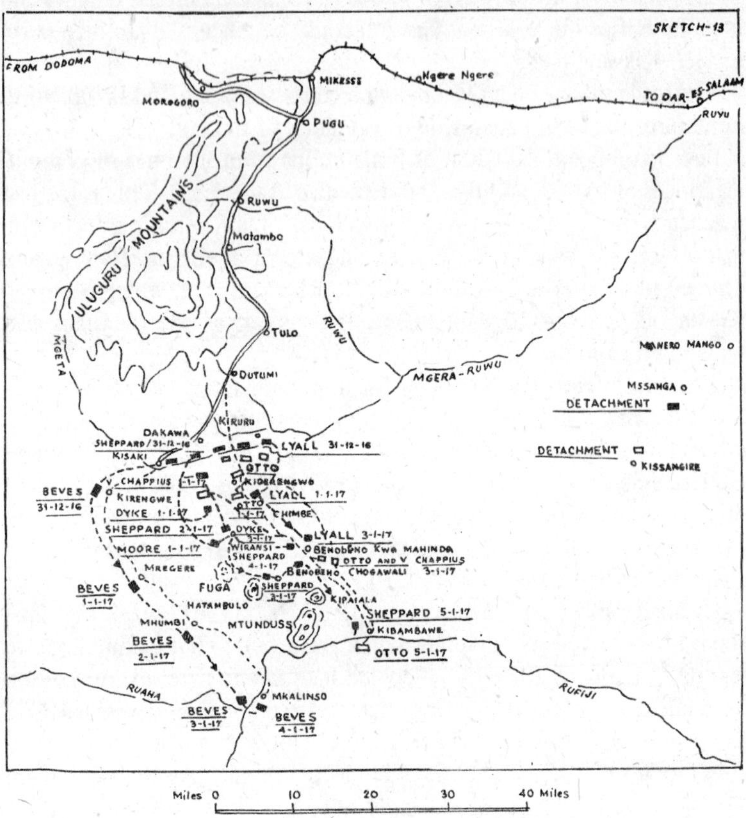

MAP TO ILLUSTRATE

GENERAL SMUTS' OPERATIONS ON THE RUFIJI, JANUARY 1917.

FORCES BRITISH (INCLUDING INDIAN).... ■

FORCES GERMAN...... □

Northey commenced his advance and reached Lupembe on December 23, while Van Deventer advanced to attack the Germans facing him in the south of Iringa the following day.[113] But Smuts' advance was held up by the heavy rains. Before resuming his advance, a regrouping of Smuts' troops was carried out as below:-

1st East African Brigade
(Sheppard)
25th Royal Fusiliers;
30th Punjabis;
130th Baluchis;
3rd Kashmir Rifles;
No. 3 Field Battery (4 Guns);
No. 6 Field Battery (2 Guns);
No. 7 Field Battery (less one section) (2 Guns);
No. 13 Howitzer Battery (1 Gun);
Half Double Company, 61st Pioneers;
One Section, East African Pioneers;
One Section, Faridkot Sappers and Miners;
No. 1 Armoured Motor Battery;
One Section, No. 5 Armoured Car Battery.

Force Reserve
(Beves)
6th South African Infantry;
Cape Corps;
Kashmir Mountain Battery (4 Guns);
Half Double Company, 61st Pioneers;
Faridkot Sappers and Miners.

Dutumi Column
(Cunliffe)
1st Nigerian Regiment;
4th Nigerian Regiment;
Cape Corps;
One Section, Nigerian Battery.

Kiburu Column
(Lyall)
2nd Kashmir Rifles;
2nd Nigerian Regiment;
One Section, Nigerian Battery.

General Headquarters Reserve
2nd Rhodesian Regiment;

African Scouts;
3rd Nigerian Regiment;
Detachment of Cape Corps;
One section, No. 7 Field Battery (2 Guns);
15th Heavy Battery (2 Guns);
134 Howitzer Battery (4 Guns).

The first object of these movements was to surround the enemy forces facing Sheppard on the Mgeta line.[115] Smuts' force resumed its advance after the heavy rains were over and by 5.30 a.m. on January 1, 1917, the leading troops under Beves were at Kirengwe, the 130th Baluchis were on the road to Wiransi and Sheppard's force was at its starting point east of Kisaki.[116] The main object of the move of the 130th Baluchis was to draw the attention of the Germans to the 130th Baluchis so that the Germans may not observe Beves' move from Mirengwe.[117] With his column, Lyall had reached Kiruru on December 31, and was on the way to Tshimbe.[118]

Lyall's column was attacked by a German force on January 1, 1917, but it successfully repulsed the attack.[119] This column remained near Tshimbe during the night.

The 130th Baluchis were attacked by three companies of Germans on the same day.[120] A severe engagement ensued in which the 130th Baluchis put up a fine fight in the course of which they sustained a loss of 36 killed and 29 wounded.[121] Many of the casualties occurred in hand to hand bayonet fighting. The German force withdrew when it learnt that Sheppard was advancing to help the 130th Baluchis.[122]

As the Germans had retired, the columns were ordered to advance further to capture them. By the evening of January 2, Lyall was moving on Beho-Beho-Kwa-Mahinda, Sheppard was advancing on Beho-Beho-Chogewali and Beves was at Mhumbi where he did not meet any resistance.[123]

On January 3, Beves reached the Rufiji river, a little south of Mkalinso, and his force seized both the banks.[124] At 4.30 p.m. on the same day, Lyall's column engaged a German force on the way, near Beho-Beho-Kwa-Mahinda.[125] Later, this German force retired after the engagement. Lyall's column was joined by the 130th Baluchis at this juncture.[126] On January 4, Sheppard's force came into contact with a German detachment and after receiving a severe drubbing, this German detachment retired through the bush.[127] On January 5, Sheppard's force reached the nothern bank of the Rufiji opposite Kibambawe and the next day found a German force was holding the southern bank.[128] The 30th Punjabis were sent to the southern bank, which they reached by the morning of the 7th .[129] The Germans attacked the 30th Punjabis who were able to retain their position with the help of the 3rd South African Battery.[130] Meanwhile, Beves' force, occupied the German position near Mkalinso on January 7, 1917.[131] Later, with the help of Cunliffe's force, Beves' men cleared Kibambawe and occupied Luhembero by January 18.[132]

In the delta of the Rufiji river, the Germans had vacated Mkamba on the night of the 8th/9th January and by January 10, a British column occupied Kibesa six miles south-west of Mkamba.[133] In the Kilwa area, Hannyngton's brigade occupied Ngarambi.[134] On the western front, Northey had advanced, and on January 16, occupied the bridge over the Rhudje at Malawis, six miles north-west of Iringa.[135]

Second Division's Action at Lukegeta

The 2nd Division, under Van Deventer, advanced from Iringa towards the south. Van Deventer had received information that a German force, estimated at 500 rifles, was holding a position 3 miles north of the Lukegeta.[136] He decided to attack the German force and for this purpose divided his troops into three columns - on the right, Colonel Haritigan with the 1st, 4th, 7th and 9th South African Horse, numbering in all about 500 rifles; on the left, under Colonel Taylor, the 4th King's African Rifles and a company of the 8th South African Infantry, numbering 750 rifles in all, with two Machine Guns; and in the centre under Brigadier General Berrange, the 7th South African Infantry and the 17th Indian Infantry with two companies of native levies. With Colonel Taylor's column was a section of the 28th Mountain Battery.[137] The whole force was concentrated at Boma Himbul on December 24. The right and the left columns were ordered to march to Muhanga via Makungwas and Boma Lukinindas, respectively.[138]

The Central column made its attack on December 25, 1916 with the 7th South African Infantry in the lead.[139] In the fight that ensued, the 17th Infantry was able to reach half way to a knoll where it dug in for the night.[140] The 17th Infantry was then ordered to wait for the flanking columns. The Germans broke up into small parties and escaped through the bush in the direction of Makungwas.[141] On the morning of the 27th, a squadron of the 7th South African Horse, of the right column, which had ben left at Makungwas, encountered a portion of the German troops and after fighting from morning to midday, the German force withdrew.[142]

The two flanking columns arrived at Muhanga on the morning of the 26th, having left detachments at Makungwas and Boma Likinindas to prevent the Germans from escaping. The idea was that the Germans, when driven out from the vicinity of the Lukegeta, would fall back on Muhanga where the flanking columns were entrenched. The flanking columns, however, left for the Lukegeta and when they were half way there, they received orders to reinforce the detachment at Makungwas. By the time they arrived, the Germans had already evacuated.[143]

At this juncture, it was decided to send back to Iringa all the white troops and with that the offensive movement of the 2nd Division came to an end.[144].

Smuts left for England to attend the Imperial Conference and Lieutenant General A.R. Hoskins took over command on January 20, 1917.[145] By then, the area up to the Rufiji had been occupied by the British and Vorbeck with his troops was retiring towards the Ruvuma river. After the departure of Smuts, the Germans were pushed southwards. The major battles being over, only minor engagements took place.

Operations Between January 1917 and November 1918

By early February 1917, the German troops had moved south of the Rufiji river and were concentrating around Madaba.[147] It was estimated that von Lettow Vorbeck was near Lindi-Kilwa with between 4000 to 5000 men.[149] An offensive was made against the German forces there under the command of Van Deventer, who at the end of May 1917, had relieved Hoskins.[150]

The Germans were holding a strong line on the Lukuledi estuary.[151] On June 10, 1917, the Germans were attacked under cover of darkness by a force consisting of one battalion of the King's African Rifles, the 25th Royal Fusiliers and the South African Field Artillery.[152] A fierce battle was fought and the Germans were routed.[153] Two German guns were captured but they were able to remove their naval gun to safety.[154]

In July 1917, the Germans evacuated Mount Shavama in the Kilwa area and retired to Narongombe.[155] On July 19, the three British columns converged at Narongombe where severe fighting took place in which both sides suffered heavy losses.[156] The Germans were forced to retire towards the Mbemkuru valley.[157] In early August, a German post at Mikumbia south-west of Lindi was attacked but the engagement proved indecisive.[158] On August 23, Tundura in the Lindi area was occupied.[159] By the end of September 1917, a German force at the Mbemkuru river in the Lindi area was defeated with heavy losses.[161] On September 25 and 26, successful efforts were made to dislodge a German force at Muta in the Lukuledi valley.[162]

On October 1, a German force under Naumann surrendered 75 miles south-east of Kondoa-Irangi.[163] It consisted of 15 Germans, 165 Askaris and 300 to 400 porters.[164] On October 10, Ruponda was captured by a British column which included the 25th Royal Fusiliers.[165] Vorbeck states that on October 18, with about 1500 men, he defeated a British force consisting of 4,000 to 6000 men at Mahiwa.[166] In this engagement, the British casualties were more than 1500 men while the German casualties were 14 Europeans and 81 Askaris killed, 55 Europeans and 367 Askaris wounded, 1 European and 1 Askari missing.[167]

In November, the British forces advanced towards Simbas, making a converging movement, to capture Vorbeck and his troops, who were reported to be holding a position there.[168] The Germans, however, escaped from Simbas.[169] Vorbeck crossed the Ruvuma on November 25.[170] He had about 2,000 rifles with him (300 Europeans and 1,700 Askaris[171]). In the same month, a German officer, Tafel surrendered unconditionally with 12 officers, 6 Medical officers, 92 Europeans, 1,220 native soldiers and 2,200 other ranks.[172] After this, Van Deventer decided to send back most of the Indian units.[173]

However, some of the Indian units remained in German East Africa till May 1919 and were utilised for repairing roads, bridges, railway lines, etc.

The campaign did not end here. The German troops under Vorbeck entered Portuguese East Africa. There, they were able to elude both the Portuguese and the British troops. In January 1918, the Portuguese placed their forces under Van Deventer with the idea of capturing the Germans. In spite of the joint efforts of the Portuguese and the British forces, Vorbeck and his troops were not captured. Vorbeck remained for about ten months in Portuguese East Africa, eluding Van Deventer's forces. At the end of September 1918, Vorbeck once again entered German East Africa,[174] where he remained for some time before going to (British) Rhodesia.

Surrender by Vorbeck

The First World War came to an end on November 11, 1918, and the German Government agreed to surrender unconditionally. On November 13, 1918, Vorbeck received this news from a motor-cyclist[175] sent to him by the British. The British Government asked for his surrender.

Accordingly, Vorbeck, with his troops, reached Abercorn on November 25, 1918 to surrender.[176] The remnants of his forces at this point of time consisted of the Governor of German East Africa, 20 officers, 5 medical officers, a doctor of the Voluntary Medical Detachment, a senior veterinary officer, a senior chemist, a field telegraph officer, 125 European other ranks, 1,156 Askaris and 1,598 porters.[177] Besides, Vorbeck surrendered 1 Portuguese gun, 37 Machine Guns (7 German and 16 heavy and 14 light British), 1,071 British and Portuguese rifles, 208,000 rounds, and 40 rounds of artillery ammunition.[178] The military operations in German East Africa during the First World War, came to an end in this manner. They had lasted more than four years.

During the period September 1916 to the end of the campaign the British forces kept on advancing on the enemy forces. The resources of the Germans were almost exhausted. The different units in different places could not contact each other, and so they could not make any concerted effort for their defence. Besides, the strength of the German forces was gradually dwindling. In face of all these difficulties Vorbeck was yet able to block the Allied forces (including the Belgian force) almost seventeen times greater than his own by adopting 'the Fabian Strategy'.

During this phase, the units of Force 'B', especially the Mountain Batteries, played a very significant role in the military operations. The engineering units of Force 'B' did useful engineering work. Some of the engineering and administrative units of Force 'B' were kept in German East Africa even after the campaign was over. The total strength of Force 'B' in German East Africa, in December 1918 was 1,597 men[179]. These Indian troops stayed there till May 1919.

NOTES

1. J.J. Collyer, *The South Africans with General Smuts in German East Africa*, Pretoria, 1939, p. 219.
2. *Ibid.*, p. 225.
3. M.D., H.S., War Diary, *IEF 'B'*, Vol. 24. pp. 54-61.
4. J.J. Collyer, *op.cit.*, p. 240.
5. *Ibid.*, p. 163.
6. *Ibid.*, p. 240.
7. *Ibid.*, p. 277.
8. M.D., H.S., War Diary, IEF 'B', Vol. 1., Map 1 (in the pocket)
9. Von L. Vorbeck, *My Reminiscences of East Africa*, London, 1920, p. 149.
10. *Ibid.*, p. 151.

11. *Ibid.*, p. 152.
12. J.J. Collyer, *op.cit.*, pp. 200-201.
13. *Ibid.*, p. 201.
14. J.H.V. Crowe, *General Smuts' Campaign in East Africa*, London, 1918, p. 196.
15. *History of the Great War, East Africa,* Vol. I, London, 1941, p. 362.
16. *Ibid.*
17. J.H.V. Crowe, *op.cit.*, p. 199, (The date in this book is given as 28th August, while in the Official History it is 29th August).
18. *History of the Great War, op.cit.*, p. 364.
19. *Ibid.*
20. J.H.V. Crowe, *op.cit.*, p. 203.
21. J.J. Collyer, *op.cit.*, p. 202.
22. *Ibid.*, p. 202.
23. *Ibid.*
24. *Ibid.*, p. 204.
25. *History of the Great War, op.cit.*, p. 365.
26. J.J. Collyer, *op.cit.*, p. 205.
27. *Ibid.*
28. *Ibid.*, p. 206.
29. *Ibid.*, p. 205.
30. *Ibid.*, p. 206.
31. *Ibid.*, p. 207.
32. *Ibid.*
33. *Ibid.*, p. 205.
34. *Ibid.*, p. 208.
35. *Ibid.*
36. *Ibid.*, p. 209.
37. *Ibid.*
38. *Ibid.*
39. *Ibid.*, p. 210.
40. *Ibid.*, p. 206.
41. *Ibid.*, p. 215.
42. *Ibid.*, p. 218.
43. *History of the Great War, op.cit.*, p. 369.
44. J.H.V. Crowe, *op.cit.*, p. 204.
45. *Ibid.*
46. *Ibid.*, p. 205.
47. J.J. Collyer, *op.cit.*, p. 217.
48. *History of the Great War, op.cit.*, p. 369.

49. *Ibid.*
50. J.H.V. Crowe, *op.cit.*, p. 205.
51. *Ibid.*
52. *Ibid.*, pp. 205-6.
53. *History of the Great War, op.cit.*, p. 369, See also J.J. Collyer, *op.cit.*, p. 217.
54. J.H.V. Crowe, *op.cit.*, p. 206.
55. *History of the Great War, op.cit.*, p. 370.
56. *Ibid.*
57. J.H.V. Crowe, *op.cit.*, p. 206.
58. *History of the Great War, op.cit.*, p. 370.
59. J.H.V. Crowe, *op.cit.*, p. 206.
60. *Ibid.*, p. 207.
61. *History of the Great War, op.cit.*, p. 370.
62. *Ibid.*, p. 370.
63. *Ibid.*
64. J.J. Collyer, *op.cit.*, p. 217.
65. *History of the Great War, op.cit.*, p. 371.
66. J.J. Collyer, *op.cit.*, p. 217.
67. *History of the Great War, op.cit.*, p. 375.
68. *Ibid.*, p. 377.
69. *Ibid.*, p. 376.
70. *Ibid.*, pp. 379-81.
71. *Ibid.*, p. 382.
72. J.J. Collyer, *op.cit.*, p. 223.
73. *History of the Great War, op.cit.*, p. 382.
74. *Ibid.*
75. *Ibid.*, p. 382 fn.
76. *Ibid.*, p. 383
77. *Ibid.*, p. 384.
78. *Ibid.*
79. *Ibid.*
80. J.J. Collyer, *op.cit.*, p. 224.
81. M.D., H.S., G.S.B., The European Crisis, Vol. 170, p. 27826.
82. *Ibid.*
83. *Ibid.*
84. *Ibid.*
85. J.J. Collyer, *op.cit.*, p. 239.
86. *Ibid.*, p. 240.
87. J.H.V. Crowe, *op.cit.*, p. 240.

88. *Ibid.*
89. J.J. Collyer, *op.cit.*, p. 240.
90. J.H.V. Crowe, *op.cit.*, p. 241.
91. J.J. Collyer, *op.cit.*, p. 241.
92. *Ibid.*
93. *Ibid.*, p. 242.
94. *Ibid.*
95. *Ibid.*
96. J.H.V. Crowe, *op.cit.*, p. 232.
97. J.J. Collyer, *op.cit,* p. 244
98. *Ibid*
99. J.H.V Crowe, *op.cit,* p. 242.
100. *Ibid.*
101. *Ibid.*
102. *Ibid.*
103. *Ibid.*, p. 243.
104. J.J. Collyer, *op.cit.*, p. 245.
105. *Ibid.*
106. J.H.V. Crowe, *op.cit.*, p. 243.
107. *Ibid.*
108. *Ibid.*
109. J.J. Collyer, *op.cit.*, p. 245.
110. *Ibid.*, p. 246.
111. *Ibid.*, p. 248.
112. *Ibid.*, p. 249.
113. *Ibid.*
114. *Ibid.*, p. 250.
115. *Ibid.*, p. 251.
116. J.H.V. Crowe, *op.cit.*, p. 252.
117. *Ibid.*
118. *Ibid.*
119. *Ibid.*
120. *Ibid.*, p. 253.
121. J.J. Collyer, *op.cit.*, p. 254.
122. *Ibid.*
123. *Ibid.*, p. 255.
124. *Ibid.*
125. *Ibid.*
126. *Ibid.*
127. *Ibid.*, p. 256.

128. *Ibid.*, p. 257.
129. J.H.V. Crowe, *op.cit.*, p. 258.
130. *Ibid.*
131. J.J. Collyer, *op.cit.*, p. 257.
132. J.H.V. Crowe, *op.cit.*, p. 264.
133. *Ibid.*, p. 259.
134. *Ibid.*, p. 260.
135. *Ibid.*
136. *Ibid.*, p. 261.
137. *Ibid.*
138. *Ibid.*
139. *Ibid.*
140. *Ibid.*, pp. 261-62.
141. *Ibid.*, pp. 262.
142. *Ibid.*
143. *Ibid.*
144. *Ibid.*, p. 262-63.
145. J.H. Collyer, *op.cit.*, p. 258.
146. After the departure of Smuts, the details of engagements are not available. The sources available cover only up to January 1917. Only summaries of operations are available for the period after Smuts departure.
147. M.D., H.S., G.S.B., The European Crisis, Vol. 242, p. 69.
148. A. Buchanan, *Three Years of War in East Africa* London, 1919, p. 175.
149. *Ibid.*, p. 176.
150. *Ibid.*
151. *Ibid.*, p. 177.
152. *Ibid.*, p. 177.
153. *Ibid.*, p. 182.
154. M.D., H.S., G.S.B., The European Crisis, Vol. 303, p. 68.
155. *Ibid.*, Vol. 326.
156. *Ibid.*
157. *Ibid.*
158. *Ibid.*, Vol. 333, p. 62.
159. *Ibid.*, Vol. 343, p. 100.
160. *Ibid.*, Vol. 349, p. 114.
161. *Ibid.*, Vol. 356, p. 117.
162. *Ibid.*, Vol. 359, p. 141.
163. *Ibid.*

164. *Ibid.*
165. Von L. Vorbeck, *op.cit.*, p. 208.
166. *Ibid.*, p. 212.
167. *Ibid.*
168. M.D., H.S., G.S.B., The European Crisis, Vol. 383. p. 43.
169. *Ibid.*
170. Von L. Vorbeck, *op.cit.*, p. 229.
171. *Ibid.*, p. 224.
172. M.D., H.S., G.S.B., *The European Crisis*, Vol. 385. p. 29.
173. *Ibid.*
174. Von L. Vorbeck, op.cit., p. 304.
175. *Ibid.*, p. 315.
176. *Ibid.*, p. 320.
177. *Ibid.*, p. 321.
178. *Ibid.*, pp. 320-21.
179. M.D., H.S., G.S.B., The European Crisis, Vol. 595, p. 21.

CONCLUSION

The German East African Campaign, in which the Indian Army played a significant role, is one of the most interesting campaigns of the First World War. The peculiar mode of warfare adopted in German East Africa was totally different to those adopted in the other theatres of the War. The terrain of this theatre of war was singularly difficult and scraggy, rendering the movement of the troops hazardous and nerve racking. In spite of great imbalance between the manpower and resources of the rival force, the weaker German forces engaged the Allied forces for more than four years, their enemy being numerically superior by nearly seventeen times (including the Belgian troops) with greater resources at their command. The most remarkable fact is that this small German force remained undefeated till the end of the First World War. Many interesting results flow from a close study of this campaign. Before analysing the final results, it is necessary to sum up the conditions under which the Indian and the German troops fought each other.

The Indian troops used by the Allies in German East Africa during the First World War had many in-built disadvantages from the beginning of the campaign; these continued through out the whole course of the campaign. The first and the most important point in this connection is that the units, which were sent to East Africa appeared to be of less importance to the Allies. The better equipped and experienced units were despatched to the more important theatres. In East Africa, only those units were sent which were found unsuitable for the other theatres of the war, which is why the 16th Poona Brigade, which had been previously destined for German East Africa, was directed "to the more important sphere of action in the Persian Gulf."[1]

Though some of the units had received battle honours before the war, yet they had no operational experience. The 63rd Palamcottah Light Infantry and the 98th Infantry had formed part of the China expedition of 1900 and had acquired honour in that expedition; in fact, it had not gone beyond Hong Kong[2], and from that year onwards until the First World War, they had never seen service in the field[3].

Second, the units which formed the force detailed for East Africa were rought from different parts of the country; hence the force lacked homogeneity. Most of the soldiers were strangers to each other[4], and lacked espirit de corps in the initial stage of the campaign. Their training was not uniform, and consequently their degree of efficiecy varied. Sheppard (later Major General) of Force 'B' inspected the units at Bombay and remarked that the campaign in German East Africa would either be a walk-over or a tragedy[5]. The Intelligence Officer of Force 'B' was also not impressed by the force and thought that the units that formed Force 'B' were the worst in India[6].

Third, the officers who had to command the force were strangers to the units. Major General Aitken saw the force only a week before it sailed for East Africa[7]. Brigadier General Wapshare came into contact with the 63rd Light Infantry and the 98th Infantry for the first time the day before embarkation while Brigadier General Tighe met the units of his brigade when they concentrated at Deolali six days before sailing[8]. In such circumstances, the qualities of the units were not known to the officers and they could not be utilized where they would have proved best. The officers too were strangers to their soldiers; hence the soldiers lacked confidence in their commanders. In such circumstances, the soldiers could not be expected to have a high morale. Besides, many officers were old and not suited for active service[9]. The net result of all these conditions was that effective coordination between the troops and their officers was lacking.

Fourth, most of the troops were not familiar with the arms they were to handle in the German East African Campaign. Before mobilization, the units in southern India were armed with the obsolete converted long M.L.E. rifles[10]. They were equipped with the standard Short Le-Enfield rifles just before the embarkation. These units were not familiar with the sighting and mechanism of this rifle and in the initial stages they could not use it efficiently and effectively.

Only two battalions (the 101st Grenadiers and the 61st Pioneers) of Force 'B' had machine guns before 1914[11]. Just before embarkation, many units were given machine guns but were not given sufficient time to practice with those guns. They had difficulty using these new guns for sometime and Force 'B' did not get the maximum advantage of the machine guns in the beginning of the campaign.

Fifth, the climatic conditions of German East Africa proved unhealthy for the Indian troops adversely affecting their efficiency. The Indian troops were not acclimatised to such climatic conditions and consequently, a considerable number of troops either became incapable of taking part in the military operations or their efficiency was much reduced.

Sixth, many types of diseases were prevalent[12]. Due to this the strength of the Indian units never remained up to their original level.

Seventh, the Indian troops had no knowledge of the topography of German East Africa. The maps available were far too inaccurate to be of any use to the Indian troops. They had no knowledge of the native tracks, nullahs, bush, etc. and faced great difficulties. This was especially so when the advance was made from Mount Kilimanjaro towards its south. They also experienced difficulty crossing streams and rivers infested with deadly fish and crocodiles. They had to make bridges over such streams and rivers to cross them. Thick bush again proved a great obstacle in their advances. As they had no knowledge of the native tracks or roads, they had to cut the bush to advance. At many places, the soil was such that became spongy during rains, making it imposible for the toops to walk over it. As the Indian troops had no knowledge of these factor, they were often held up in such circumstances, resulting in considerably reducing the mobility of the Indian troops.

And last the Indian troops had difficulty in sending supplies to the forward units. As there was a lack of proper roads on which wheeled traffic could pass, supplies were sent by pack animals. The pack animals very frequently succumbed to the stings of the Tsetse flies. Consequently, there was always a dearth of animals. This difficulty persisted throughout the campaign. To overcome this, many new railway lines and roads were constructed to enable wheeled traffic to move to the forward units. The Ushambara Railway line was linked with the Uganda Railway. Many roads were constructed in the south of Mount Kilimanjaro. On several occasions, the troops had to wait until the roads were constructed. This was one of the reasons that delayed the advance of the Indian troops.

Though it is true that the Indian troops suffered many disadvantages in this campaign, it cannot be denied that they enjoyed certain advantages, too. First, the number of the Indian troops was considerably larger than the German troops. The total number of the Indian troops was more than the German troops even when the latter touched its maximum number during the campaign. Therefore, it was possible for the Indian troops to spare those soldiers, who were unable to take part in the military operations because of sickness and injury.

Also the Indian troops had no difficulty in receiving reinforcements (provided the Indian Government could spare more units). During the campaign many Indian units were sent to reinforce Force 'B'[13]. There was no blockade of German East Africa by the Germans due to lack of resources and the ships carrying the Indian units could reach East Africa without any resistance. This was of great advantage to the Indian troops as fresh units could be employed in the battles and the tired ones could be relieved. In addition, the Indian troops had the support of the South African, British and K.A.R. units.

The Indian units also had no difficulty obtaining arms and ammunition from India or England. During the campaign, the Indian units received large quantities of arms and ammunition and were never in a short supply. Some of the Indian artillery units were given Howitzers in German East Africa.

The Indian units had the support of the British Navy. In most of the coastal operations Naval help was given. Even in Tanga, in November 1914, the Navy had deployed her ships to assist Force 'B'. All the coastal towns like Dar-es-Salaam, Kilwa and Lindi were captured with the help of the British Navy. In the later years, aeroplanes were also used for making aerial surveys and for bombarding.[14] Besides, from February 1916, onwards, a large number of the South African units were sent to take offensive action against the Germans and the overall command was given to Smuts, who was familiar with the tropical warfare. The Belgians and the Portuguese also cooperated with the British forces from the western and southern sides, respectively.

Vorbeck's force had started the operations in German East Africa with many disadvantages. First, the Protective Force could not get reinforcements from the mother country mainly for two reasons. The first was that German East Africa was surrounded on three sides by the Allies and the coastal belt was guarded by the British Navy. Hence, there was hardly any route left by which the Germans could receive reinforcements. The second reason was that Germany was busy in the other theatres of the First World War which were more important for her. It had to meet the requirements in these theatres and its resources were less compared to the resources at the command of Great Britain. Hence, it could not be expected to send more men and materials to reinforce the Protective Force in German East Africa. Actually, Vorbeck received very little help from Germany. He had mainly to rely upon the local resources. During the campaign, he recruited the natives and Europeans available in German East Africa and trained them to fight against the Allied Forces.

The Protective Force was armed with the old pattern of artillery. Many of the German companies were armed with 1871 pattern rifles and machine guns of 1873 pattern which discharged smoke on firing.[15] The disadvantage with such rifles and guns was that they disclosed their positions and the enemy could fire upon them accurately.[16] Besides, these old pattern guns and rifles had low rates of fire. It is true that the Protective Force had the *Königsberg* guns, which had a long firing range and did not discharge smoke on firing, but they could only be moved with great difficulty as they had no wheels and fired from a fixed point.[17] Hence, the Germans could use these guns only at such places where they could be brought up by wheeled traffic.

The Protective Force had certain advantages as well. First, the bulk of the Protective Force was composed of native inhabitants of German East Africa. The climate did not pose any problem for them. The bulk of the Askaris belonged to the declared martial races, who were well versed in bush warfare. During the campaign, these natives gave a very good performance. Moreover, these natives were immune to the diseases which were prevalent in German East Africa. Vorbeck remarks, "Generally speaking the native is in a great measure immune against malaria and it does not often happen that an Askari gets really ill with it."[18]

Second, the German troops carried their wives and children with them. Due to this, the German soldiers never felt homesick. Besides, their families proved useful as the ladies cooked their meals thus reducing one of the responsibilities of the soldiers.[19]

Third, the German forces has a thorough knowledge of the topography of the theatre which greatly helped them. They knew the native track and so were more mobile. That is why the Protective Force was able to withdraw quickly whenever required and could make surprise attacks on enemy detachments.

Fourth, the Protective Force had many good officers including Vorbeck. The officers had full knowledge of bush warfare and knew the country well. Besides, they knew how to tackle the natives and that is why a considerable number of the natives remained with the Protective Force throughout the campaign.

Fifth, the Protective Force had always maintained a number of porters to carry rations, and the arms and ammunition of the force so that the German soldiers did not find their movements very tiring and always remained prepared for offensive action. Besides, the porters formed a reserve force.[20]

Sixth, each German company carried a portable boat and so the streams, rivers or nullahs presented no obstacles to them.[21] This factor also increased the mobility of the Protective Force.

Seventh, the Germans had been able to manufacture ammunition with local materials. "Ammunition of all natures, including 10.5 and 8.8 cm.

was manufactured at Dar-es-Salamm. They had about 30,000 pounds of sulphur in the country at the outbreak of war, by chance or design and there was no difficulty as to saltpetre or charcoal."[22] This factor, to some extent, solved the problem of obtaining ammunition for the Protective Force.

And last, one of the factors which greatly helped the Germans in the campaign was the luckly coincidence of the Dar-es-Salaam Exhibition which was to be opened in August, 1914. The preparations for this had begun a few months earlier and before the outbreak of the war, German East Africa had received great supplies of machinery, stores, and exhibits which were swiftly adapted to the making of rifles and ammunitions of war.[23] The famous German ship *Königsberg*, whose guns were utilised on land after it had been destroyed was also brought to German East Africa for the purpose of this exhibition.[24]

The campaign had some special features which are not generally found elsewhere. In this theatre, the geographical factors led the dance while strategy and tactics acted as docile partners. The wide variation of climate and the insect pests detrimentally affected the troops. The area between the plateau and the sea, where the military operations mainly took place, has an average height of 3,000 feet. This is an area of great heat and humidity, with an unhealthy climate, wherein a foreigner finds it impossible to keep fit. The temperature also varied from place to place. At some places, the temperature falls below the freezing point at night and rises upto boiling point during the day. At such places, it was difficult for troops to march during the day and also to sleep at night without proper clothing. Besides, the numerous waterless tracts in German East Africa played their own role in the military operations.

Another telling factor of this theatre was the thick bush. It was difficult for one unit to observe the movements of other units because of the thick bush, and in most of the engagements the 'Principle of Cooperation' could not be properly applied. In the thick ush it was very difficult for one to know where exactly the hostile forces were holding their positions. At many times hostile datachments passed through almost the same place without noticing each other. The bush also provided a good shelter to the German forces when they began their retreat southwards.[25] It proved a boon in tactical defence, especially for the Germans, who were familiar with the country.

During the rains, the whole country became swampy and impassable. The troops had to curtail their movements in marshy land. Often at places it rained so heavily that small nullahs became gushing streams and the troops had to wade through breast deep water in order to reach a point where they could remain for some time.[26] In those conditions it was impossible to move the mechanical transport and often the troops had to remain where they were before the rains came.

The supply problem was beyond complete solution because there were only two railway lines and a few roads. The roads, whatever their condition, did not prove of much value. The bush grew so quickly that it was difficult to pass without clearing it. Often, it was difficult to trace the roads because of the bush.

One of the most interesting features of this campaign was that more casualties occurred because of diseases than in actual battle. From the records showing the effective strength of the Indian units at various times, it is evident that they mostly remained at a much lower level than their actual strength. The total number of deaths in the campaign was 10,001 of which only 3,443 were battle casualties,[27] the rest dieing of diseases. Even the transport animals died of these diseases. Collyer mentions that about 28,000 oxen died in a short time.[28]

While on the one hand, the use of the natives was of advantage, on the other it often created complications. From the sources available, it appears that native messengers, who used to take messages from one unit to another, were unable to distinguish between the German whites and the British and gave messages to the wrong parties, specially because they knew neither English nor German.

Another interesting feature of this campaign was that in spite of the fact that Smuts and Vorbeck were commanding hostile forces, Smuts appreciated the achievements of Vorbeck's force on many occasions.[29] Smuts congratulated Vorbeck when he was awarded the Second Class of the Order of the Crown with Swords.[29] Vorbeck later sent a letter, thanking him, in reply.[30]

The kind of warfare which the troops fought in German East Africa is usually termed 'Guerilla Warfare'. Guerilla warfare in the wider sense has come to mean the art of combat waged by the weak to overcome the strong. It is a highly intelligent form and not wild cat scrimmage. In such warfare, the weaker party avoids pitched battles as far as possible and looks out for opportunities to ambush the enemy. Through ambushes, the weaker party tries to exhaust the enemy. Besides, the weaker party turns the hazards of the terrain to its advantage by making an ally of tropical rains, heavy snow, intense heat and freezing cold. Guerilla strategy is primarily based on alertness, mobility and attack. It lays emphasis on surprise attack, hit and run tactics and harassing techniques.

Vorbeck had adopted the essential ingredients of Guerilla Warfare. However, the more appropriate term for the mode of warfare that Vorbeck adopted is the 'Fabian Strategy'[31]. Though most of the techniques in 'Fabian Strategy' and 'Guerilla Strategy' are common, yet there is a difference. Both of them are meant for the weaker party and based on the fundamental principle of avoiding pitched battles with the stronger party. Surprise attacks and hit and run tactics form the essential ingredients of the 'Fabian Strategy' as well as the 'Guerilla Strategy'. The only difference between the two is that 'Guerilla Warfare' is based on the support of the masses and that is why, it is called 'the Peoples' War', while 'Fabian Strategy' does not depend upon the support of the masses. The latter is a strategy meant for conventional forces.

The German force adopted the Fabian Strategy in German East Africa. This was essential as the Protective Force was much less in number and was equipped with inferior weapons. In March 1916, the British forces were about three times the German force. By the end of the year 1916, the total strength of the Allied force was fifteen times the strength of the German force. Besides, the German force had to face a Belgian force, which was roughly one and a half times greater than the former. Had Vorbeck fought pitched battles his force would have been defeated within a short time. But by adopting the Fabian Strategy he was able to continue the military operations until the end of the First World War and remained uncaptured. Considering the meagre resources of the German force, this was a great achievement. Mao Tse-tung, the master of Guerilla Warfare, says that the weaker party must exhaust her enemy by prolonging the war. This is what Vorbeck did.

This campaign clearly shows the importance of morale in war. It has been rightly said that in wars 'morale is to force as three is - to one'. The maintenance of morale is recognized in miltary circles as the most important single factor in war though outside these circles there is sometimes difficulty in appreciating this. Military historians lacking the experience of actual command during wartime make the mistake of attributing too much importance to tactics. Tactics are relatively less important than morale. The truth is that a brilliant plan of battle in the tactical sense can be a complete failure if morale is bad, while a poor plan can be made to work well if morale is good. High morale is the most important quality of a soldier. It is a quality of mind and spirit which combines courage, self-discipline and endurance. It manifests itself in the soldier's absolute determination to do his duty to the best of his ability under all circumstances. It was because of high morale that the German forces continued the fight for such a long period, and at times even defeated the British force despite the latter's large numerical strength (as was the case at Tanga in November 1914). Brigadier General S.H. Sheppard once remarked about this Campaign: "I have never known any campaign in which 'spirit' played so large a part as in East Africa. It may almost be taken for granted that after a year or eighteen months service out here every man is potentially 'sick' and unless he has the 'will to keep going' he will be sick."[32] It was indeed a war of human endurance.

This campaign also demonstrates the importance of good leadership in military operations. The creative military leader can originate and use ingenious techniques to achieve success in military operations. The Protective Force, which was commanded by an able commander, was able to achieve its objective in spite of heavy odds. Vorbeck utilized all the local resources to meet the war time requirements. He raised the morale of his soldiers who continued to fight till the end of the war. In the military operations, he turned the irregular terrain to his advantage. Force 'B', on the other hand, was not led by good commanders in the beginning. They failed to utilize all the available resources to their advantage. The situation was favourable for Force 'B' but still it met disaster at the beginning of the campaign. Most of the principles of war were ignored in the early stages. To win war proper planning is essential, and for the formulation of a proper plan collection of topographical and other factual data about the enemy is indispensable. Aitken, the Commander of Force 'B' did not collect the necessary data for the formulation of a proper plan before hand, and hence Force 'B' met with disaster at Tanga. In the later operations also, sometimes the suggestions of the Intelligence Officer of Force 'B' were not taken into account, which led to faulty planning.

According to Mao Tse-tung in such wars, the weaker party must have the support of the civilian population. The main advantage of this is that the latter provide shelter and rations to the fighting soldiers. Vorbeck had procured the support of the natives upto some extent and that is why he did not face difficulty in obtaining rations for his troops. At most places, Vorbeck and his troops received a warm welcome. Until the end of the campaign, many of the natives remained loyal to him. He had to decline the offer of services by a large number of the natives, because of lack of supplies, when he crossed the Ruvuma river and entered Portuguese East Africa.[33] Without the support of the civilian population, the Protective Force could not have prolonged the war for such a long duration.

Considering Vorbeck's objective in this campaign, it would be correct to say that he achieved it. His main objective was to pin down as many British troops as possible in German East Africa thereby denying the British all their available troops against Germany in the decisive sectors in Europe. In this objective, Vorbeck was fully successful. He kept large forces of the Allied Powers tied down in German East Africa with his meagre forces and resources till the end of the First World War.

The Indian Army in this campaign did commendable service for the British cause. The Indian troops were in the thick of the fighting. The most important role was played by the Mountain Artillery units. In most of the engagements and battles their support to the advancing units proved invaluable. One of the reasons for the defeat of the Indian troops at Tanga was that the services of these Mountain Batteries were not properly utilized. The Indian cavalry unit served as the advance guard at many places in the campaign, e.g., at Longido in March 1915,[34] and in the south of the Kilimanjaro in April 1916.[35] The Infantry units, too, played a significant part in the campaign. Many of these units were employed for the protection of the lines of communication. The engineering units like the Railway Companies, the Faridkot Sappers and Miners and the 61st Pioneers deserve special mention. Many new railway lines, roads and bridges were constructed by them which were essential for the movement of the troops. The work done by the medical units was also of great importance. They gave much needed relief to the wounded and and sick soldiers.

The campaign cost the Indians 4,934 casualties (2,865 killed, 2002 wounded, 46 missing and 21 prisoners).[36] On the whole, the role of the Indian troops was appreciated by the commanders of Force 'B'. However, two units of the Imperial Service Troops got adverse reports.[37]

General Smuts remarked: "The Indians in may army proved them selves gallant and skilful soldiers and in many hardwon fights earned the respect and admiration of their European colleagues".[38] Van Deventer on the termination of his command of the East African Force, wrote to the Commander-in-Chief of India. "The troops sent from India have borne their full share of the hardship of a campaign in which the fighting has been severe and the physical difficulties enormous and have played a gallant part in the conquest of German East Africa. I am proud to have had them under my command".[39]

In spite of defective organisation and unprecedented difficulties, the Indian Army played a significant role in the East African Campaign. In the early phase of the campaign, the Indian Army could not do well as it was not properly led, but later, under able commanders like Smuts and Van Deventer, it proved invaluable to the Allies.

NOTES

1. *History of the Great War, East Africa*, Vol.I, London, 1941, p. 62.
2. *Ibid.*, p. 68 fn.
3. *Ibid.*, p. 68.
4. *Ibid.*
5. *Ibid.*, p. 69 fn.
6. R. Meinertzhagen *Army Diary, 1899-1926* London, 1926, p. 82.
7. *History of the Great War, op.cit.*, p. 68.
8. *Ibid.*, p. 68 fn.
9. R. Meinertzhagen, *op.cit.*, p. 68.
10. See Chapter II.
11. *History of the Great War, op.cit.*, p. 70.
12. See Chapter III.
13. See Chapter II.
14. *History of the Great War, op.cit.*, pp. 216 217.
15. See Chapter II.
16. Von L. Vorbeck, *My Reminiscences of East Africa*, London, 1920, p. 47.
17. *Ibid.*, p. 111.
18. *Ibid.*
19. This information is given by Lt Col M.A. Singh (attached to 57th Rifles) who participated in the campaign, in an interview with the author on 10 June 1972 at Kanpur.
20. See Chapter II.
21. J.H.V, Crowe, *op.cit.*, p. 32.
22. R.V. Dolbey, *Sketches of East African Campaign*, London, 1918, pp. 12-13.
23. *Ibid.*
24. See Chapter III.
25. A. Buchanan, *Three Years of War in East Africa*, London, 1919, p. 10.
26. J.H.V. Crowe, *op.cit.*, p. 263.

27. J.J. Collyer, *The South Africans with General Smuts in German East Africa,* Pretoria, 1939, p. 277
28. *Ibid.*, p. 275.
29. Von L. Vorbeck, *op.cit.*, p. 170.
30. *Ibid.*
31. This strategy is named after the Roman General Quintus Fabius Maximus, who applied it against the Carthigian General Hannibal in 217 B.C. Fabius's force was not only weaker than Hannibal's force but was also armed with inferior weapons. Fabius avoided direct confrontation. Maneuvering among the hills, where Hannibal's cavalry was useless, he cut off his supplies, harassed him incessantly and did everything except engage battle. In this way, Fabius was able to exhaust his enemy's force which was greater in strength and equipped with better weapons, without suffering much loss.
32. M.D., H.S. *War Diary, IEF 'B'*, Vol. 29, p. 216.
33. Von L. Vorbeck, *op.cit.*, p. 224.
34. *History of the Great War, op.cit.*, p. 238.
35. *Ibid.*, p. 291 fn.
36. M.B.L. Bhargava, *India's Services in the War*, Lucknow, 1919, p. 87.
37. M.D., H.S., *War Diary, IEF 'C'*, Vol. 4, p. 12.
38. Foreword by J.C. Smuts to the book by J.J. Collyer, *op.cit.*, p. vii.
39. M.D., H.S., G.S.B., The European Crisis, Vol. 602, p. 103.

Appendix A

AFTERMATH : THE SETTLEMENT OF VERSAILLES

After the First World War, the Allies were confronted with the problem of making peace. For this purpose, a Conference was summoned, which met at Paris on January 18, 1919, and the terms for peace were settled. The terms of peace with Germany contained in the Treaty of Versailles, comprising 440 articles and almost a score of annexes. By Article 119 of this treaty, Germany was stripped off all its colonies. Germany renounced "in favour of the Principal Allied and Associated Powers all her rights and titles over her overseas possessions", being later apportioned among Great Britain, France, Belgium, Japan, the Union of South Africa, Australia and New Zealand as mandatees of the League. German East Africa no longer remained a German colony. It was given to Great Britain as a 'B' class mandate and renamed Tanganyika.

Appendix B
ORDER OF BATTLE, MARCH 5, 1916[1]

	I Division (Major-General Stewart)	II Division (Major-General Tighe)	Force . Reserve (Brigidier-General Beves)	Flanking Force (Brigadier-General Van Deventer
MOUNTED TROOPS	B.A. Mtd. Rifles Sqdn. 17th Cavalry K.A.R. M.I. Coy	4 S.A. Horse Belfield's Scouts M.I Boy (L.N. Lancs) No. 10 (R.N.) Armed Car Bty.		1st S.A. Mtd. Br. 1st S.A. Hore 2nd S.A. Horse 3rd S.A. Horse
INFANTRY	2nd East African Brigade 25th Royal Fusiliers 29th Punjabis 129th Baluchis Cape Corps Bn Attached: 1/K.A.R. (4 Coys) B.A.M.G. Coy	Ist East African Brigade 2/ Loyal North Lancashire 2nd Rhodesia Regt. 130th Baluchis 3/K.A.R. (5 coys) Attached: Kashmir Rifles (Composits Bn) Volunteer M.G. Coy.	2nd South African Brigade 5th S.A. Infantry 6th S.A. Infantry 7th S.A. Infantry 8th S.A. Infantry	3rd South African Brigade 9th S.A. Infantry 10th S.A. Infantry 11th S.A. Infantry 12th S.A. Infantry
ARTILLERY	No. 1 Group 1st S.A. Field Bde. (Nos. I and 3 Btys) No. 7 Field Bty. 27th Mountain Bty. Ist Div. Ammunition Column	No.2 Group 4th Indian Mountain Arty. Bde. (excluding 27th & 28th Btys) No. 6 Field Bty. No. 8 Field Bty. No. 9 Field Bty No. 10 Howitzer Bty. 134th Howitzer Bty. 2nd Div. Ammunition Column	No.5 S.A. Field Bty. No. 12 Howitzer Bty.	2nd S.A. Field Bde. (Nos. 2 and 4 Btys.) 28th Mountain Bty. S.A. Div. Ammunition Column

OTHER UNITS	Div. Signal Coy Half Coy. Faridkot S. and M.	Div. Signal Coy. Half Coy. Faridkot S. and M	Order G.H.Q. No. 26 Sqn. R.F.C. 61st Pioneers
	4,000 Men (18 guns and 22 m.gs)	8,500 Men (25 guns and 61 m.gs)	5,900 men (14 guns and 16 m.gs)
		18,400 men (57 guns and 99 m/gs)	

1. History of the Great War, Vol. 1. *op. cit.*, p. 248.

Appendix C

NAMES OF VETERANS WHO SERVED THE INDIAN ARMY DURING THE FIRST WORLD WAR, INTERVIEWED BY THE AUTHOR

1. Lieutenant Colonel M.A. Singh of the 57th Rifles (participated in the German East African Campaign). 4/276, Parvati Bagla Road, District Kanpur (U.P)
2. Major Narain Singh of the 23rd Sikh Pioneers,
   Village Urmar,
   Tehsil Dasuya,
   District Hoshiarpur (Punjab).
3. Captain B.L. Dubey of the Ist Gwalior
   119/469 Darshanpurva,
   District Kanpur (U.P.).
4. Subedar Major & Honorary Captain Hazara Singh of the 30th Punjabis (participated in the German East African Campaign)
   Village Thakkar,
   Tehsil Dasuya,
   District Hoshiarpur (Punjab).
5. Subedar Major & Honorary Lieutenant Manmohan Singh of the 76th Punjabis
   Village Mahilpur,
   Tehsil Garhshankar,
   District Hoshiarpur (Punjab).
6. Subedar Major & Honorary Lieutenant Sunehra Singh of the 4th Rajputs
   Village Rampur,
   Tehsil Karnal,
   District Karnal (Haryana).
7. Havildar Sunder Singh of the 59th Punjabis
   Village Singhpur,
   Tehsil Dasuya,
   District Hoshiarpur (Punjab).

8. Sepoy Roshan Singh of the 95th Infantry
   Village Bhadesa,
   Tehsil Ghatampur,
   District Kanpur (U.P).
9. Sepoy Sahu Singh of the 2nd Rajputs
   Village Rampura,
   Tehsil Karnal,
   District Karnal (Haryana).
10. Sepoy Yadu Singh of the 2nd Rajputs
    Village Charaunda,
    Tehsil Karnal,
    District Karnal (Haryana).

Bibliography

A. *Original Unpublished Sources*

I. *Records of the Historical Section, Ministry of Defence*

1. Annual Report on Imperial Service Troops for 1919-1920, File No. 1311/H/I.
2. Army Department Report on Organization of Indian Army, 1921, File No. M.O. 82.
3. Collection of Army Department (General Staff Branch) Correspondence relating to The European Crisis *1914* (769 Volumes). Case No.9576/Field Operation (Confidential).
4. Copies of Reports by General Officer Commanding Troops. East Africa and Uganda Protectorates on Operations in East Africa during September and October 1914. Case No. 10838 (Secret).
5. Copy of Report on the Operations of IEF 'B' during the tenure of Command of Major General R. Wapshare, December 1914-April 1915. Case No. 11707 (Secret).
6. Correspondence between the GOC Troops, British East Africa and Uganda Protectorate and HE the Governor and C in C British East Africa Protectorate. File No. WWI/1485/H (Secret).
7. Plans of Operations against Germany, General Staff Branch, 1914. Case No.101162 (Secret).
8. Preparation for the Army in India for War. File No. M.O.18 (Secret).
9. Proceedings of the Advisory Council, October 1917-September 1918 (5 Volumes). Case No. 18328.
10. Report of a Committee on Sappers and Miners Organization, Equipment and Transport etc., September 1920. File No. M.O. 224.
11. Report on Army Headquarters, 1922, File No. M.O. 231.
12. Summary of the Distribution of the Army in India, Ist July 1914. Case No.2626 Official, Q.M.G.I.

13. War Diary, Army Headquarters, 'FRONTIER OPERATIONS' (56 Volumes). From 29th November 1914 to 29th February 1920 (Confidential).
14. War Diary, Army Headquarters, 'GENERAL' (28 Volumes). From 9th October 1914 to 30th April 1916 (Confidential).
15. War Diary, Indian Expeditionary Force 'B', (34 Volumes). From 8th August 1914 to 31st May 1919 (Confidential).
16. War Diary, Indian Expeditionary Force 'C', (4 Volumes). From 8th August 1914 to 4th December 1914 (Confidential).
17. Recruiting in India Before and During the War of 1914-1918 (Army Headquarters, India, 1919).

ii. *Records of the Ministry of Defence*

18. Correspondence of the General Staff Branch, during 1914-1918 (Geographical Section).
19. Correspondence of the Adjutant General's Branch during 1914-1918.
20. Correspondence of the Military Secretary's Branch during 1914-1918.
21. Correspondence of the Quartermaster General's Branch during 1914-1918.

iii. *Records of the National Archives of India*

21. Papers of Joseph A. Chamberlain, Secretary of State for India (1915-1917). Micro-film Reel Nos. 1738 to 1741.

B. *Official Published Reports and Books*

1. *Report of the Army India Committee*, 1919-1920. (Esher Committee).
2. *Report on Indianisation of the India Army*, 1922 (Shea Committee).
3. *Army Quarterly List*, October 1914.
4. *The Army in India and its Evolution*, Calcutta, 1924.
5. *History of the Great War, Military Operations, East Africa*, London, 1941, Official History.

C. *Contemporary and Secondary Sources*

Addison, C., *Politics From Within*, 1911-1918 (2 Volumes), London, 1924.

Albertini, L., *The Origins of the War of 1914,* (3 Volumes), New York, 1929.

Bhargava, M.B.L., *India's Services in the War,* Lucknow, 1919.

Birnie, A., *The Art of War,* London Edinburgh Paris-Melbourne-Toronto-New York, 1942.

Buchan, J.A., *A History of the Great War,* Boston, 1922.

Buchan, J., *Nelson's History of the War* (22 Volumes), London-Edinburg-New York (Year of publication not mentioned).

Buchanan, A., *Three Years of War in East Africa,* London, 1919.

Chapman, C., *Vain Glory,* London, 1937.

Chaudhury, J.N., *Arms, Aims and Aspects,* Bombay, 1966.

Churchill, W.S., *The Great War* (4 Volumes), London, 1933.

--------------------- *The Unknown War,* London, 1923.

--------------------- *The World Crisis,* London, 1923

Clausewitz, K., *On War* (3 Volumes), Washington, 1950.

Cohen, S.P., *The Indian Army,* London, 1971.

Cole, D.H., *Imperial Military Geography,* London, 1963.

Cole, D.H., and Priestley, E.C., *An Outline of British Military History, 1660-1937,* London, 1937.

Collen, E., *The Indian Army : A Sketch of its History and Organization,* London, 1907

Collyer, J.J., *The South Africans with General Smuts in German East Africa,* Pretoria, 1939.

Creagh, Sir O Moore, *Indian Studies,* London, n.d.

Crowe, J.H.V., *General Smuts' Campaign in East Africa,* London, 1918.

Cruttwell, C.R.M.P., *A History of the Great War,* Oxford, 1934.

Cunea, J.R., *The Air Weapon, 1914-16,* Harrisburg, 1960.

Dane, E., *British Campaigns in Africa and the Pacific,* London, 1919.

Das, S.T., *Indian Military,* New Delhi, 1969.

Dixon, C.A., and Heilbrunn,O, *Communist Guerilla Warfare,* London, 1954.

Dolby, R.V., *Sketches of the East African Campaign,* London, 1918.

Dorling, T., *Endless Story,* London, 1931.

Dorpalen, A., *The World of General Haushofer, Geopolitics in Action,* New York, 1942

Downes, W.B., *With the Nigerians in German East Africa,* London, 1919.

Earle, H.M.(Ed), *Makers of Modern Strategy,* Prince, 1943.

Eddmons, J., *A Short History of World War I,* London Fairlawn, 1951.

Ellinwood, D.C., and Pradhan, S.D. (Eds), *India and World War I,* New Delhi, 1978.

Esposito, V.J. (Ed), *A Concise History of World War, I,* New York, 1964.

Falls, C., *A Hundred Years of War,* London, 1963.

--------------------- *The Great War,* New York, 1959

--------------------- *The Nature of Modern Warfare,* London, 1941.

Fay, S.B., *Origins of the War,* New York, 1929.

Fendall, C.P., *The East African Field Force,* 1915-19, London, 1921.

Fitzgerald, W., *Africa,* London, 1934.

Fortesque, J.W., *A History of the British Army* (12 Volumes), London, 1899-1927.

Forthingham, T.G., *The Naval History of the World War,* (3 Volumes), Cambridge-Mass, 1924-26.

Fuller, J.F.C., *The Decisive Battle of the Western World and their Influence upon History,* London, 1956.

Gardner, B., *German East,* Africa, London, 1963.

George, D.L., *War Memoirs* (6 Volumes), London, 1933-37.

Gooch, G.P., *Before the War,* London, 1936-38.

Graham, C.A.D., *The History of the Indian Mountain Artillery,* Aldershot, 1957.

Greene. T.N., *The Guerilla and How to Fight Him,* New York, 1962.

Greener, W.W., *The Gun and its Development,* London-Paris-New York, 1884

Griffith, S.B. (trans), *Mao-Tse-tung on Guerilla Warfare,* New York, 1961.

Guest, F., *The Indian Cavalryman,* London, 1959.

Guichard, L., *The Naval Blockade 1914-1918,* New York.

Halevy, E., *The World Crisis,* 1914-18, Oxford, 1930.

Hance, W.A., *The Geography of Modern Africa,* New York-London, 1964

Hardrach, G., *The First World War I, 1914-1918,* London, 1977.

Hart, B.H.L., *A History of the World War,* 1914-1918, London, 1934

--------------------- *Strategy : The Indirect Approach,* London, 1967.

--------------------- *The Revolution in Warfare,* London, 1943.

--------------------- *Thoughts on War,* London, 1943.

--------------------- *Through the Fog of War,* New York, 1938.

Hayes, C.J.H., *A Brief History of the Great War,* New York, 1931.

Hoyt, E.P. (Jr), *The Germans Who Never Lost,* London, 1969.

Jackson, D., *India's Army,* London, 1940.

Jones, H.A., and Raleigh, W., *The War in the Air* (6 Volumes), Oxford, 1922-1937.

Kautsky, K., *Outbreak of the World War : German Documents;* Oxford, 1924

Kennedy, J.R., *Modern War and Defence Reconstruction,* London, 1936.

Lether, O., *Cohort of the Tropics,* London, 1930.

Lucas, C., *The Empire at War* (IV Volume), London, 1926.

Ludendorff, General, *My War Memories,* London, 1919.

Mackinder, H.J., *Britain and the British Seas,* New York, 1902

Macmunn, G.F., *The Armies of India,* London, 1911.

Mansergh, N., *The Coming of the First World War,* London-New York-Toronto, 1949.

Martin, K., *A Military History of Germany,* London, 1975.

McEntee, G.L., *Military History of the World War,* New York, 1937.

Meinertzhagen, R., *Army Diary, 1899-1926,* London, 1926.

Montross, L., *War Through the Ages,* New York, 1960.

Mosely, L., *Duel for Kilimanjaro,* London, 1963.

Mountjoy, A.B., and Embleton, C., *Africa: Geographical Study,* London, 1966.

Naution, A.B., *Fundamentals of Guerilla Warfare,* New Delhi.

Newbolt, H., *Naval History of the Great War,* 1914-1918, London, 1920

Paget, S., *A Guide to the Study of the War,* London, 1918.

Palit, D.K., *The Essentials of Military Knowledge,* Aldershot, 1947.

Panichas, C.A. (ed), *Promise of Greatness,* London, 1968.

Peltier, L.C., and Pearcy, G.E. *Military Geography,* Princeton, 1966.

Pendlebury, J.W., *Tactics,* Allahabad, 1930.

Phillips, T.R. (ed), *Roots of Strategy,* Pennsylvania, 1940.

Pollard, A.F., *A Short History of the Great War,* London, 1920.

Pollock, N.C., *A Systematic Regional Geography,* Vol. IX, London, 1968.

Portway, D., *Science and Mechanisation in Land Warfare,* Cambridge, 1938.

Patter, E.B., and Nimitz, C.W. (eds), *See Power: A Naval History,* Englewood, 1960.

Pritchard, J.M., *A Geography of East Africa,* London, 1962.

Pruitt, D.G. and Synder, R.C., *Theory and Research on the Causes of War,* Englewood Cliffs, 1969.

Rivett-Carnac., *The Presidential Armies of India,* London, 1890.

Roberts, Lord F.S. *Forty-One Years in India (2 Volumes),* London, 1897.

Robertson, W., *Soldiers and Statesman, 1914-1918 (2 Volumes),* London-Toronto-Melbourneo-Sydney, 1926.

Ropp, T., *War in the Modern World,* New York-London, 1962.

Schnee, H., *Deutsch-Ostafrika in Weltkriege,* Leipzig, 1919 (in German).

Sculard, H.H., *A History of the Roman World,* New York-London, 1962.

Shackleton, W.S., *East African Experiences,* 1916, Knox-Durban, 1940.

Sharma, G., *Indian Army Through the Ages,* Bombay-New Delhi-Calcutta-Madras, 1966.

Sims, W.S., *The Victory at Sea,* London, 1923.

Singh, R., *Organization and Administration in the Indian Army,* Aldershot, 1952.

Stamp, L.D., *Africa : A Study in Tropical Development,* New York-London, 1953.

Synder, G.H., *Deterrence and Defence : Toward a Theory of National Security,* Princetion, 1961.

--------------------- *The Times History of the War* (14 Volumes) Printed and Published by the *Times, London.*

Thoumin, R., *The First World War,* London, 1963.

Vorbeck, Von Lettow, *My Reminiscences of East Africa,* London, 1920.

Whittall, W., *With Botha and Smuts in Africa,* London, 1917.

Williams, B., *Botha, Smuts and South Africa,* London, 1946

Wilson, H.W., *Battleships in Action,* Boston, 1926.

Wright, O., *A Study of War* (2 Volumes), Boston, 1942.

Young, F.B., *Marching on Tanga,* London, 1917.

D. *Journals and Newspapers*

Journal of the Royal United Service Institution July 1911.

Journal of the United Service Institution, January 1916.

Journal of the United Service Institution, January 1917.

Journal of the United Service Institution July 1918.

Journal of the United Service Institution April 1919.

Sketch 14
GERMAN EAST AFRICA
Scale 1:4,000,000
50 0 50 100 Miles
UGANDA
BRITISH EAST AFRICA
BELGIAN CONGO
RHODESIA
NYASALAND
PORTUGUESE EAST AFRICA
Victoria Nyanza
Lake Tanganyika
Lake Nyasa
Kivu
RUANDA
MASSAI STEPPE
CENTRAL RAILWAY
Nairobi
Bukoba
Shirati
Mwanza
Kigali
Biaramulo
Bujombe
Gitega
Usumbura
Mariahilf
St Michel
Kahama
Iwingo
Tinde Hills
Kigoma
Ujiji
Ruchugi
Tabora
Igalula
Sikonge
Karema
Itunda
Bismarckburg
Abercorn
New Utengule
New Langenburg
Ilembule
Ubena
Lupembe
Wiedhafen
Songea
Tunduru
Newala
Liwale
Lindi
Kilwa
Kilwa Kisiwani
Mombasa
Tanga
Pangani
Bagamoyo
Dar es Salaam
Zanzibar I.
Pemba
Mafia I.
Kilimanjaro
Moshi
Taveta
Voi
Tsavo
Longido
Kampfontein
Arusha
Mbulu
Ufiome
Kondoa Irangi
Singida
Saranda
Dodoma
Kilimatinde
Kikombo
Iringa
Mahenge
Madibira
Malangali
Kidete
Kilosa
Morogoro
Uleia
Kidodi
Kidatu
Kissaki
Tulo
Kissangire
Mohoro
Kibata
Handeni
Kangata
Korogwe
Mkalamo
Wilhelmstal
Amani
Nguru Mts
Dakawa
Mkata
Mpapua
Tschunjo
Njangalo
Ngomini
Mtumbi
Lukuledi
Mpotora
R. Kagera
R. Malagarasi
R. Ulanga
R. Ruaha
R. Rufiji
R. Luwegu
R. Mbemkuru
R. Rovuma
R. Athi
R. Wami
R. Umba

INDEX